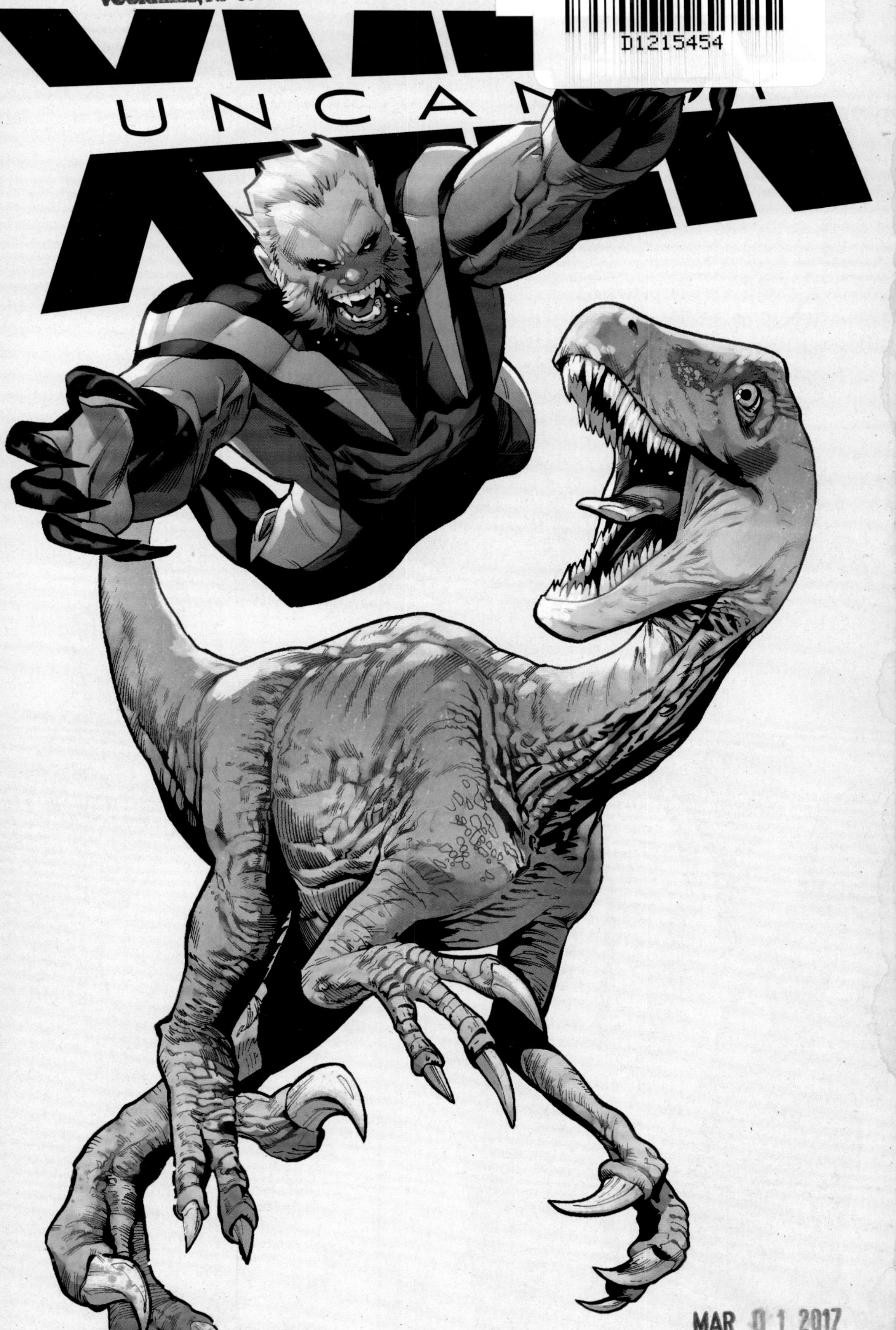
UNCANNY

PREVIOUSLY

RECENTLY, MAGNETO AND PSYLOCKE TRAVELED TO COLORADO TO AID THEIR TEAMMATE, ARCHANGEL, ONLY TO DISCOVER HE WAS A PAWN OF GENOCIDE AND CLAN AKKABA. IN THE COURSE OF BATTLE, PSYLOCKE DISCOVERED THAT MAGNETO HAD BEEN SECRETLY EMPLOYING MYSTIQUE AND FANTOMEX IN CLANDESTINE X-MEN OPERATIONS.

MEANWHILE, TO SAVE A NEW SOCIETY OF MORLOCKS, MONET WAS FORCED TO ABSORB HER BROTHER EMPLATE'S ESSENCE AT GREAT PERSONAL COST...

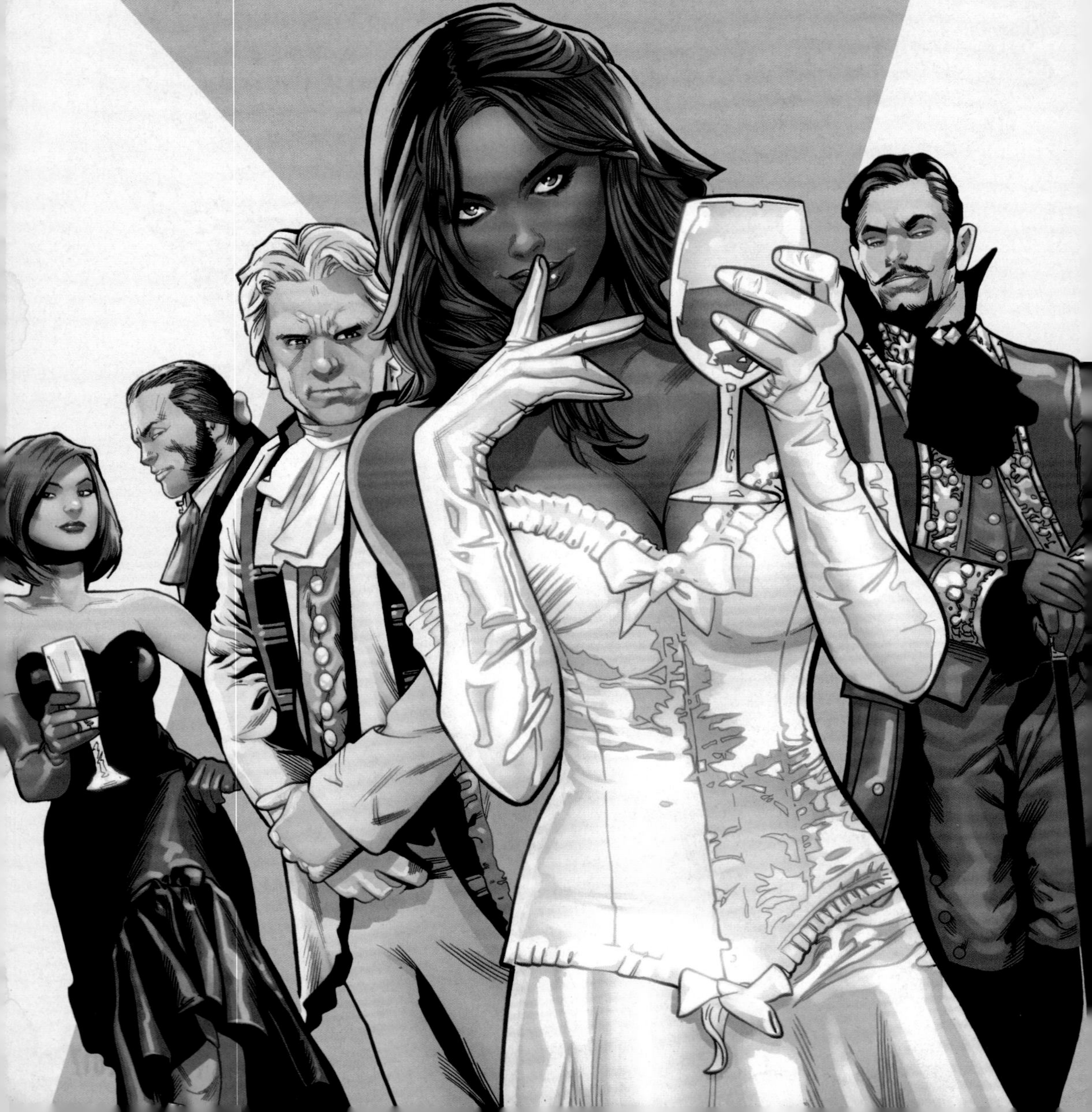

TERRIGEN MISTS CIRCLE THE GLOBE, WHITTLING DOWN MUTANTKIND'S NUMBERS AND SUPPRESSING ANY NEW MUTANT MANIFESTATIONS. BELIEVING BIGGER THREATS REQUIRE MORE THREATENING X-MEN, MAGNETO IS JOINED BY A TEAM OF THE MOST RUTHLESS MUTANTS ALIVE TO STEM THE THREAT OF EXTINCTION...

UNCANNY X-MEN

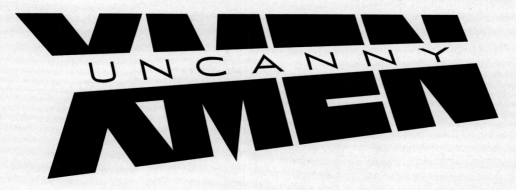

WAKING FROM THE DREAM

CULLEN BUNN
WRITER

GREG LAND WITH **IBRAIM ROBERSON** (#15)
PENCILERS

JAY LEISTEN WITH **WADE VON GRAWBADGER** (#15)
INKER

NOLAN WOODARD (#11) & **DAVID CURIEL** (#12-15) WITH **JAY DAVID RAMOS** (#15)
COLORIST

VC's JOE CARAMAGNA
LETTERER

GREG LAND WITH **NOLAN WOODARD** (#11-13) & **DAVID CURIEL** (#14-15)
COVER ART

CHRIS ROBINSON
ASSISTANT EDITOR

DANIEL KETCHUM
EDITOR

MARK PANICCIA
X-MEN GROUP EDITOR

X-MEN CREATED BY ***STAN LEE & JACK KIRBY***

COLLECTION EDITOR: ***JENNIFER GRÜNWALD***
ASSOCIATE MANAGING EDITOR: ***KATERI WOODY***
ASSOCIATE EDITOR: ***SARAH BRUNSTAD***
EDITOR, SPECIAL PROJECTS: ***MARK D. BEAZLEY***
VP PRODUCTION & SPECIAL PROJECTS: ***JEFF YOUNGQUIST***
SVP PRINT, SALES & MARKETING: ***DAVID GABRIEL***
BOOK DESIGNER: ***JAY BOWEN***

EDITOR IN CHIEF: ***AXEL ALONSO***
CHIEF CREATIVE OFFICER: ***JOE QUESADA***
PUBLISHER: ***DAN BUCKLEY***
EXECUTIVE PRODUCER: ***ALAN FINE***

;ANNY X-MEN: SUPERIOR VOL. 3 — WAKING FROM THE DREAM. Contains material originally published in magazine form as UNCANNY X-MEN #11-15. First printing 2017. ISBN# 978-1-302-90313-8. Published MARVEL WORLDWIDE, INC., a subsidiary of MARVEL ENTERTAINMENT, LLC. OFFICE OF PUBLICATION: 135 West 50th Street, New York, NY 10020. Copyright © 2017 MARVEL No similarity between any of the names, racters, persons, and/or institutions in this magazine with those of any living or dead person or institution is intended, and any such similarity which may exist is purely coincidental. **Printed in Canada.** ALAN FINE, sident, Marvel Entertainment; DAN BUCKLEY, President, TV, Publishing & Brand Management; JOE QUESADA, Chief Creative Officer; TOM BREVOORT, SVP of Publishing; DAVID BOGART, SVP of Business Affairs & rations, Publishing & Partnership; C.B. CEBULSKI, VP of Brand Management & Development, Asia; DAVID GABRIEL, SVP of Sales & Marketing, Publishing; JEFF YOUNGQUIST, VP of Production & Special Projects; DAN RR, Executive Director of Publishing Technology; ALEX MORALES, Director of Publishing Operations; SUSAN CRESPI, Production Manager; STAN LEE, Chairman Emeritus. For information regarding advertising in Marvel nics or on Marvel.com, please contact Vit DeBellis, Integrated Sales Manager, at vdebellis@marvel.com. For Marvel subscription inquiries, please call 888-511-5480. **Manufactured between 12/2/2016 and 1/9/2017 SOLISCO PRINTERS, SCOTT, QC, CANADA.**

987654321

11

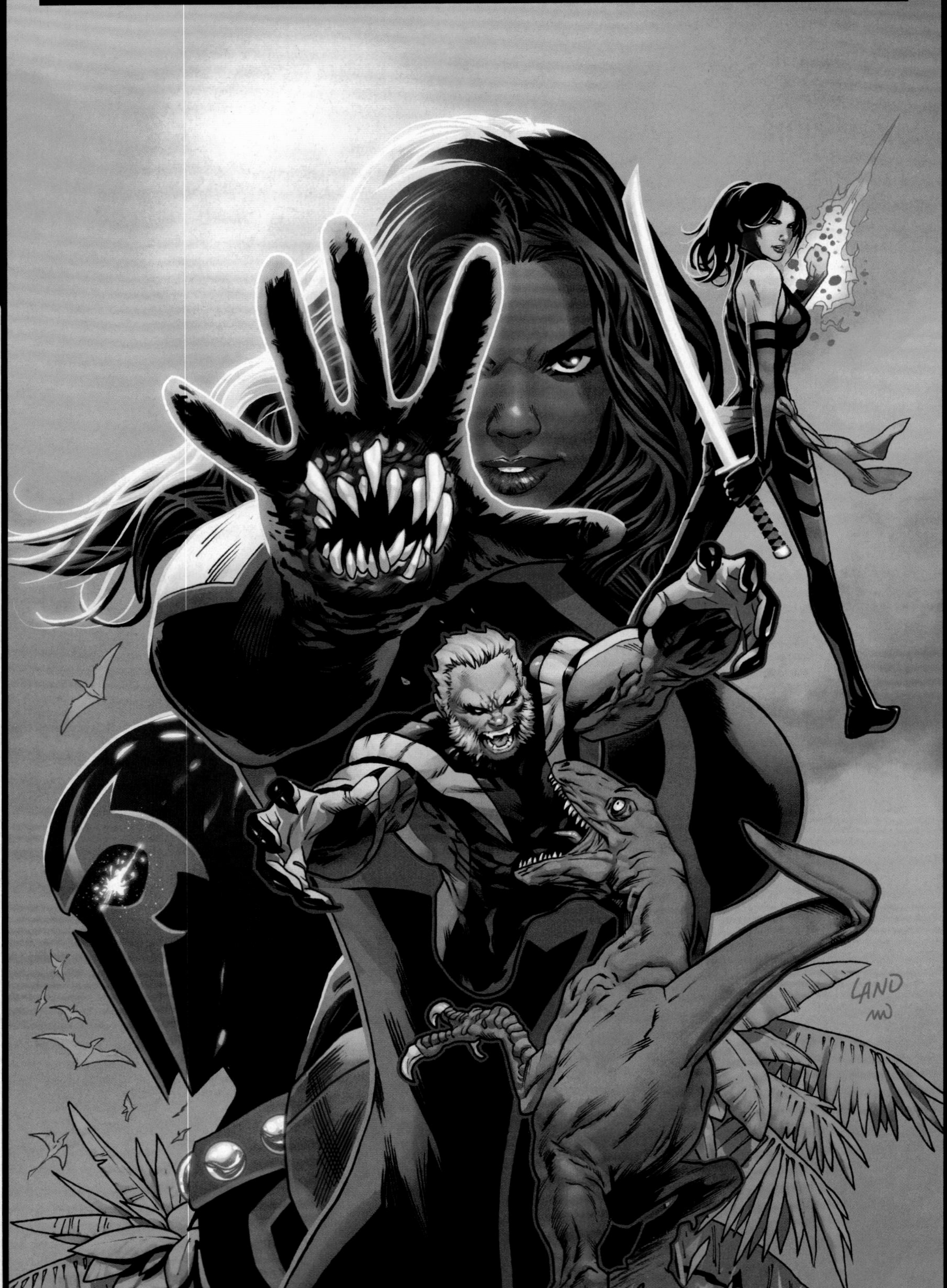
LAND

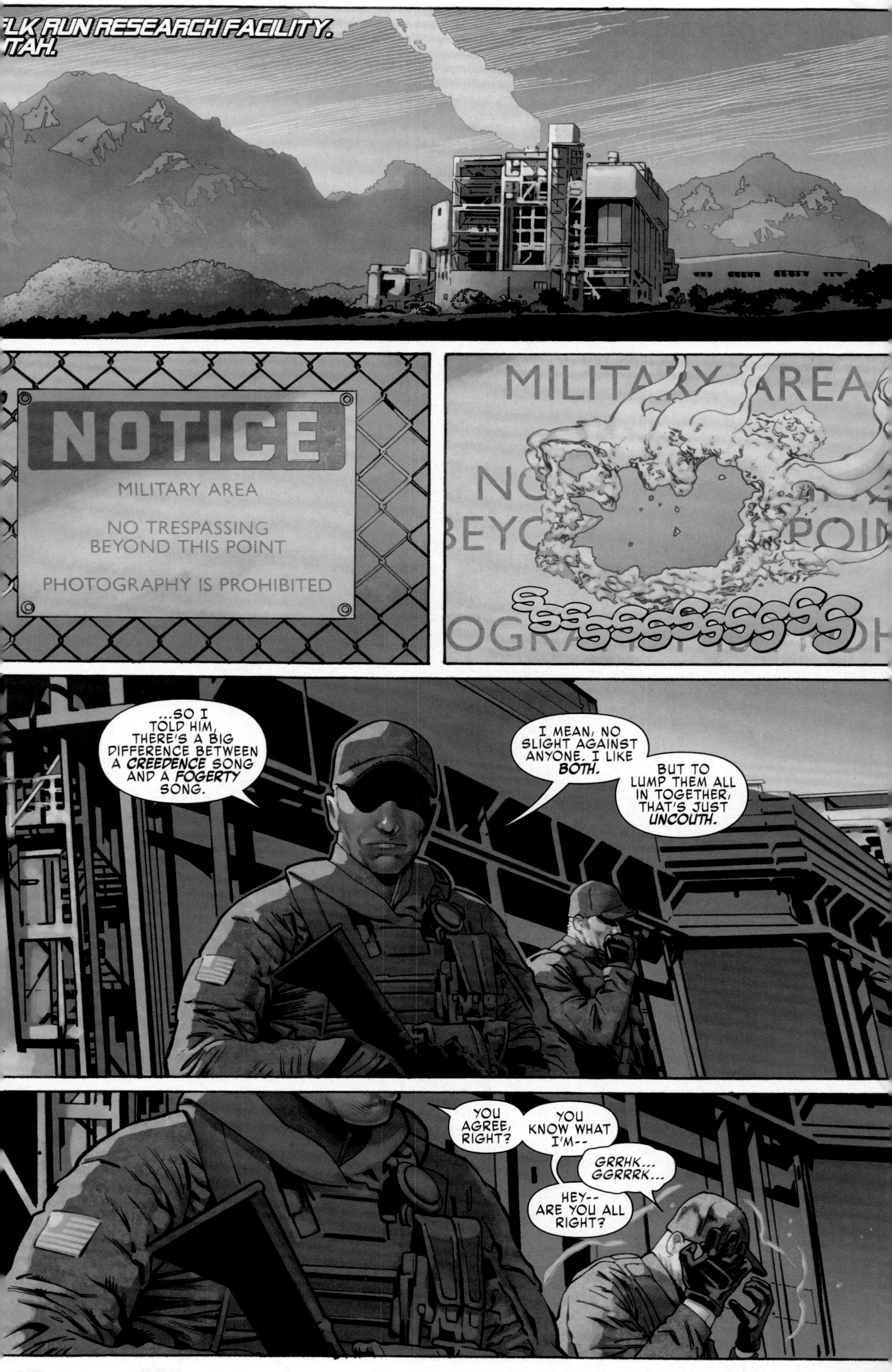
ELK RUN RESEARCH FACILITY. UTAH.
NOTICE
MILITARY AREA
NO TRESPASSING BEYOND THIS POINT
PHOTOGRAPHY IS PROHIBITED
SSSSSSSSSSSSS
...SO I TOLD HIM, THERE'S A BIG DIFFERENCE BETWEEN A CREEDENCE SONG AND A FOGERTY SONG.
I MEAN, NO SLIGHT AGAINST ANYONE. I LIKE BOTH.
BUT TO LUMP THEM ALL IN TOGETHER, THAT'S JUST UNCOUTH.
YOU AGREE, RIGHT?
YOU KNOW WHAT I'M--
GRRHK... GGRRRK...
HEY-- ARE YOU ALL RIGHT?

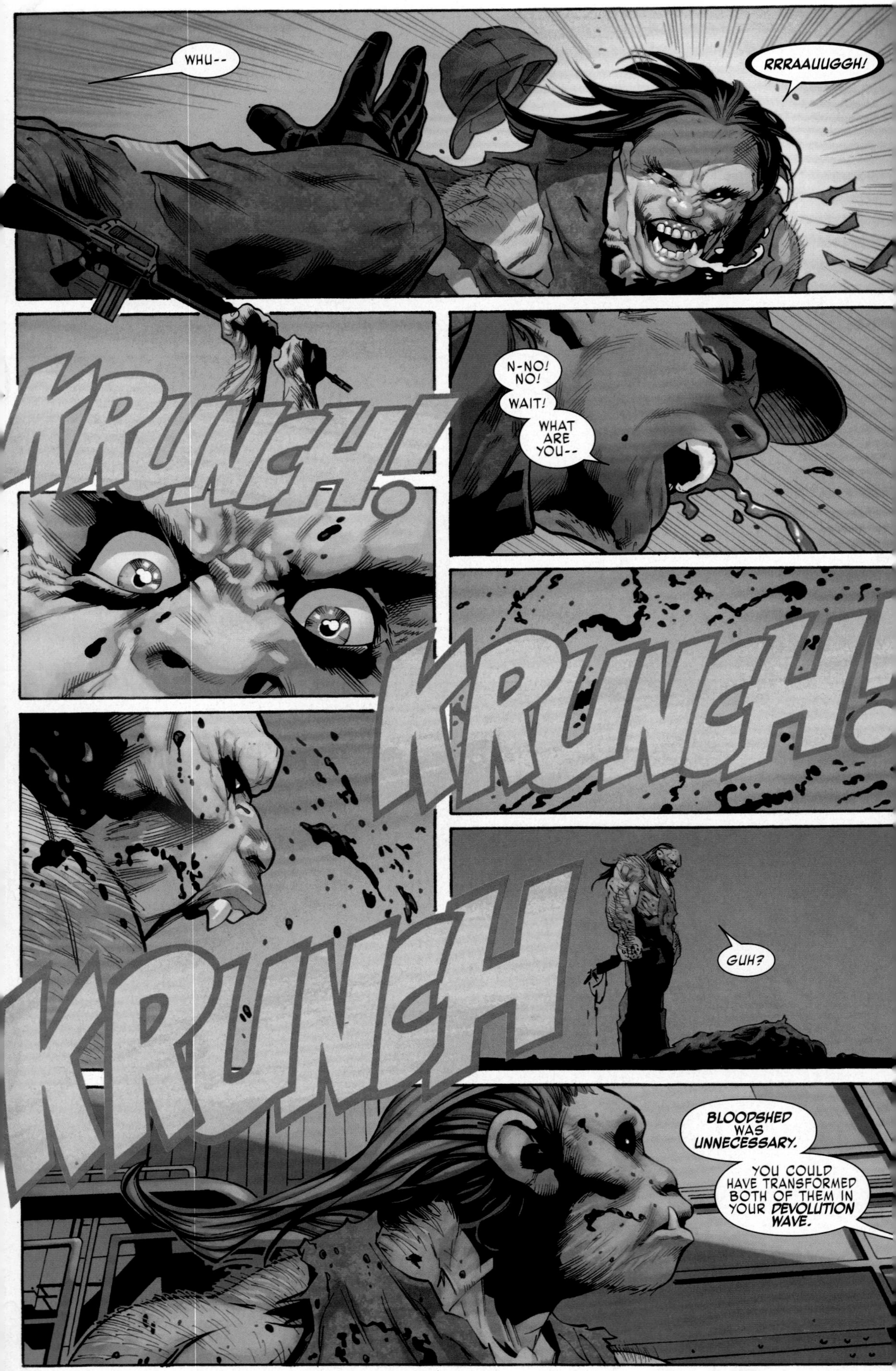
WHU--
RRRAAUUGGH!
KRUNCH!
N-NO! NO!
WAIT!
WHAT ARE YOU--
KRUNCH!
KRUNCH
GUH?
BLOODSHED WAS UNNECESSARY.
YOU COULD HAVE TRANSFORMED BOTH OF THEM IN YOUR DEVOLUTION WAVE.

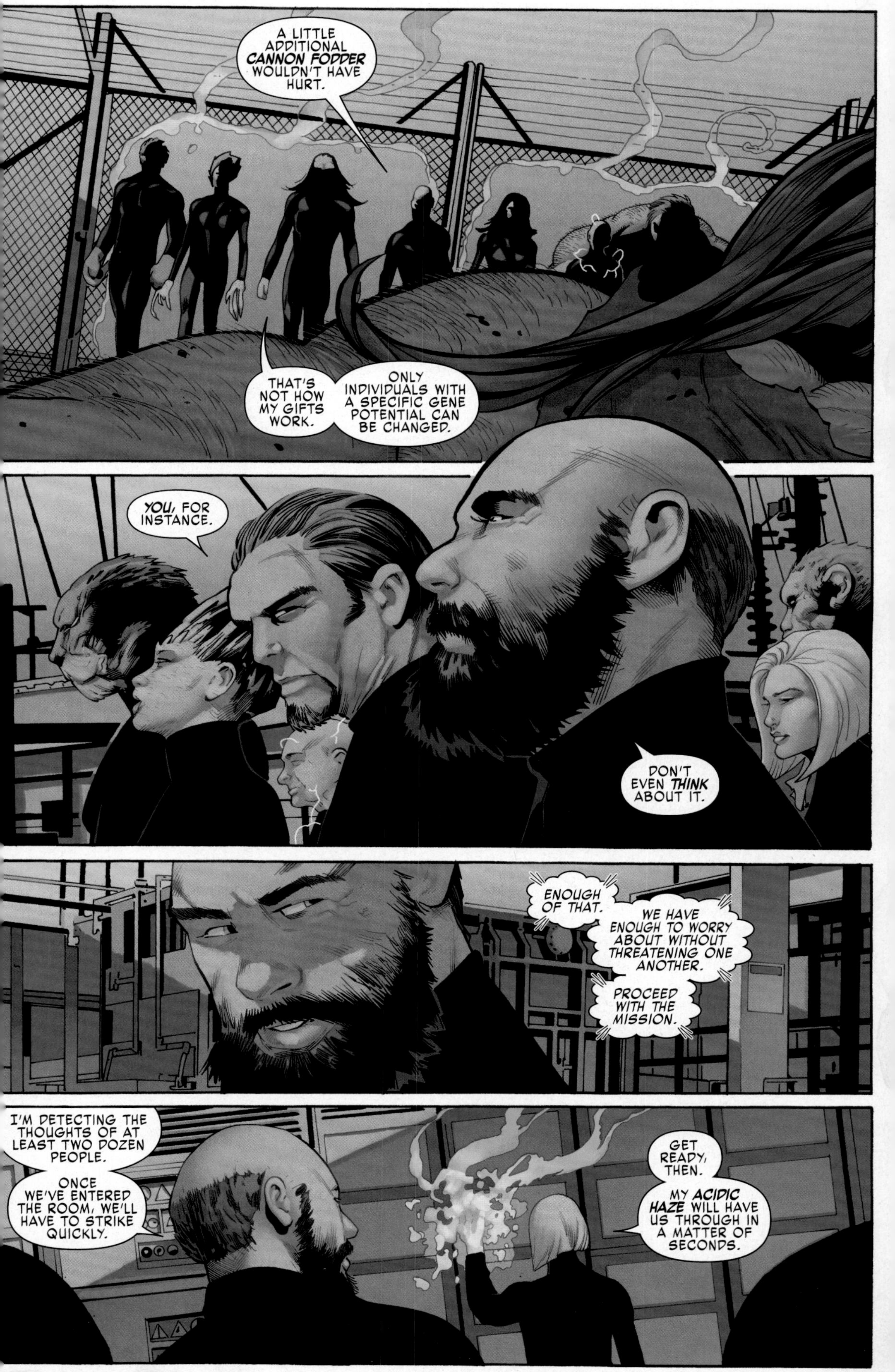
A LITTLE ADDITIONAL CANNON FODDER WOULDN'T HAVE HURT.
THAT'S NOT HOW MY GIFTS WORK.
ONLY INDIVIDUALS WITH A SPECIFIC GENE POTENTIAL CAN BE CHANGED.
YOU, FOR INSTANCE.
DON'T EVEN THINK ABOUT IT.
ENOUGH OF THAT.
WE HAVE ENOUGH TO WORRY ABOUT WITHOUT THREATENING ONE ANOTHER.
PROCEED WITH THE MISSION.
I'M DETECTING THE THOUGHTS OF AT LEAST TWO DOZEN PEOPLE.
ONCE WE'VE ENTERED THE ROOM, WE'LL HAVE TO STRIKE QUICKLY.
GET READY, THEN.
MY ACIDIC HAZE WILL HAVE US THROUGH IN A MATTER OF SECONDS.

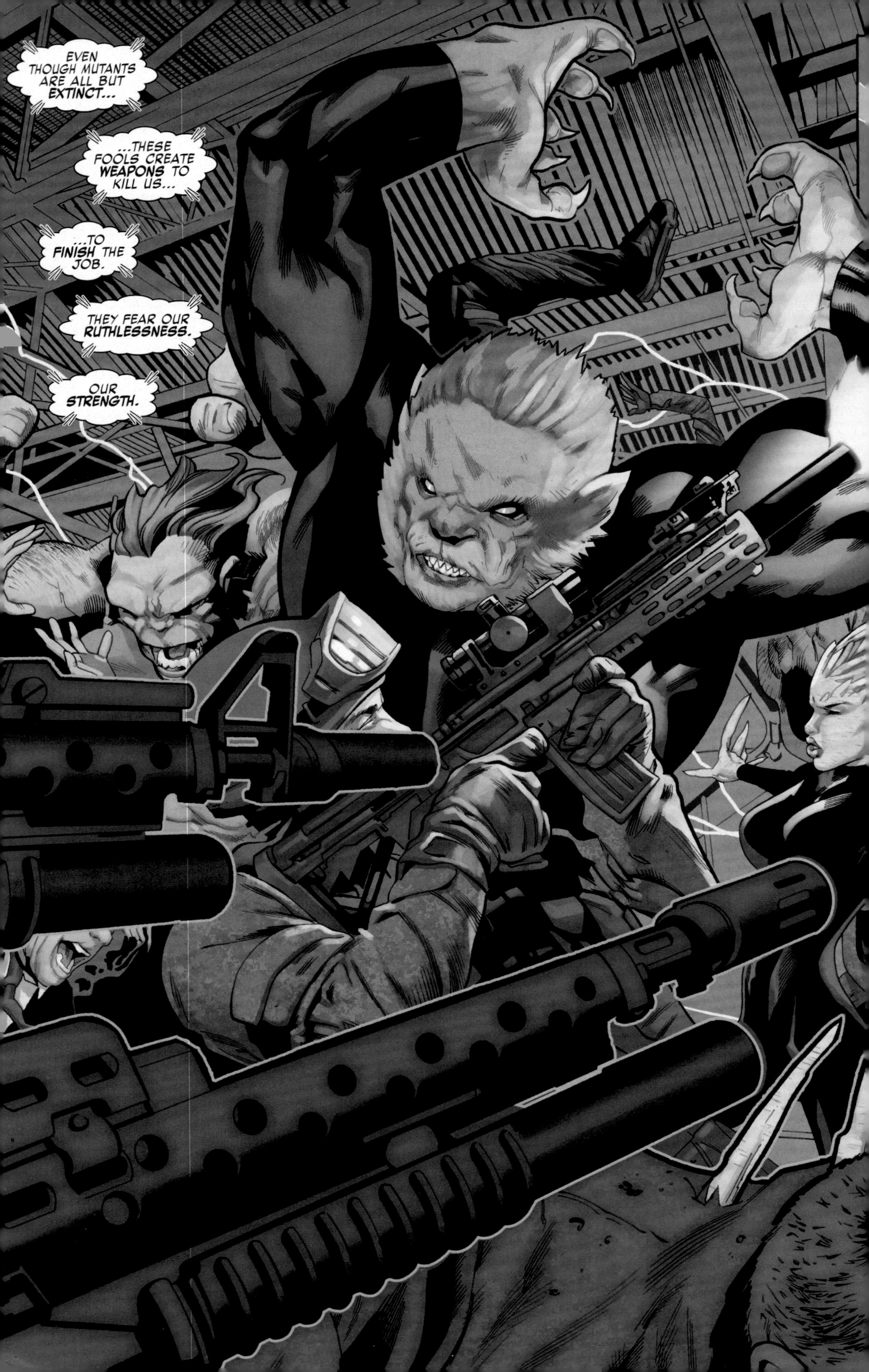
EVEN THOUGH MUTANTS ARE ALL BUT EXTINCT...
...THESE FOOLS CREATE WEAPONS TO KILL US...
...TO FINISH THE JOB.
THEY FEAR OUR RUTHLESSNESS.
OUR STRENGTH.

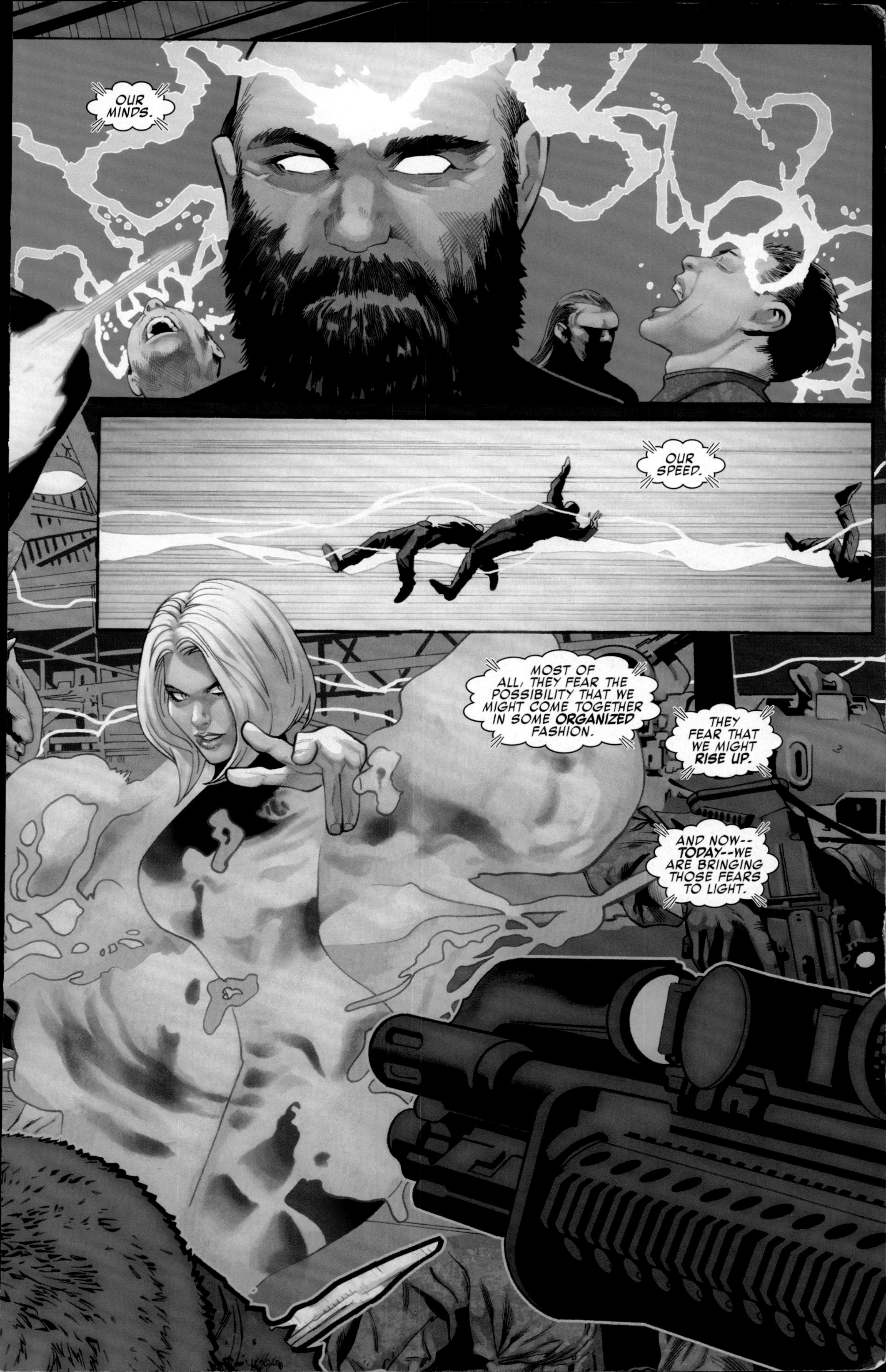
OUR MINDS.
OUR SPEED.
MOST OF ALL, THEY FEAR THE POSSIBILITY THAT WE MIGHT COME TOGETHER IN SOME ORGANIZED FASHION.
THEY FEAR THAT WE MIGHT RISE UP.
AND NOW-- TODAY--WE ARE BRINGING THOSE FEARS TO LIGHT.

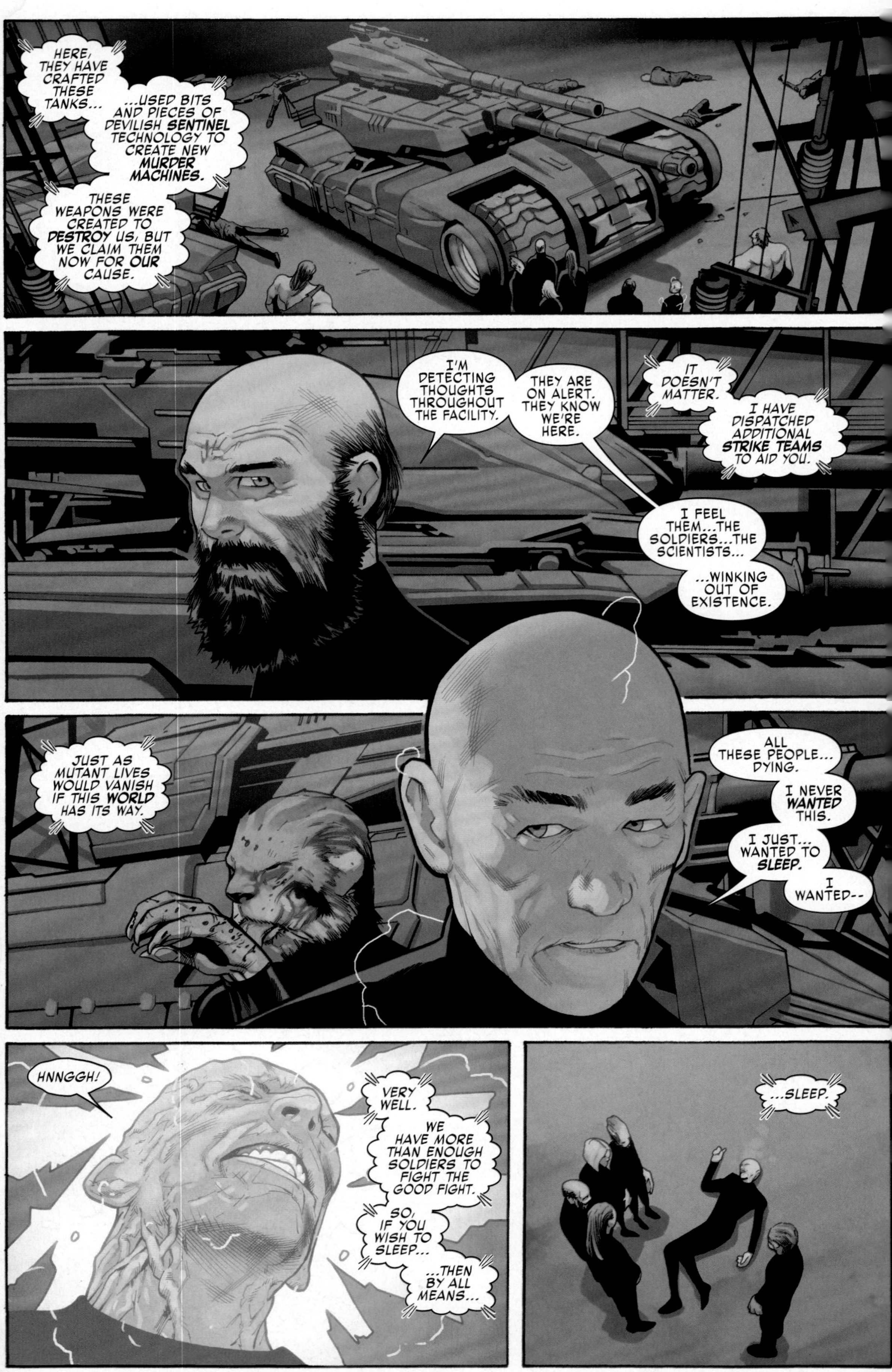
HERE, THEY HAVE CRAFTED THESE TANKS...
...USED BITS AND PIECES OF DEVILISH SENTINEL TECHNOLOGY TO CREATE NEW MURDER MACHINES.
THESE WEAPONS WERE CREATED TO DESTROY US, BUT WE CLAIM THEM NOW FOR OUR CAUSE.
I'M DETECTING THOUGHTS THROUGHOUT THE FACILITY.
THEY ARE ON ALERT. THEY KNOW WE'RE HERE.
IT DOESN'T MATTER.
I HAVE DISPATCHED ADDITIONAL STRIKE TEAMS TO AID YOU.
I FEEL THEM...THE SOLDIERS...THE SCIENTISTS...
...WINKING OUT OF EXISTENCE.
JUST AS MUTANT LIVES WOULD VANISH IF THIS WORLD HAS ITS WAY.
ALL THESE PEOPLE... DYING.
I NEVER WANTED THIS.
I JUST... WANTED TO SLEEP.
I WANTED--
HNNGGH!
VERY WELL.
WE HAVE MORE THAN ENOUGH SOLDIERS TO FIGHT THE GOOD FIGHT.
SO, IF YOU WISH TO SLEEP...
...THEN BY ALL MEANS...
...SLEEP.

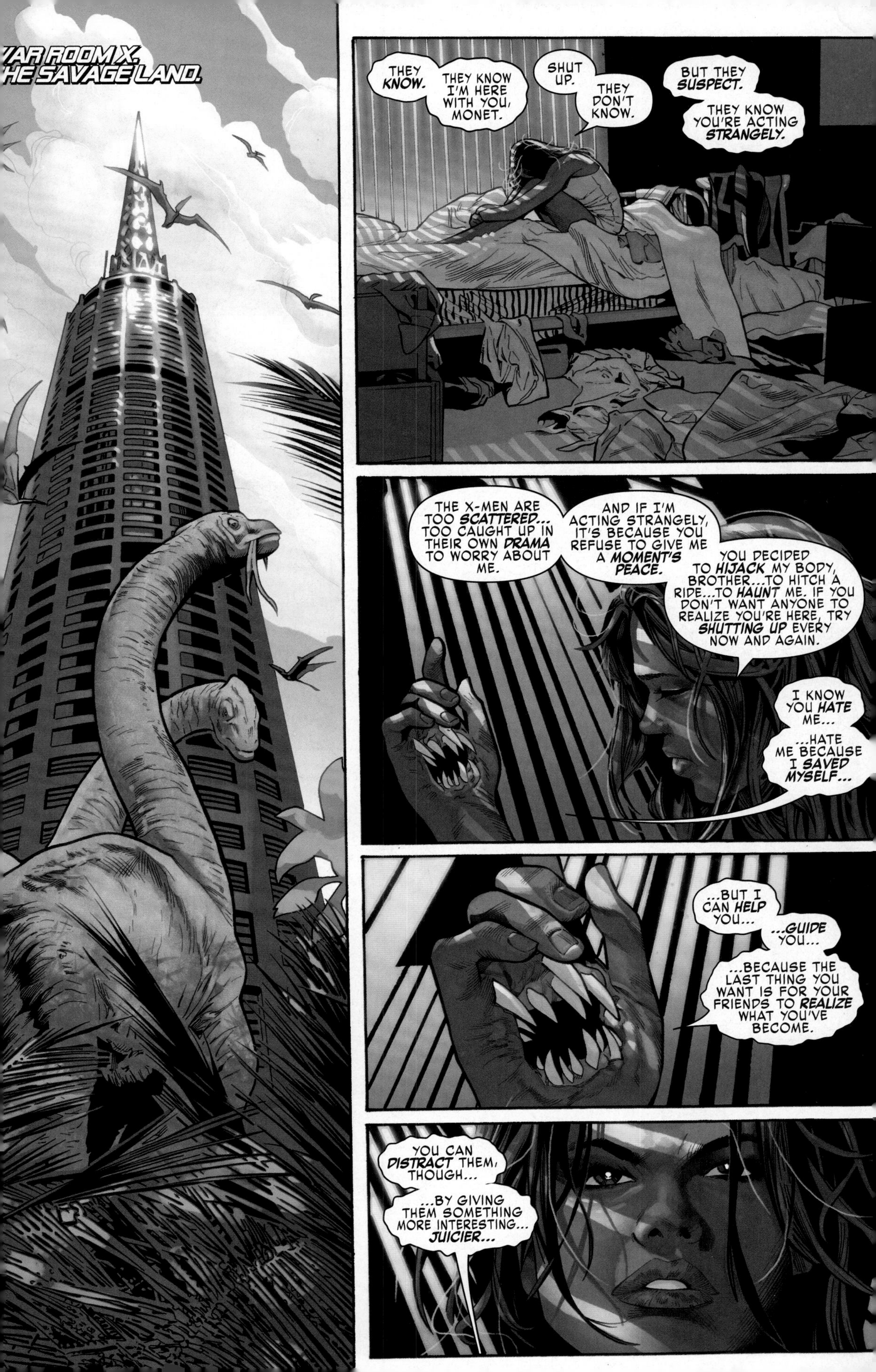

WAR ROOM X. THE SAVAGE LAND.
THEY KNOW.
THEY KNOW I'M HERE WITH YOU, MONET.
SHUT UP.
THEY DON'T KNOW.
BUT THEY SUSPECT.
THEY KNOW YOU'RE ACTING STRANGELY.
THE X-MEN ARE TOO SCATTERED... TOO CAUGHT UP IN THEIR OWN DRAMA TO WORRY ABOUT ME.
AND IF I'M ACTING STRANGELY, IT'S BECAUSE YOU REFUSE TO GIVE ME A MOMENT'S PEACE.
YOU DECIDED TO HIJACK MY BODY, BROTHER...TO HITCH A RIDE...TO HAUNT ME. IF YOU DON'T WANT ANYONE TO REALIZE YOU'RE HERE, TRY SHUTTING UP EVERY NOW AND AGAIN.
I KNOW YOU HATE ME...
...HATE ME BECAUSE I SAVED MYSELF...
...BUT I CAN HELP YOU...
...GUIDE YOU...
...BECAUSE THE LAST THING YOU WANT IS FOR YOUR FRIENDS TO REALIZE WHAT YOU'VE BECOME.
YOU CAN DISTRACT THEM, THOUGH...
...BY GIVING THEM SOMETHING MORE INTERESTING... JUICIER...

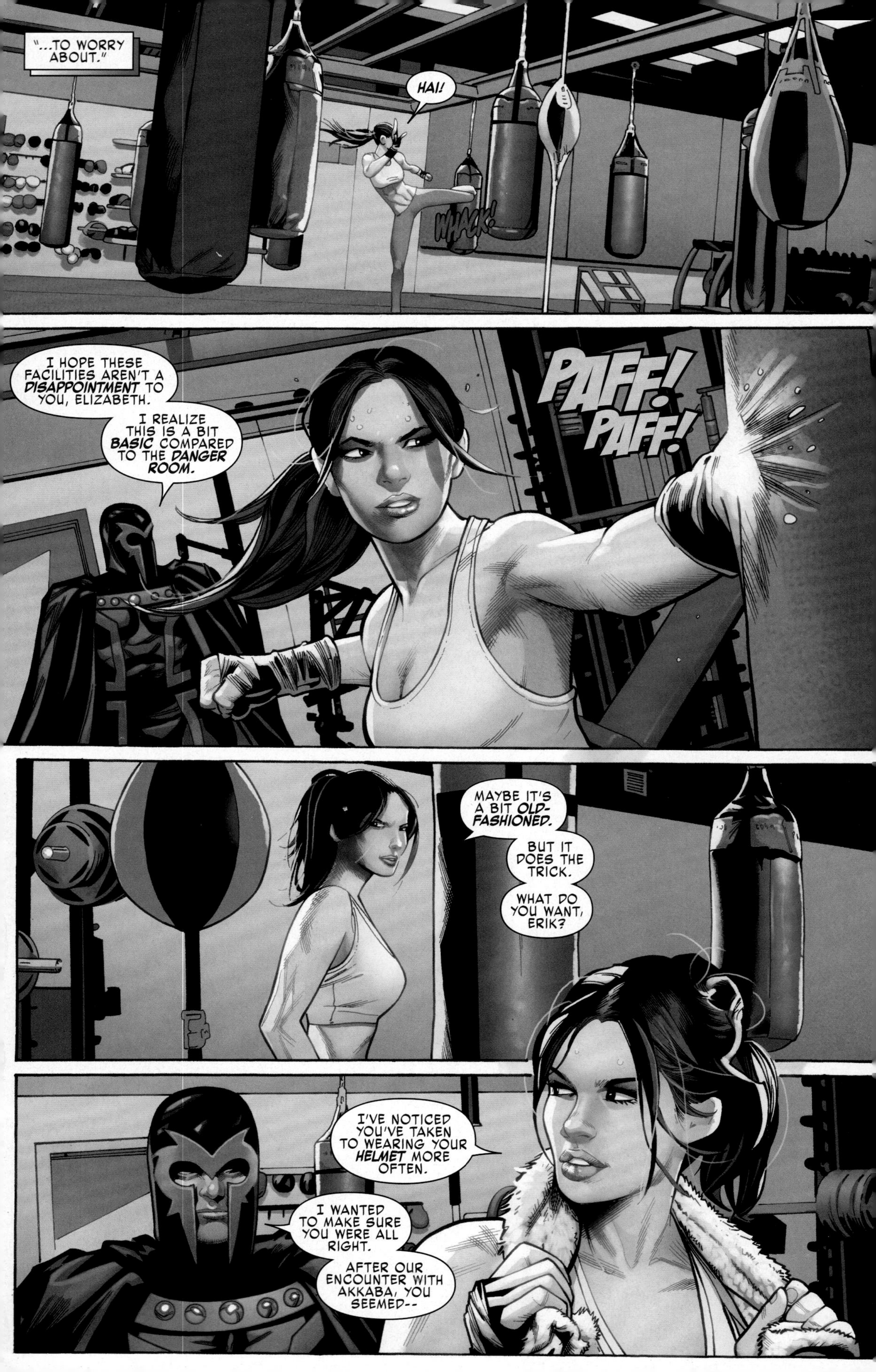

"...TO WORRY ABOUT."
HAI!
WHACK!
I HOPE THESE FACILITIES AREN'T A DISAPPOINTMENT TO YOU, ELIZABETH.
I REALIZE THIS IS A BIT BASIC COMPARED TO THE DANGER ROOM.
PAFF! PAFF!
MAYBE IT'S A BIT OLD-FASHIONED.
BUT IT DOES THE TRICK.
WHAT DO YOU WANT, ERIK?
I'VE NOTICED YOU'VE TAKEN TO WEARING YOUR HELMET MORE OFTEN.
I WANTED TO MAKE SURE YOU WERE ALL RIGHT.
AFTER OUR ENCOUNTER WITH AKKABA, YOU SEEMED--

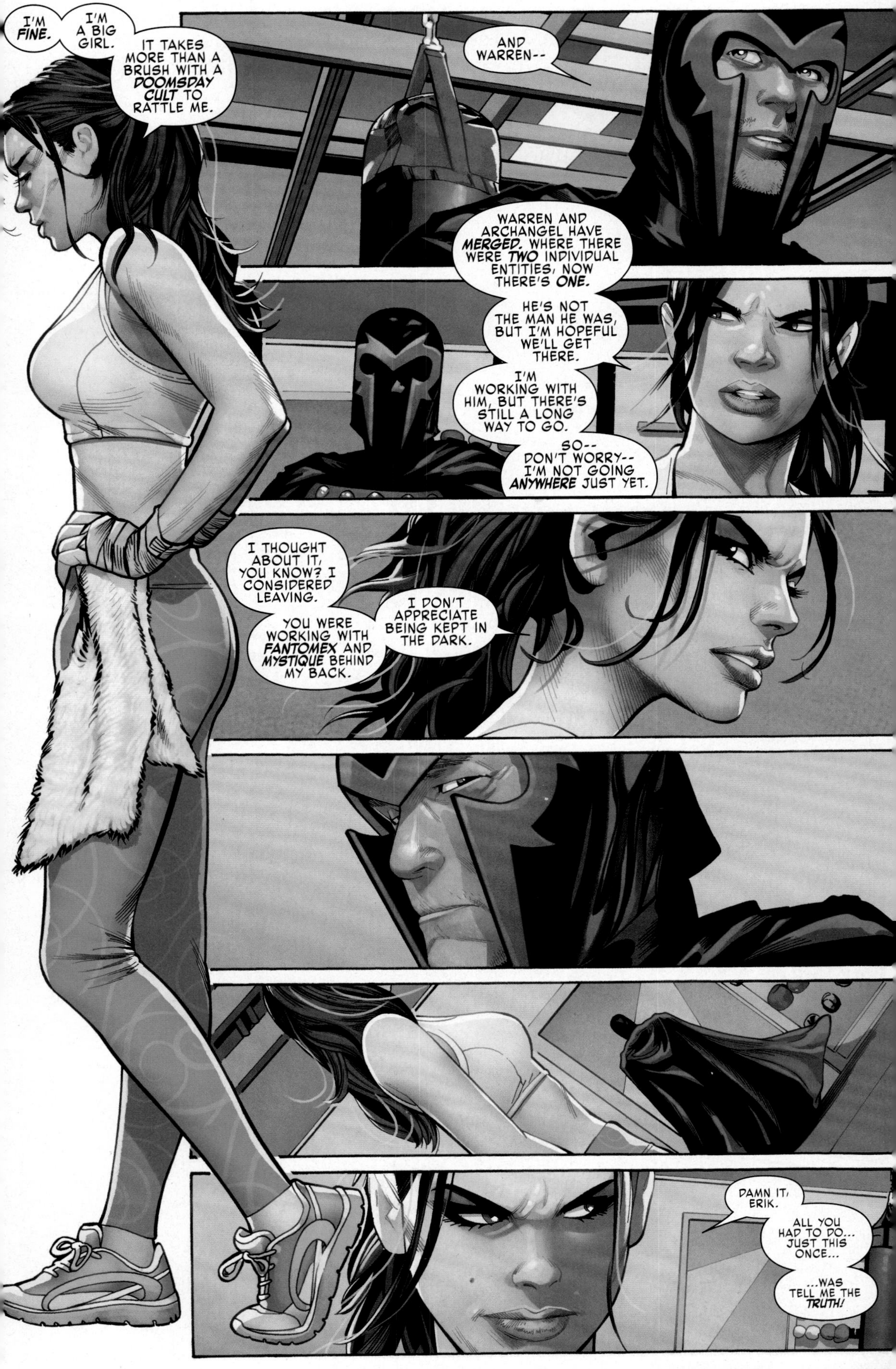
I'M FINE.
I'M A BIG GIRL.
IT TAKES MORE THAN A BRUSH WITH A DOOMSDAY CULT TO RATTLE ME.
AND WARREN--
WARREN AND ARCHANGEL HAVE MERGED. WHERE THERE WERE TWO INDIVIDUAL ENTITIES, NOW THERE'S ONE.
HE'S NOT THE MAN HE WAS, BUT I'M HOPEFUL WE'LL GET THERE.
I'M WORKING WITH HIM, BUT THERE'S STILL A LONG WAY TO GO.
SO-- DON'T WORRY-- I'M NOT GOING ANYWHERE JUST YET.
I THOUGHT ABOUT IT, YOU KNOW? I CONSIDERED LEAVING.
YOU WERE WORKING WITH FANTOMEX AND MYSTIQUE BEHIND MY BACK.
I DON'T APPRECIATE BEING KEPT IN THE DARK.
DAMN IT, ERIK.
ALL YOU HAD TO DO... JUST THIS ONCE...
...WAS TELL ME THE TRUTH!

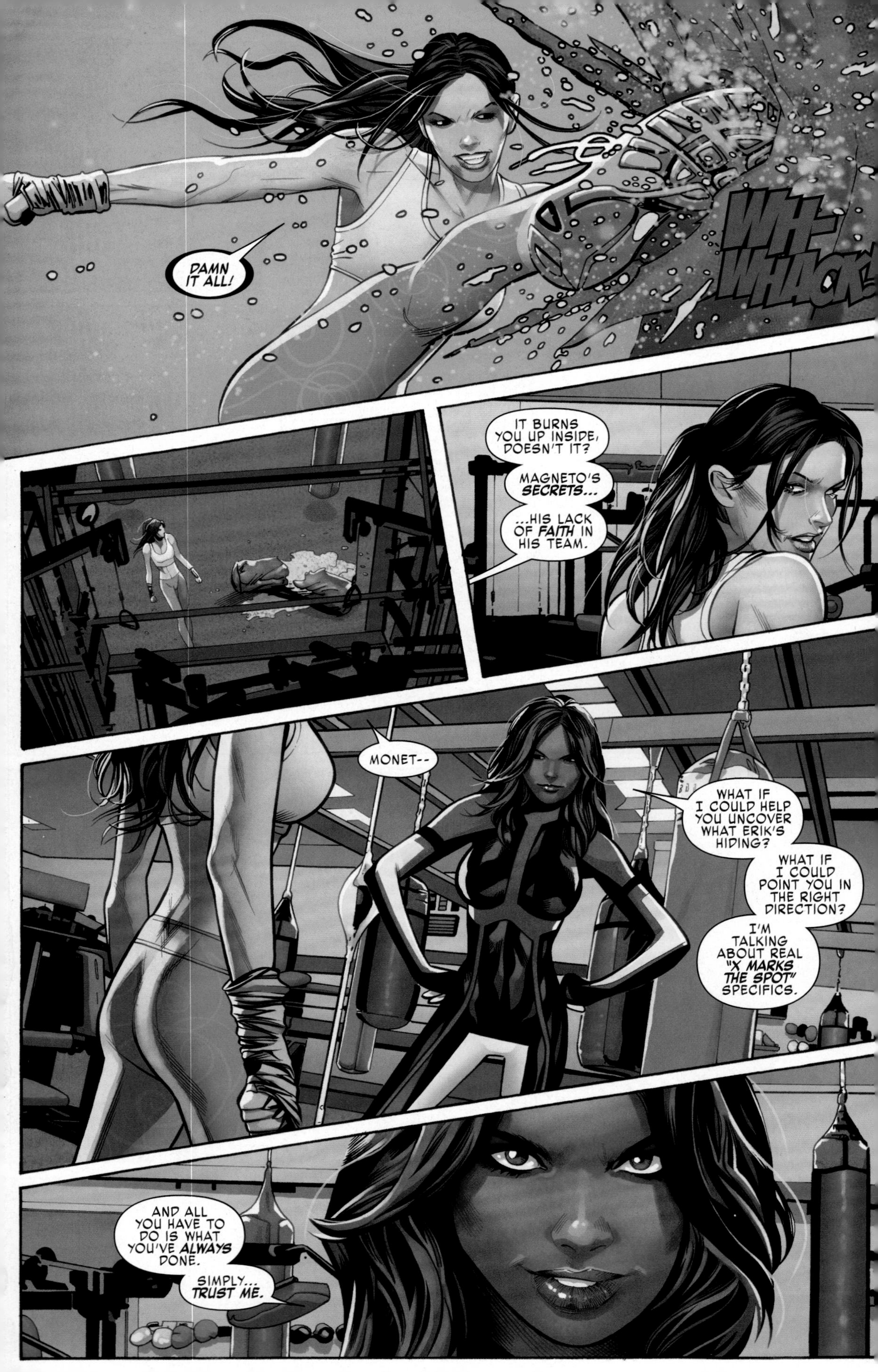
DAMN IT ALL!
WH-WHACK!
IT BURNS YOU UP INSIDE, DOESN'T IT?
MAGNETO'S SECRETS...
...HIS LACK OF FAITH IN HIS TEAM.
MONET--
WHAT IF I COULD HELP YOU UNCOVER WHAT ERIK'S HIDING?
WHAT IF I COULD POINT YOU IN THE RIGHT DIRECTION?
I'M TALKING ABOUT REAL "X MARKS THE SPOT" SPECIFICS.
AND ALL YOU HAVE TO DO IS WHAT YOU'VE ALWAYS DONE.
SIMPLY... TRUST ME.

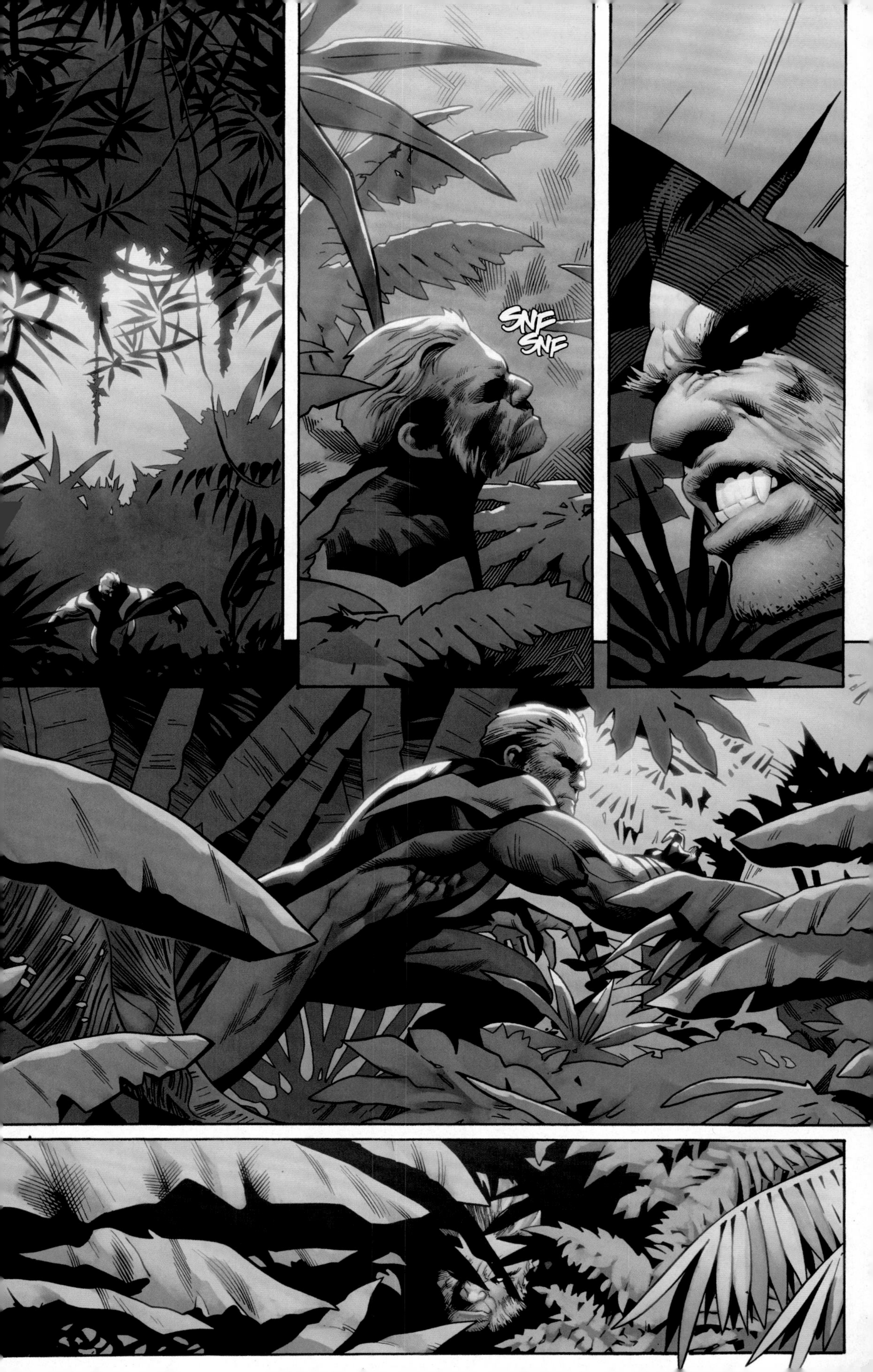
SNF
SNF

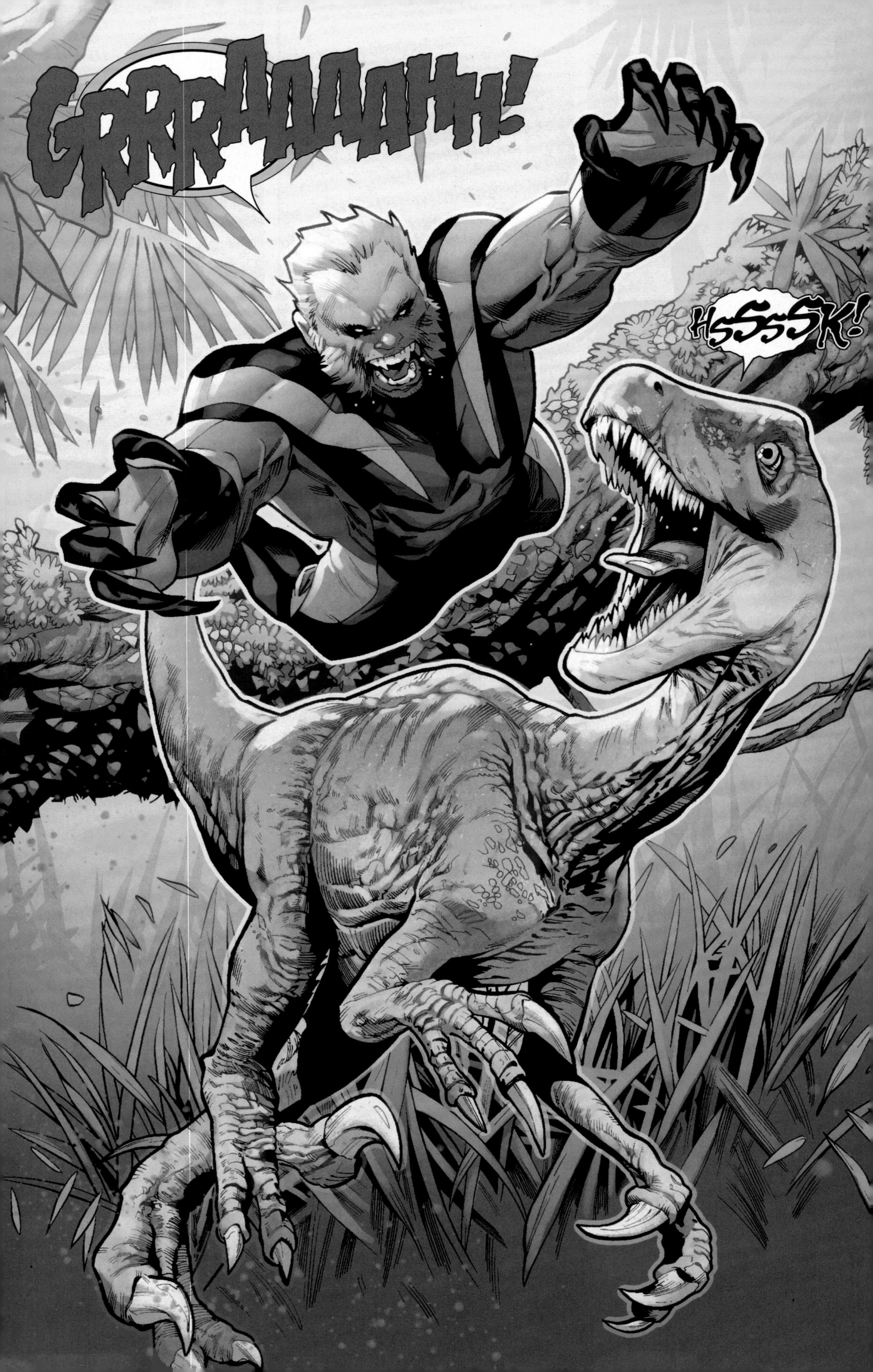
GRRRAAAAHH!
HSSSSK!

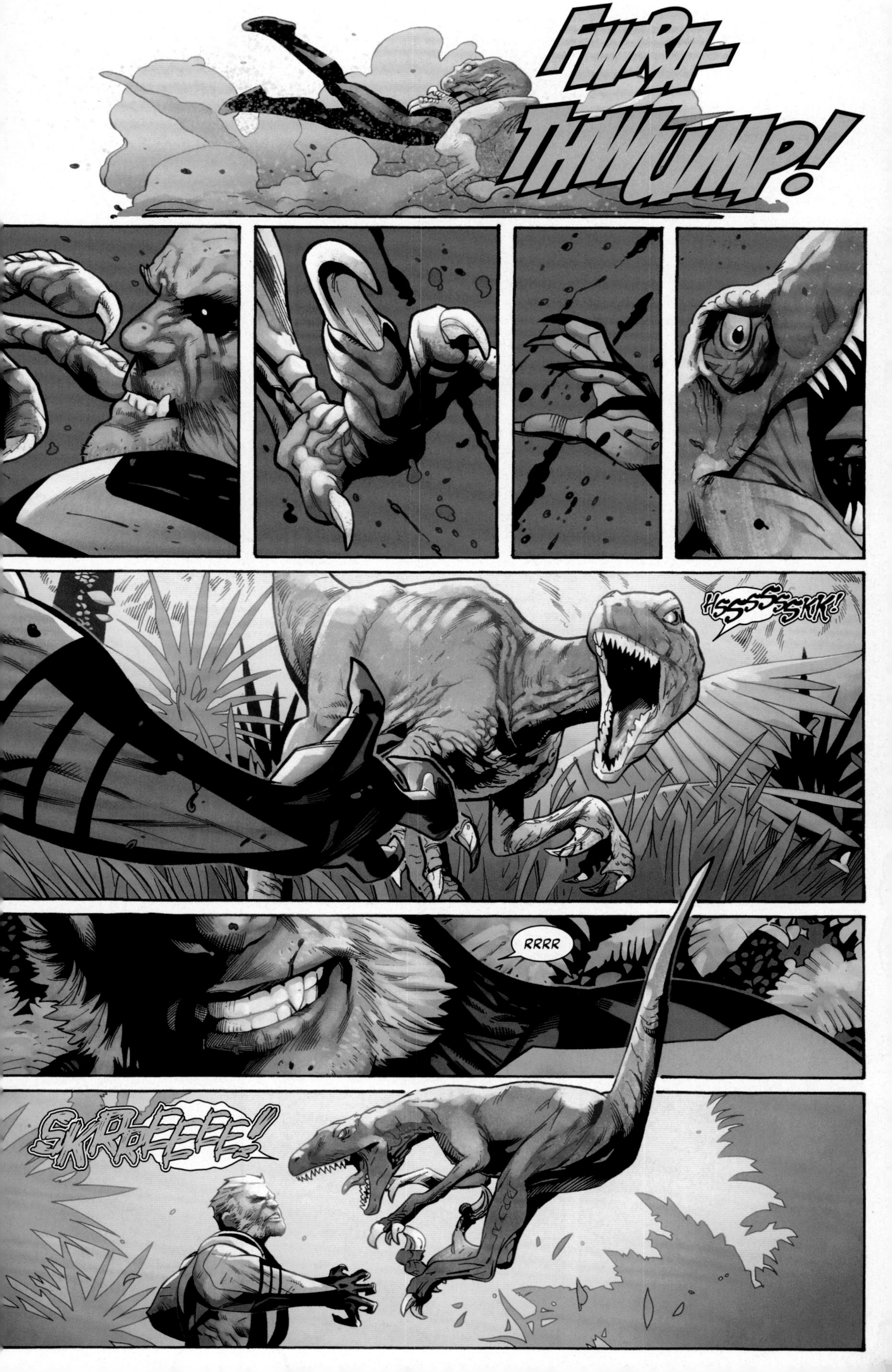
FWRA-THWUMP!
HSSSSSSKK!
RRRR
SKRREEEE!

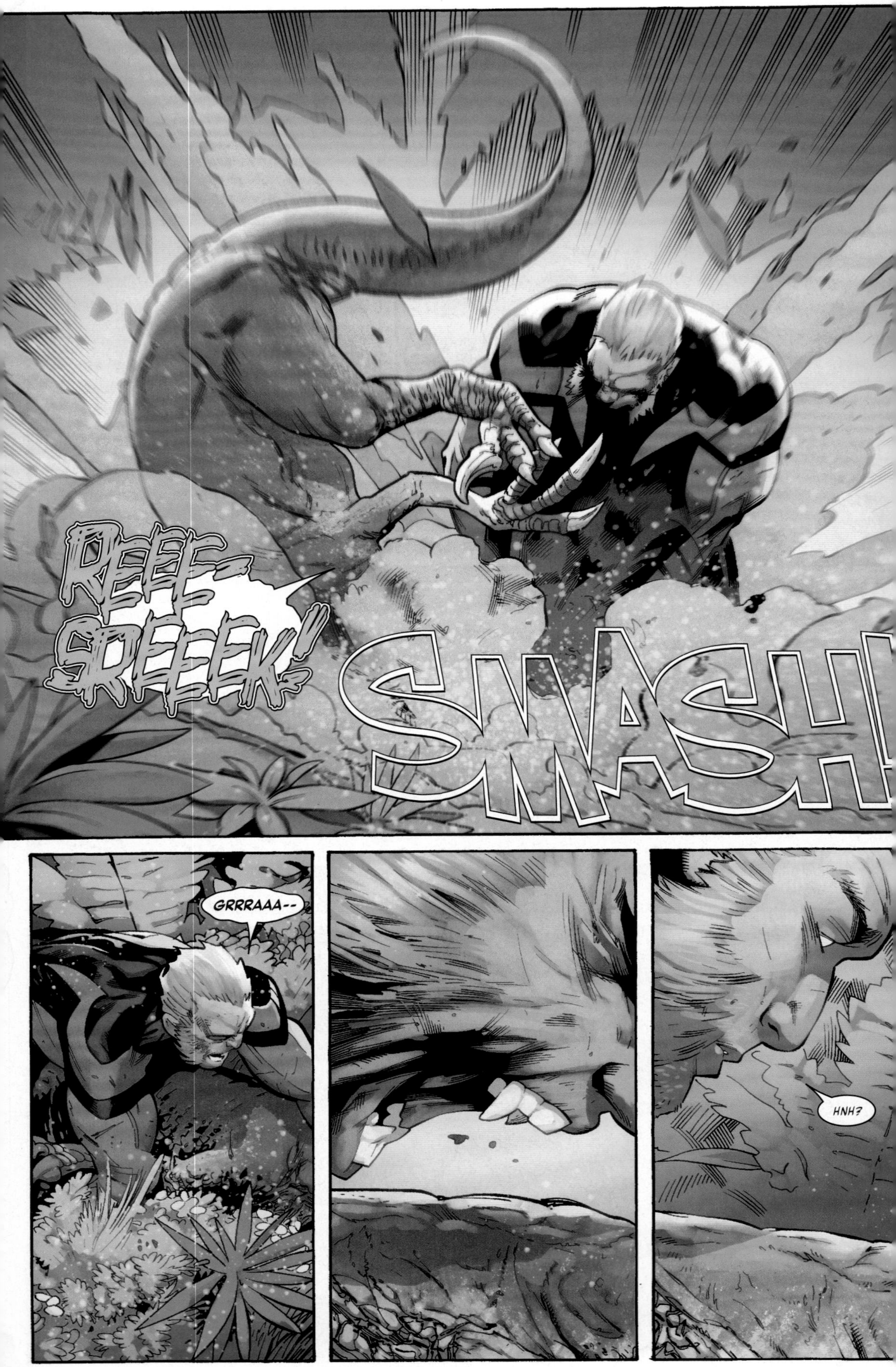
REEE-SREEEK!
SMASH!
GRRRAAA--
HNH?

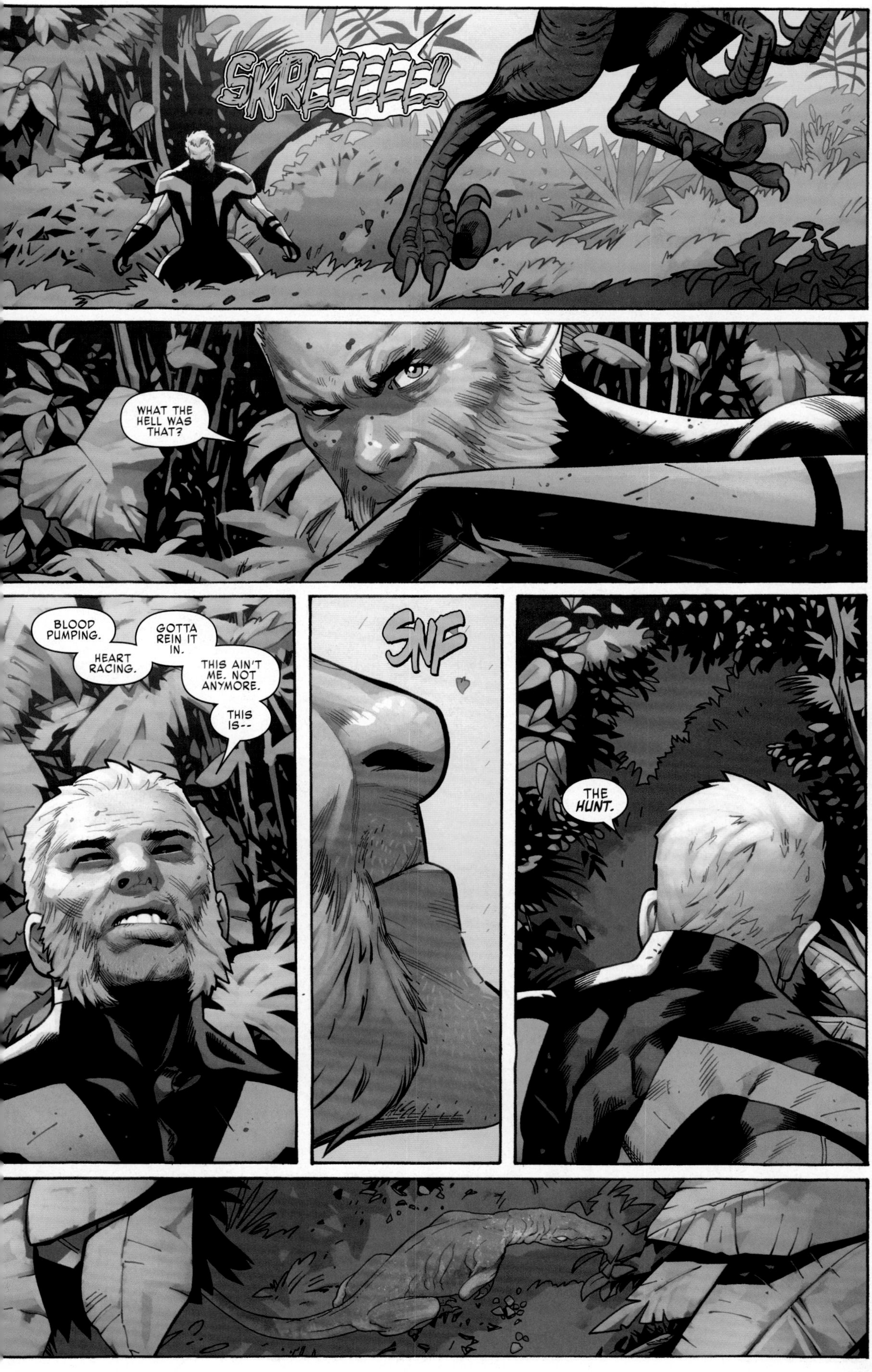
SKREEEEEE!
WHAT THE HELL WAS THAT?
BLOOD PUMPING.
HEART RACING.
GOTTA REIN IT IN.
THIS AIN'T ME. NOT ANYMORE.
THIS IS--
SNF
THE HUNT.

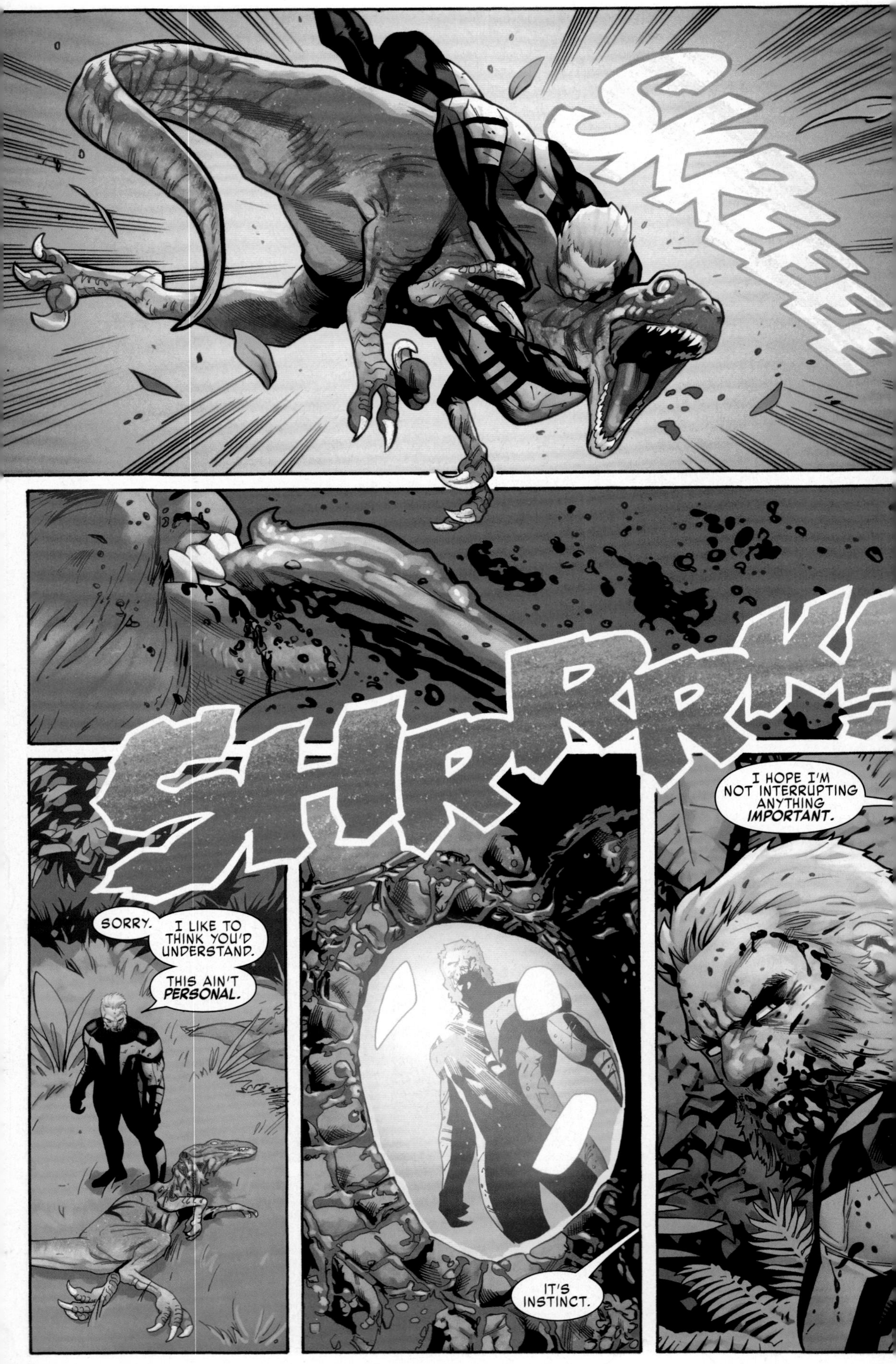
SKREEEE
SHRRRK
SORRY.
I LIKE TO THINK YOU'D UNDERSTAND.
THIS AIN'T *PERSONAL.*
IT'S INSTINCT.
I HOPE I'M NOT INTERRUPTING ANYTHING *IMPORTANT.*

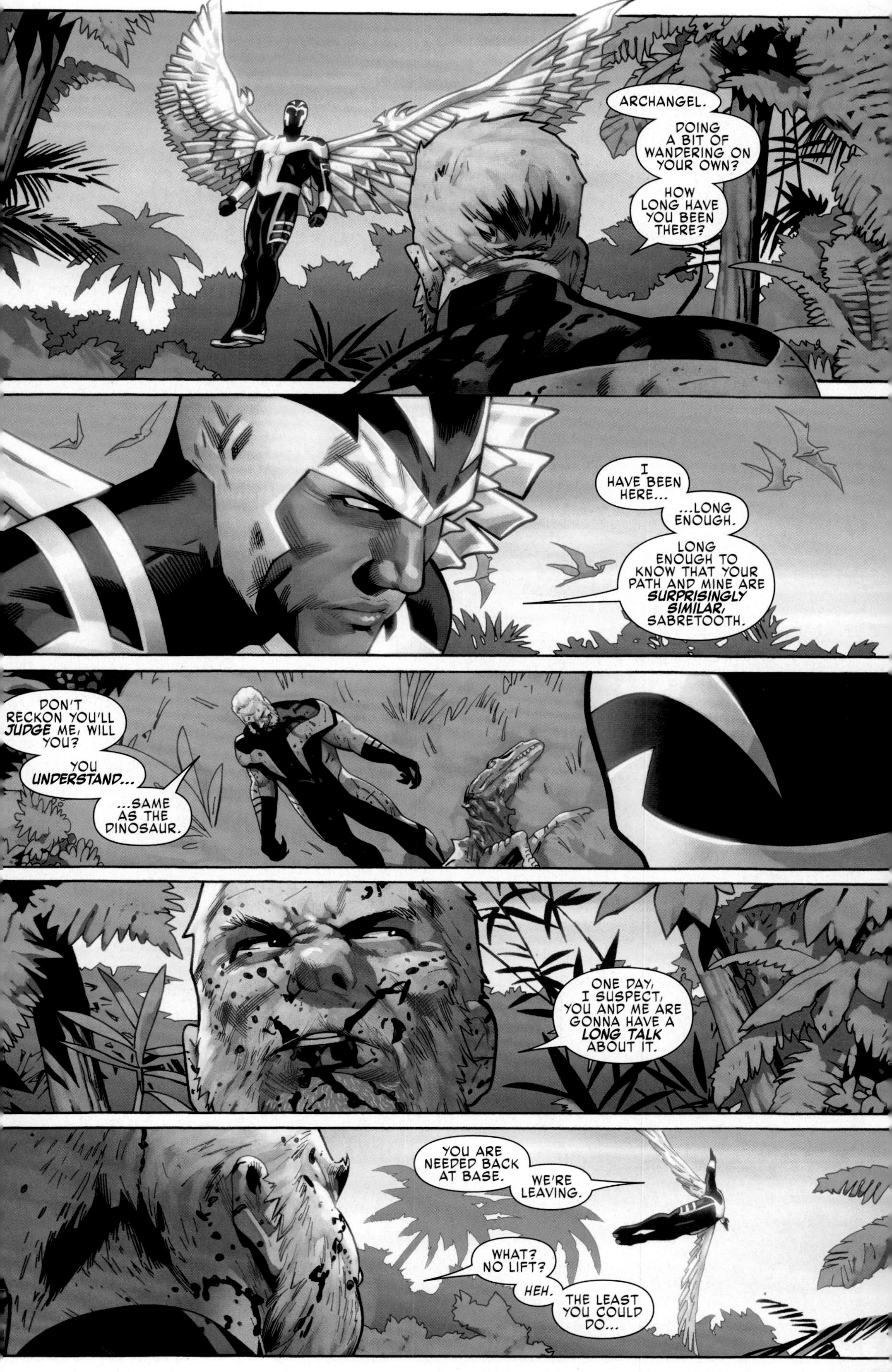
ARCHANGEL.
DOING A BIT OF WANDERING ON YOUR OWN?
HOW LONG HAVE YOU BEEN THERE?
I HAVE BEEN HERE...
...LONG ENOUGH.
LONG ENOUGH TO KNOW THAT YOUR PATH AND MINE ARE SURPRISINGLY SIMILAR, SABRETOOTH.
DON'T RECKON YOU'LL JUDGE ME, WILL YOU?
YOU UNDERSTAND...
...SAME AS THE DINOSAUR.
ONE DAY, I SUSPECT, YOU AND ME ARE GONNA HAVE A LONG TALK ABOUT IT.
YOU ARE NEEDED BACK AT BASE.
WE'RE LEAVING.
WHAT? NO LIFT?
HEH.
THE LEAST YOU COULD DO...

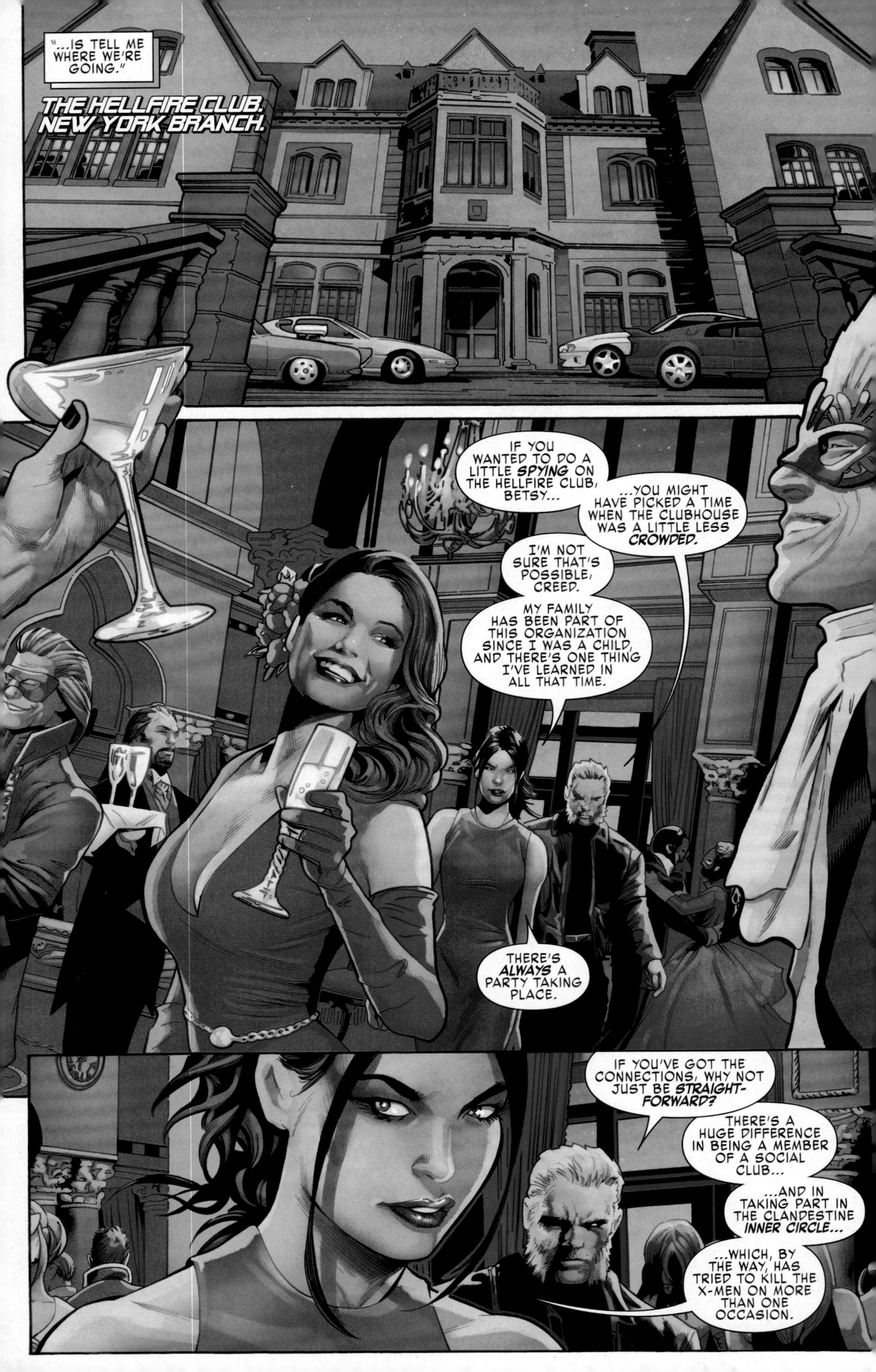

"...IS TELL ME WHERE WE'RE GOING."
THE HELLFIRE CLUB. NEW YORK BRANCH.
IF YOU WANTED TO DO A LITTLE SPYING ON THE HELLFIRE CLUB, BETSY...
...YOU MIGHT HAVE PICKED A TIME WHEN THE CLUBHOUSE WAS A LITTLE LESS CROWDED.
I'M NOT SURE THAT'S POSSIBLE, CREED.
MY FAMILY HAS BEEN PART OF THIS ORGANIZATION SINCE I WAS A CHILD, AND THERE'S ONE THING I'VE LEARNED IN ALL THAT TIME.
THERE'S ALWAYS A PARTY TAKING PLACE.
IF YOU'VE GOT THE CONNECTIONS, WHY NOT JUST BE STRAIGHT-FORWARD?
THERE'S A HUGE DIFFERENCE IN BEING A MEMBER OF A SOCIAL CLUB...
...AND IN TAKING PART IN THE CLANDESTINE INNER CIRCLE...
...WHICH, BY THE WAY, HAS TRIED TO KILL THE X-MEN ON MORE THAN ONE OCCASION.

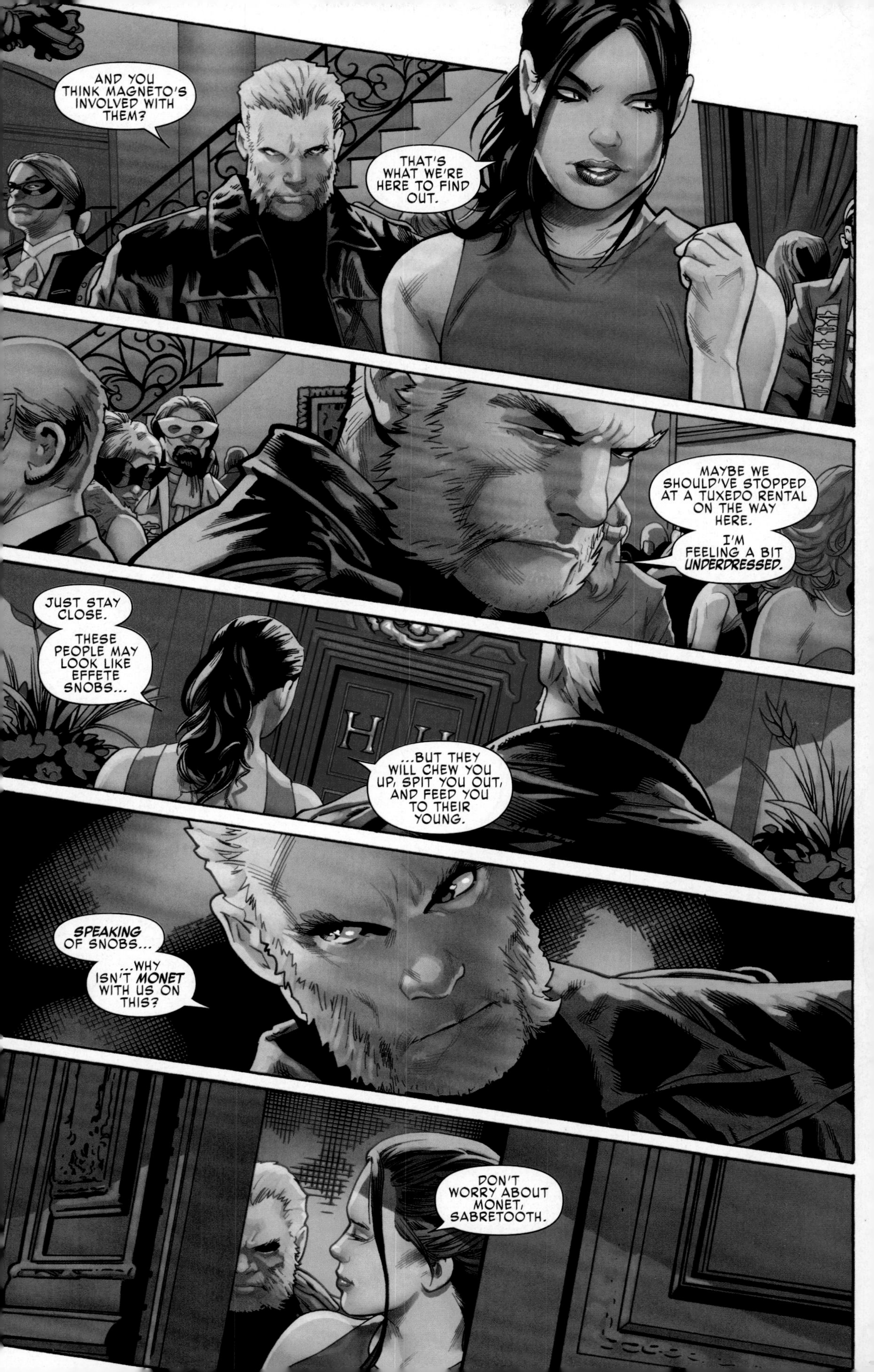
AND YOU THINK MAGNETO'S INVOLVED WITH THEM?
THAT'S WHAT WE'RE HERE TO FIND OUT.
MAYBE WE SHOULD'VE STOPPED AT A TUXEDO RENTAL ON THE WAY HERE.
I'M FEELING A BIT UNDERDRESSED.
JUST STAY CLOSE.
THESE PEOPLE MAY LOOK LIKE EFFETE SNOBS...
...BUT THEY WILL CHEW YOU UP, SPIT YOU OUT, AND FEED YOU TO THEIR YOUNG.
SPEAKING OF SNOBS...
...WHY ISN'T MONET WITH US ON THIS?
DON'T WORRY ABOUT MONET, SABRETOOTH.

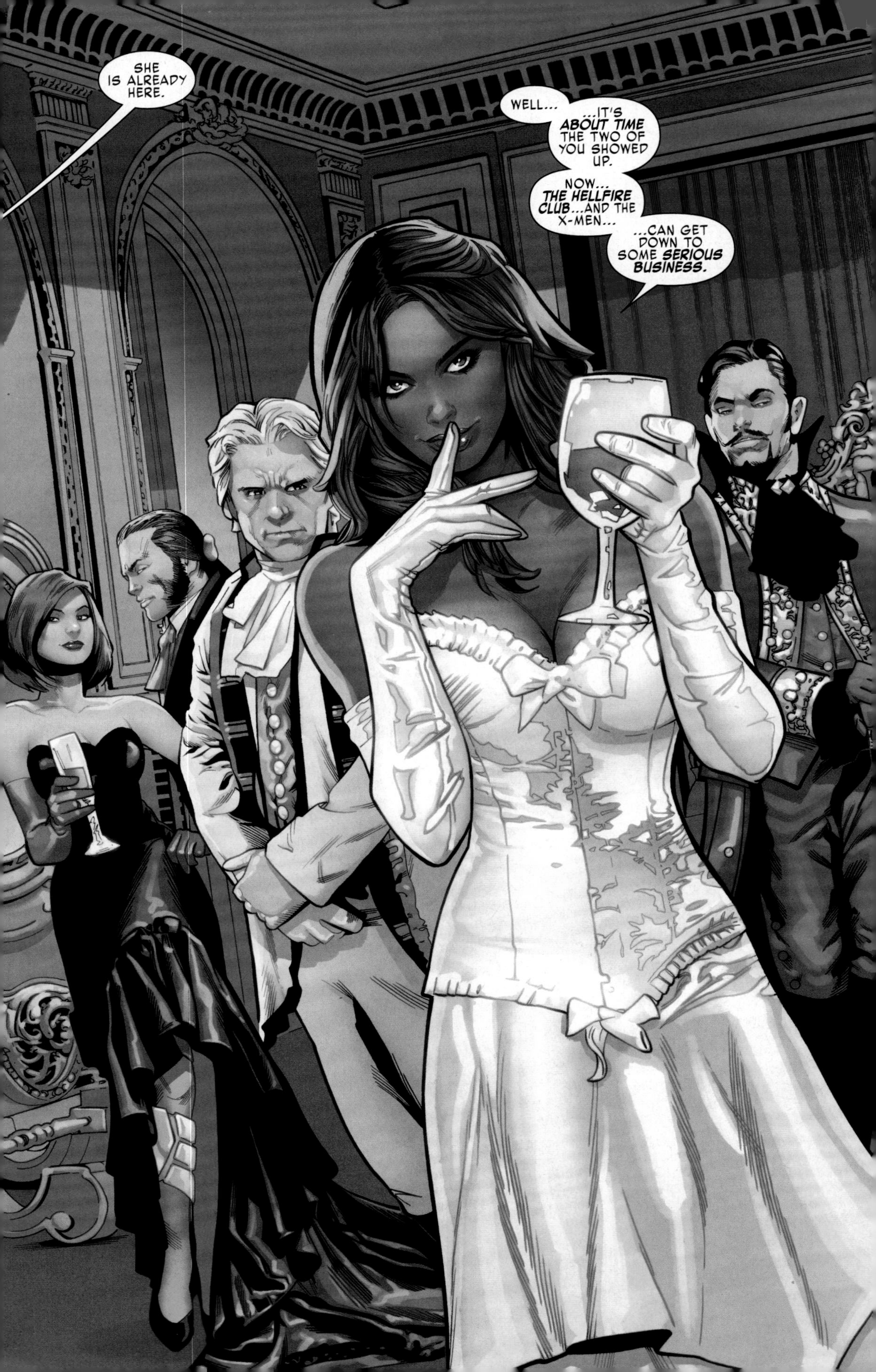
SHE IS ALREADY HERE.
WELL...
...IT'S ABOUT TIME THE TWO OF YOU SHOWED UP.
NOW... THE HELLFIRE CLUB...AND THE X-MEN...
...CAN GET DOWN TO SOME SERIOUS BUSINESS.

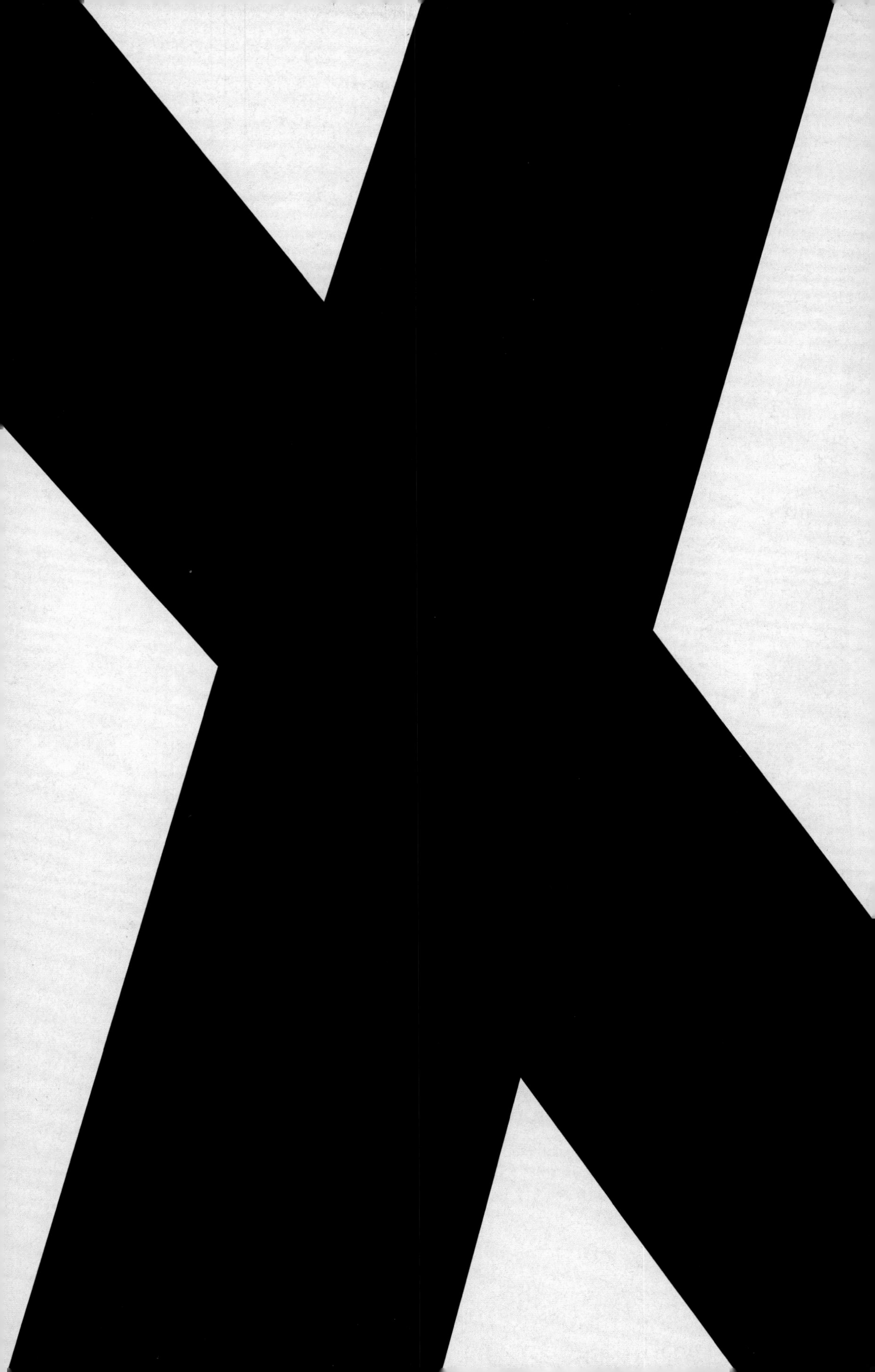

12

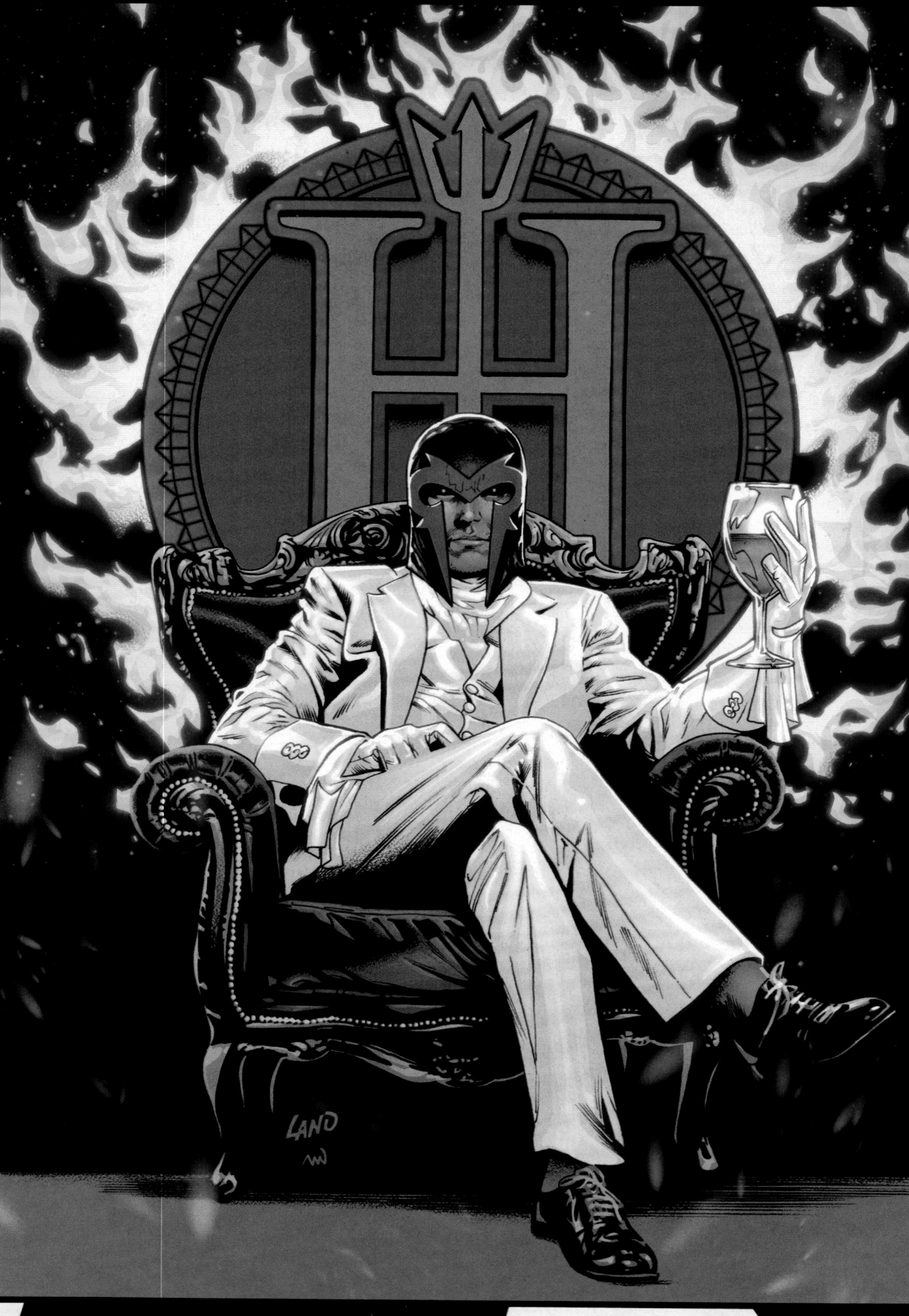
LAND

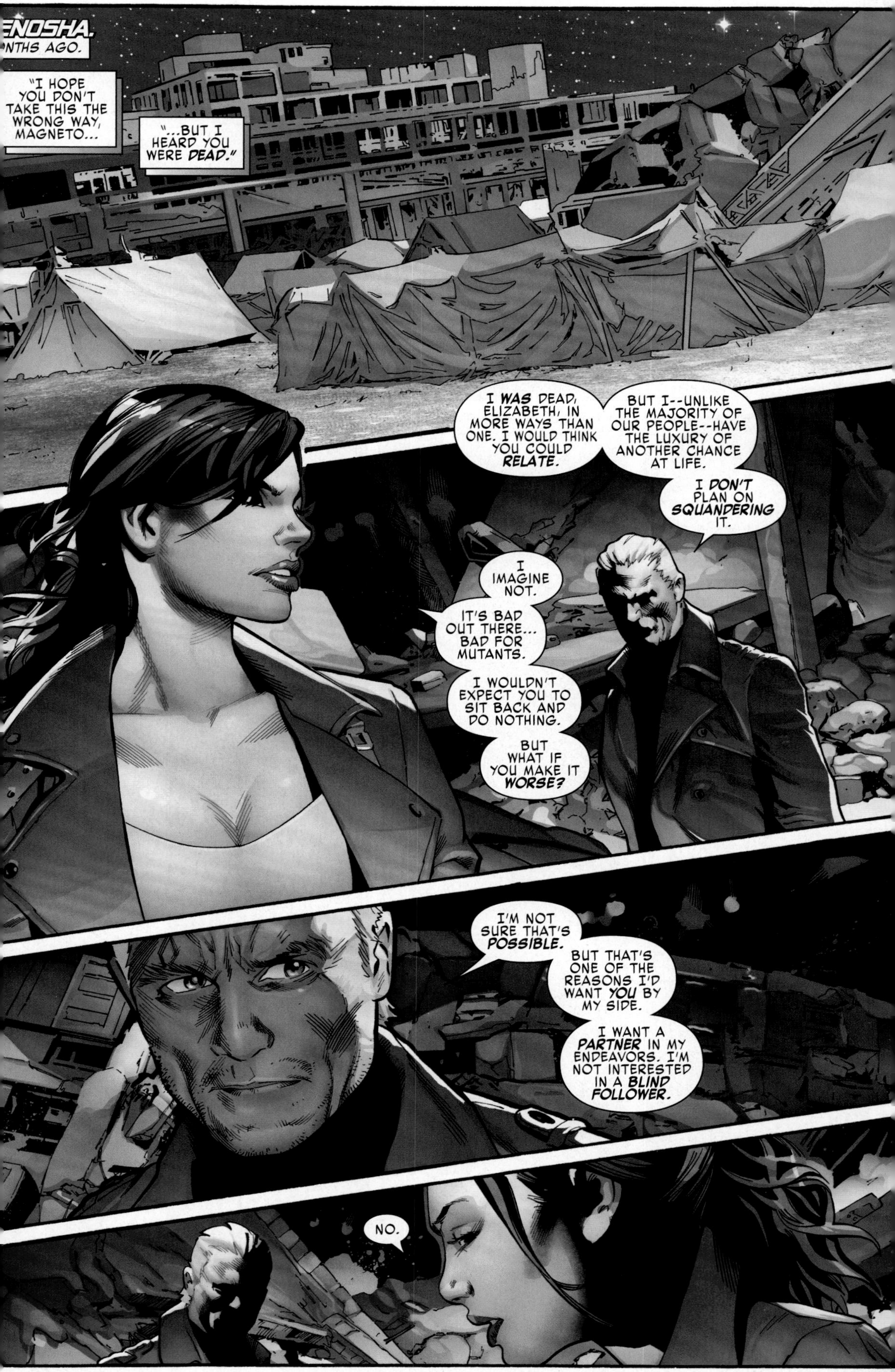

ENOSHA.
NTHS AGO.
"I HOPE YOU DON'T TAKE THIS THE WRONG WAY, MAGNETO...
"...BUT I HEARD YOU WERE DEAD."
I WAS DEAD, ELIZABETH, IN MORE WAYS THAN ONE. I WOULD THINK YOU COULD RELATE.
BUT I--UNLIKE THE MAJORITY OF OUR PEOPLE--HAVE THE LUXURY OF ANOTHER CHANCE AT LIFE.
I DON'T PLAN ON SQUANDERING IT.
I IMAGINE NOT.
IT'S BAD OUT THERE... BAD FOR MUTANTS.
I WOULDN'T EXPECT YOU TO SIT BACK AND DO NOTHING.
BUT WHAT IF YOU MAKE IT WORSE?
I'M NOT SURE THAT'S POSSIBLE.
BUT THAT'S ONE OF THE REASONS I'D WANT YOU BY MY SIDE.
I WANT A PARTNER IN MY ENDEAVORS. I'M NOT INTERESTED IN A BLIND FOLLOWER.
NO.

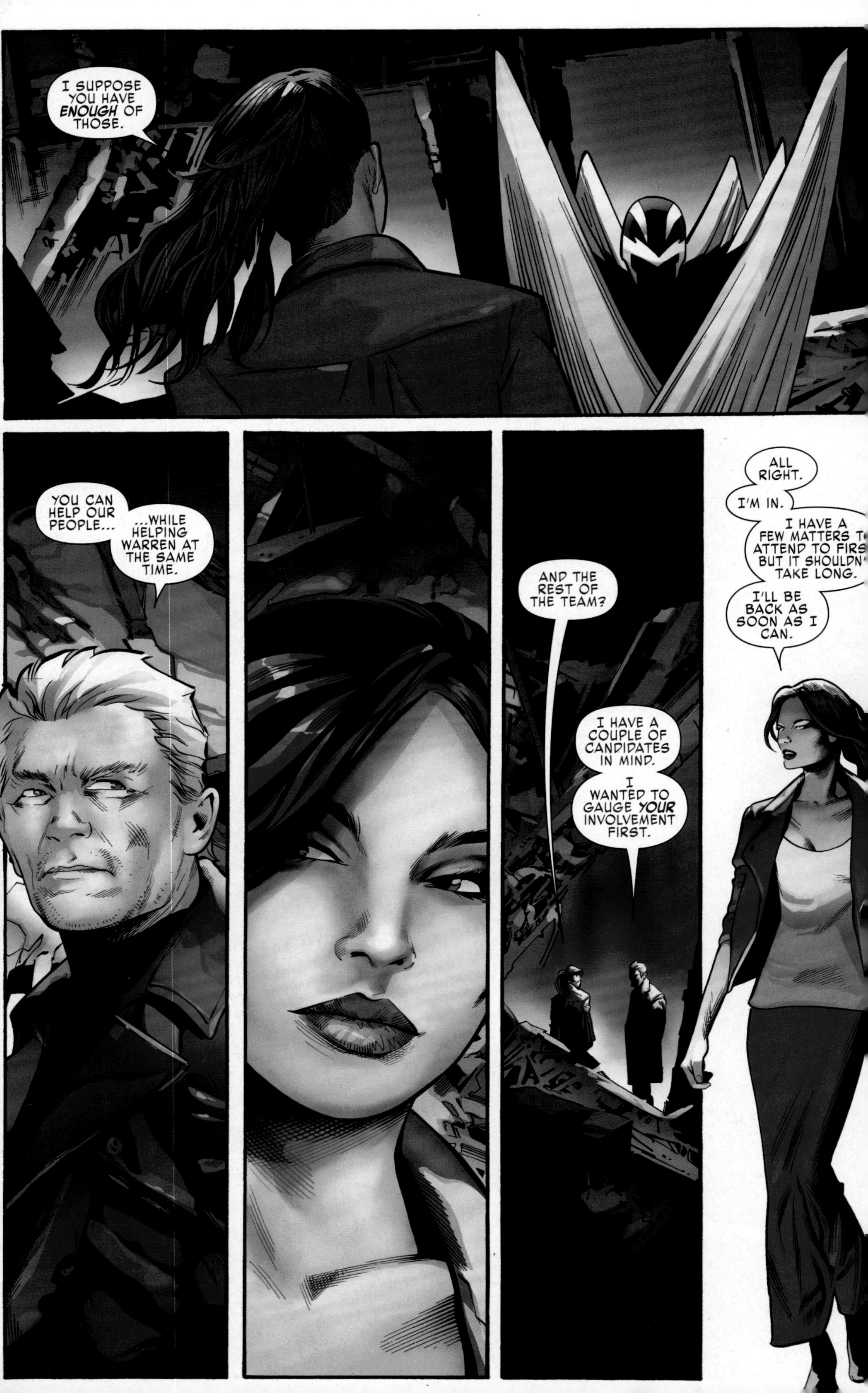

I SUPPOSE YOU HAVE ENOUGH OF THOSE.
YOU CAN HELP OUR PEOPLE...
...WHILE HELPING WARREN AT THE SAME TIME.
AND THE REST OF THE TEAM?
I HAVE A COUPLE OF CANDIDATES IN MIND.
I WANTED TO GAUGE YOUR INVOLVEMENT FIRST.
ALL RIGHT.
I'M IN.
I HAVE A FEW MATTERS TO ATTEND TO FIRS
BUT IT SHOULDN' TAKE LONG.
I'LL BE BACK AS SOON AS I CAN.

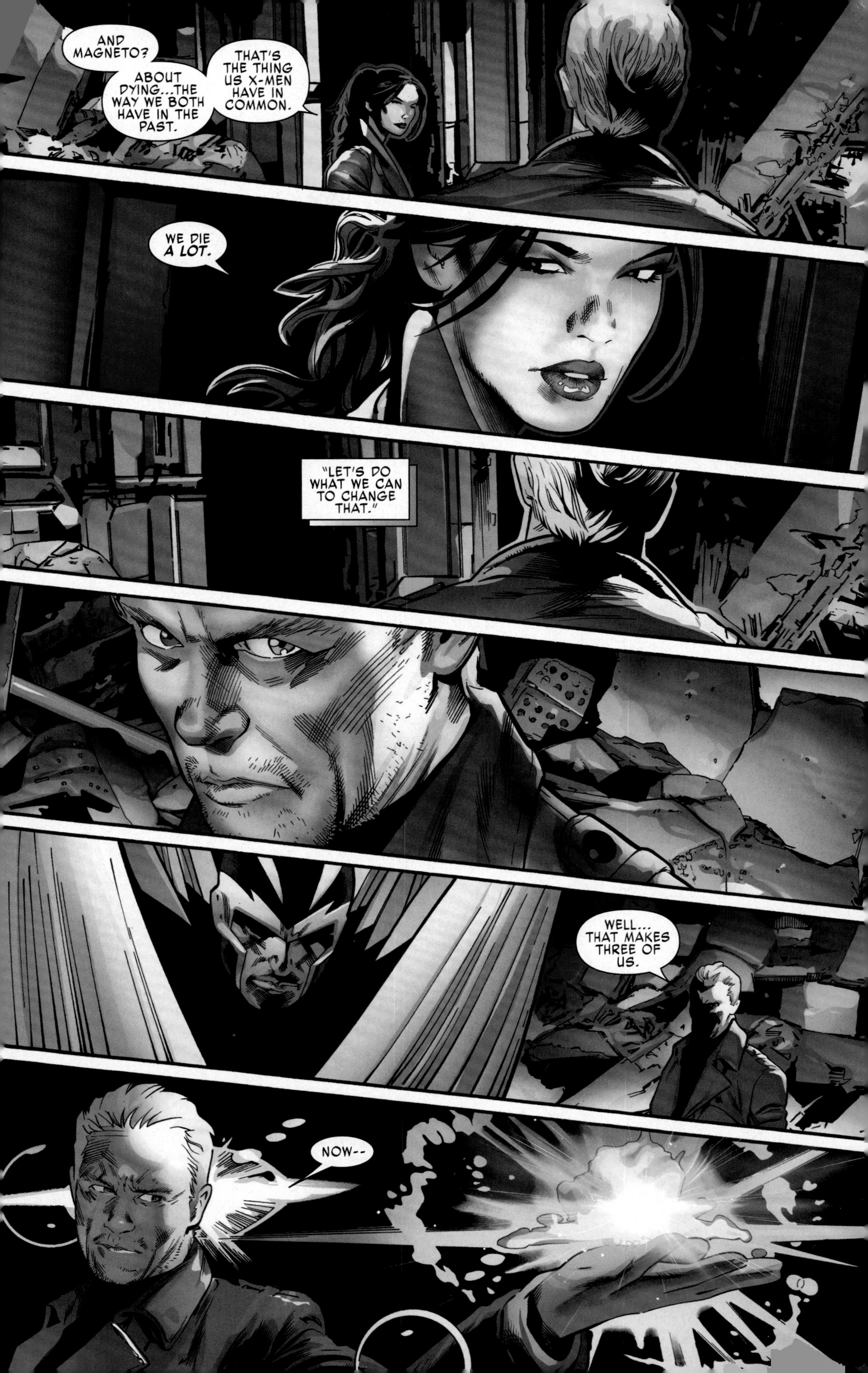
AND MAGNETO?
ABOUT DYING...THE WAY WE BOTH HAVE IN THE PAST.
THAT'S THE THING US X-MEN HAVE IN COMMON.
WE DIE A LOT.
"LET'S DO WHAT WE CAN TO CHANGE THAT."
WELL... THAT MAKES THREE OF US.
NOW--

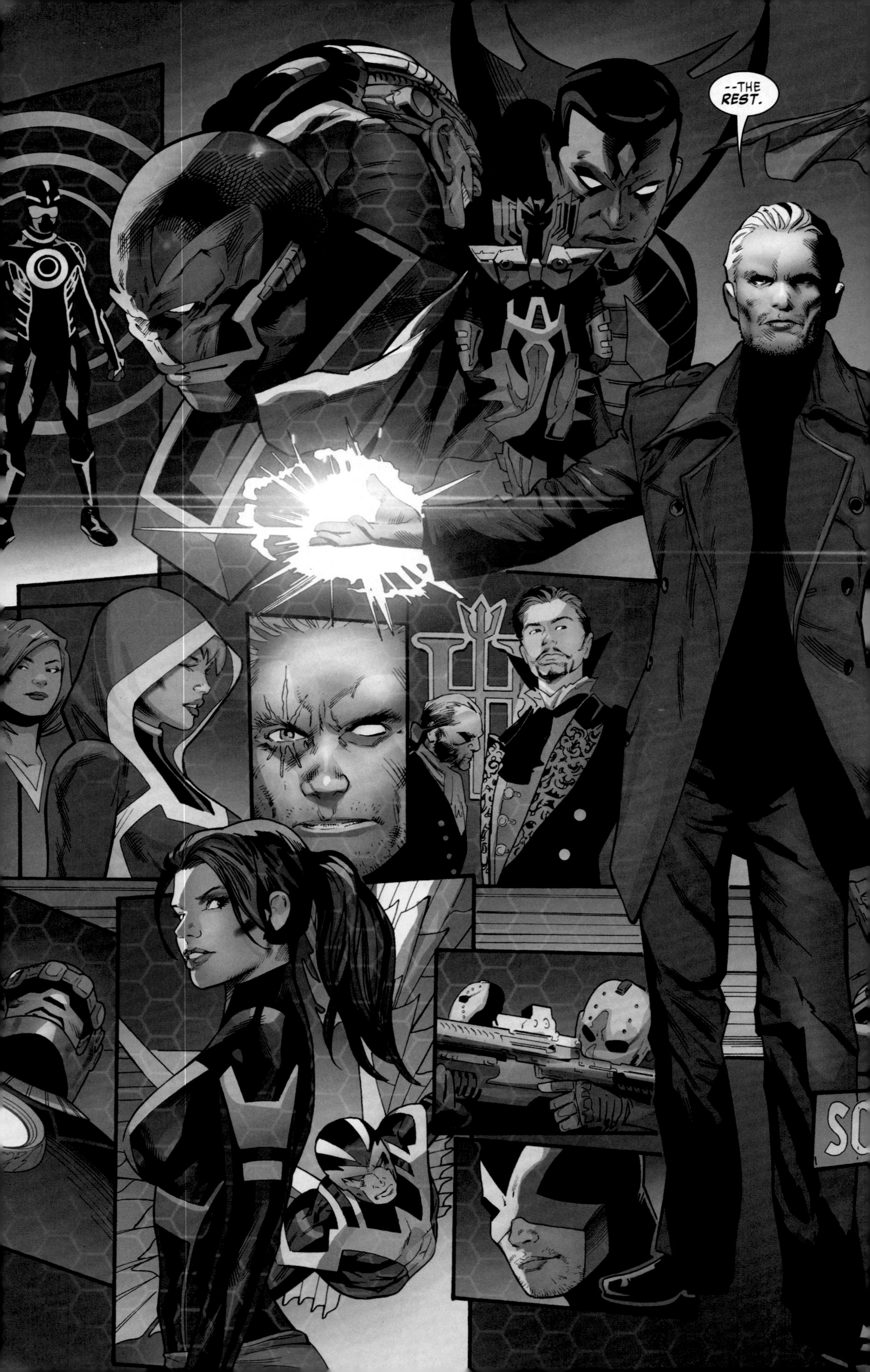
--THE REST.

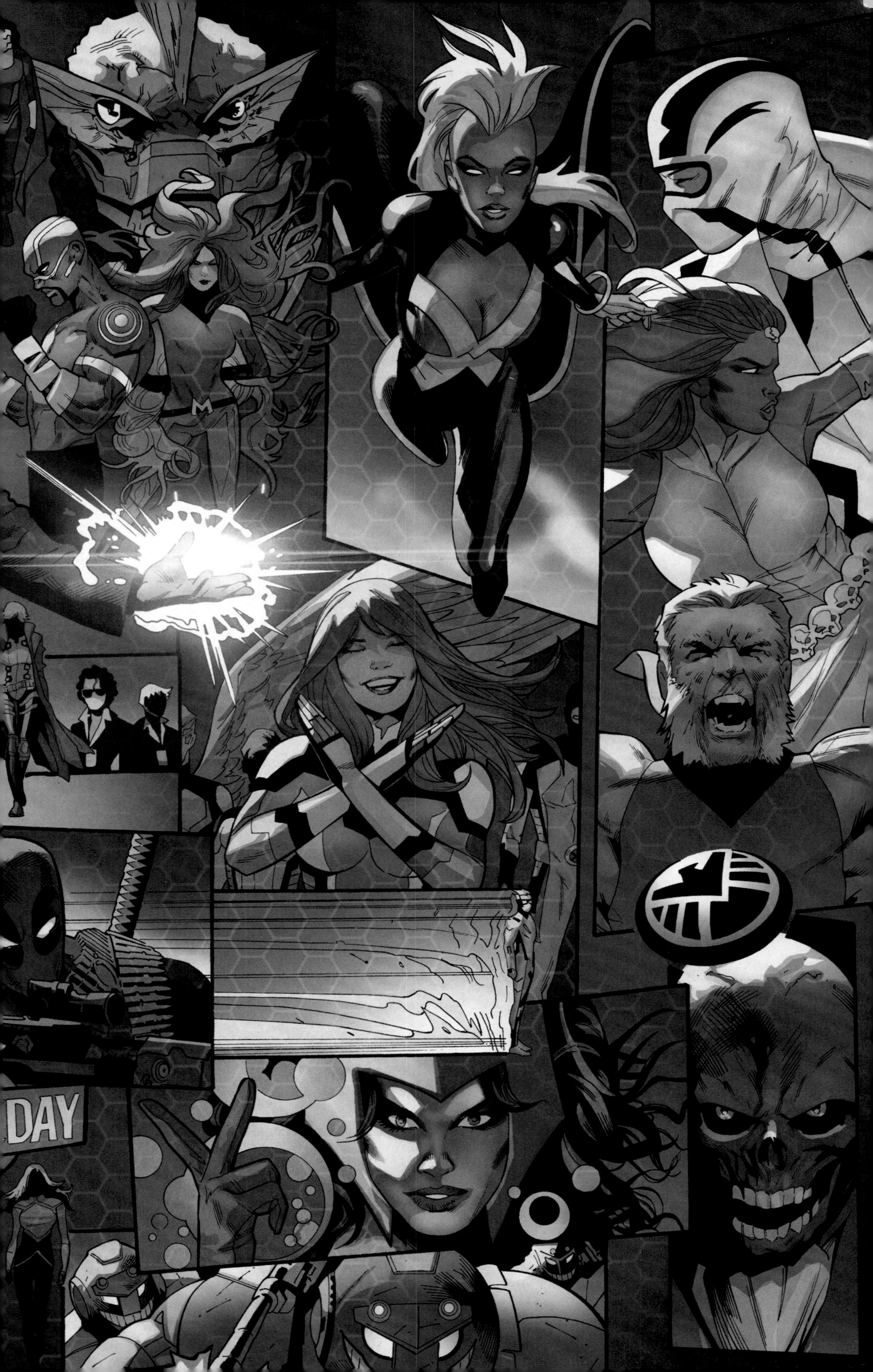
DAY

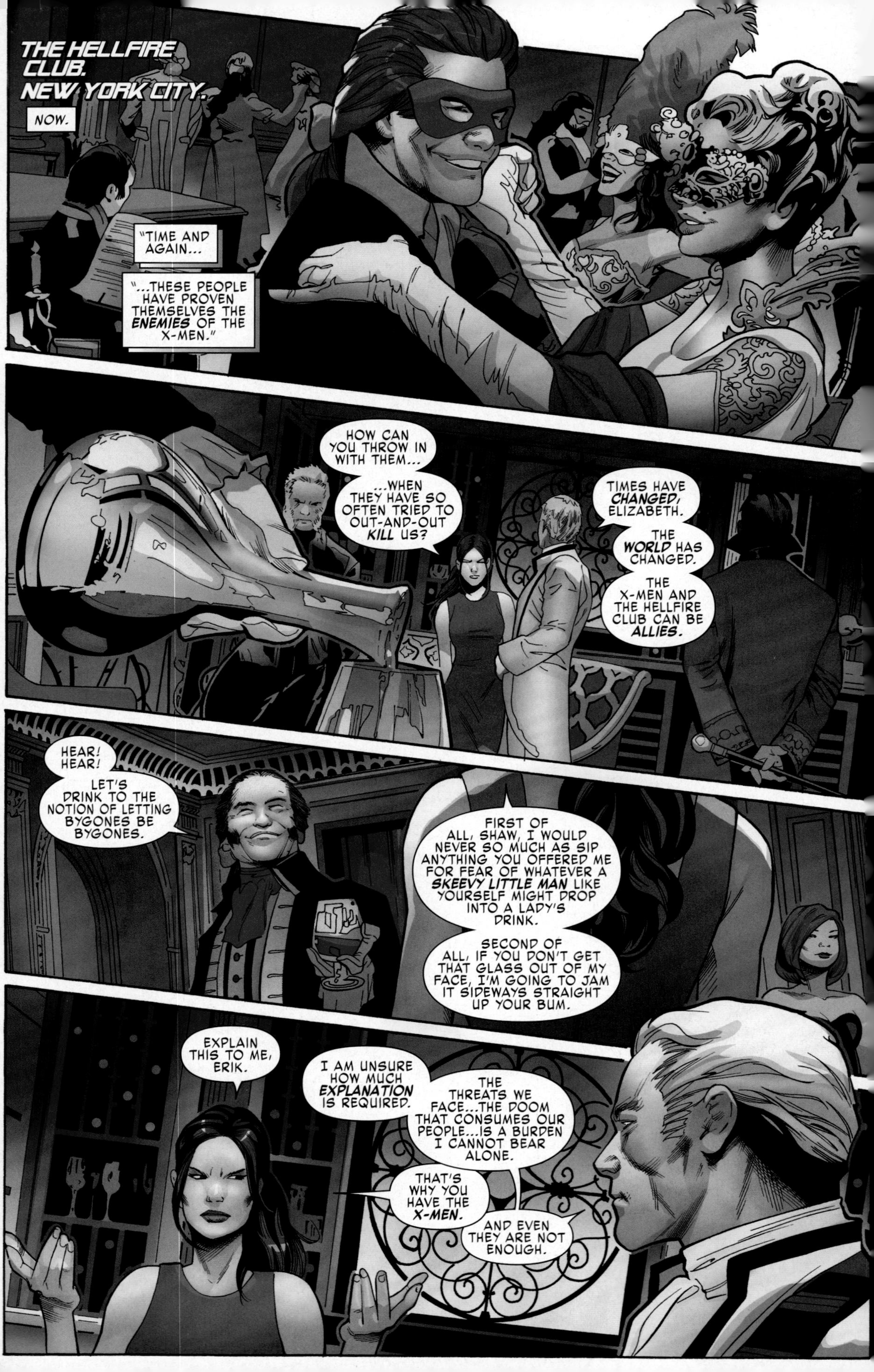
THE HELLFIRE CLUB. NEW YORK CITY.
NOW.
"TIME AND AGAIN...
"...THESE PEOPLE HAVE PROVEN THEMSELVES THE ENEMIES OF THE X-MEN."
HOW CAN YOU THROW IN WITH THEM...
...WHEN THEY HAVE SO OFTEN TRIED TO OUT-AND-OUT KILL US?
TIMES HAVE CHANGED, ELIZABETH.
THE WORLD HAS CHANGED.
THE X-MEN AND THE HELLFIRE CLUB CAN BE ALLIES.
HEAR! HEAR!
LET'S DRINK TO THE NOTION OF LETTING BYGONES BE BYGONES.
FIRST OF ALL, SHAW, I WOULD NEVER SO MUCH AS SIP ANYTHING YOU OFFERED ME FOR FEAR OF WHATEVER A SKEEVY LITTLE MAN LIKE YOURSELF MIGHT DROP INTO A LADY'S DRINK.
SECOND OF ALL, IF YOU DON'T GET THAT GLASS OUT OF MY FACE, I'M GOING TO JAM IT SIDEWAYS STRAIGHT UP YOUR BUM.
EXPLAIN THIS TO ME, ERIK.
I AM UNSURE HOW MUCH EXPLANATION IS REQUIRED.
THE THREATS WE FACE...THE DOOM THAT CONSUMES OUR PEOPLE...IS A BURDEN I CANNOT BEAR ALONE.
THAT'S WHY YOU HAVE THE X-MEN.
AND EVEN THEY ARE NOT ENOUGH.

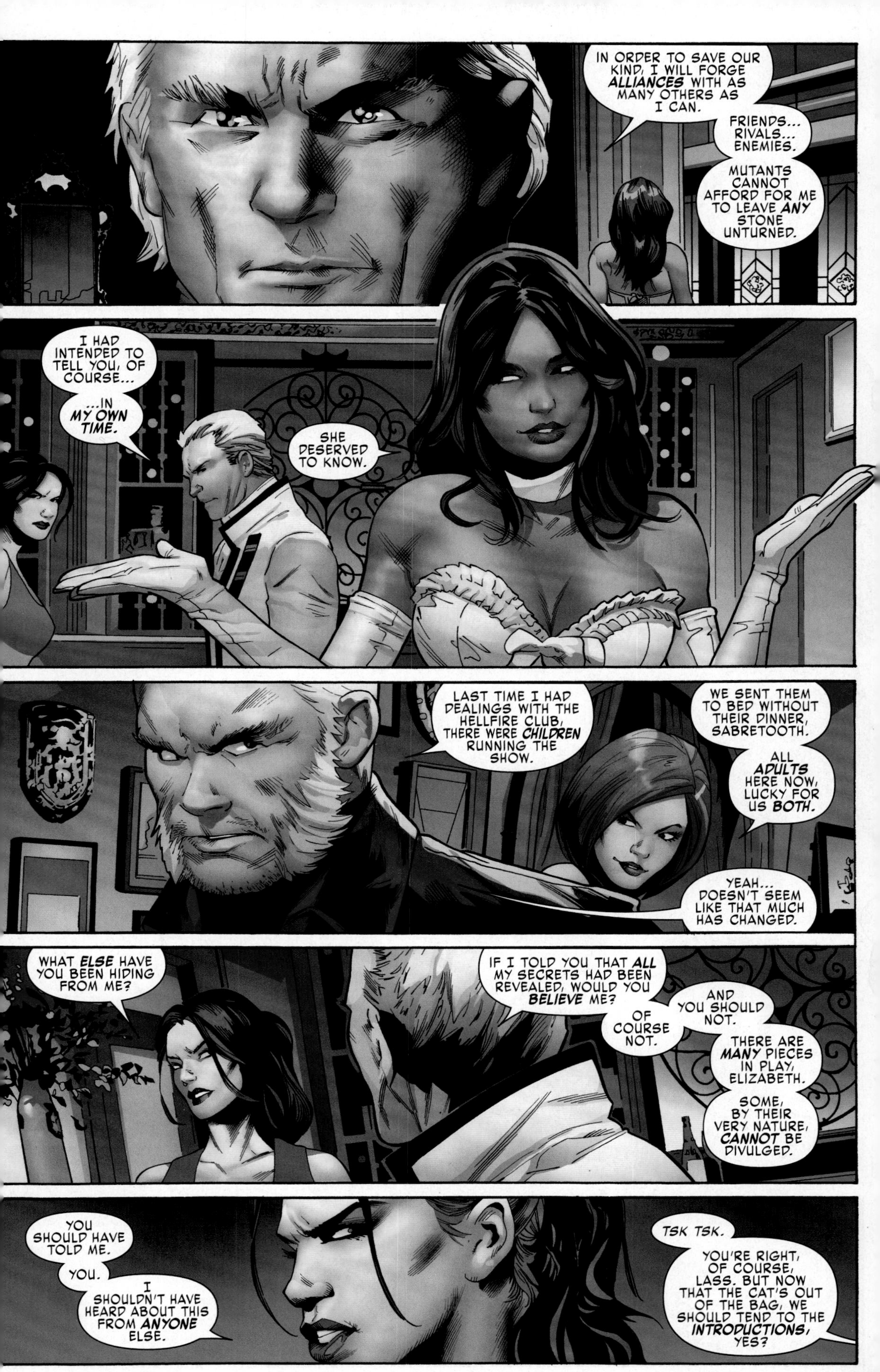
IN ORDER TO SAVE OUR KIND, I WILL FORGE ALLIANCES WITH AS MANY OTHERS AS I CAN.
FRIENDS... RIVALS... ENEMIES.
MUTANTS CANNOT AFFORD FOR ME TO LEAVE ANY STONE UNTURNED.
I HAD INTENDED TO TELL YOU, OF COURSE...
...IN MY OWN TIME.
SHE DESERVED TO KNOW.
LAST TIME I HAD DEALINGS WITH THE HELLFIRE CLUB, THERE WERE CHILDREN RUNNING THE SHOW.
WE SENT THEM TO BED WITHOUT THEIR DINNER, SABRETOOTH.
ALL ADULTS HERE NOW, LUCKY FOR US BOTH.
YEAH... DOESN'T SEEM LIKE THAT MUCH HAS CHANGED.
WHAT ELSE HAVE YOU BEEN HIDING FROM ME?
IF I TOLD YOU THAT ALL MY SECRETS HAD BEEN REVEALED, WOULD YOU BELIEVE ME?
OF COURSE NOT.
AND YOU SHOULD NOT.
THERE ARE MANY PIECES IN PLAY, ELIZABETH.
SOME, BY THEIR VERY NATURE, CANNOT BE DIVULGED.
YOU SHOULD HAVE TOLD ME.
YOU.
I SHOULDN'T HAVE HEARD ABOUT THIS FROM ANYONE ELSE.
TSK TSK.
YOU'RE RIGHT, OF COURSE, LASS. BUT NOW THAT THE CAT'S OUT OF THE BAG, WE SHOULD TEND TO THE INTRODUCTIONS, YES?

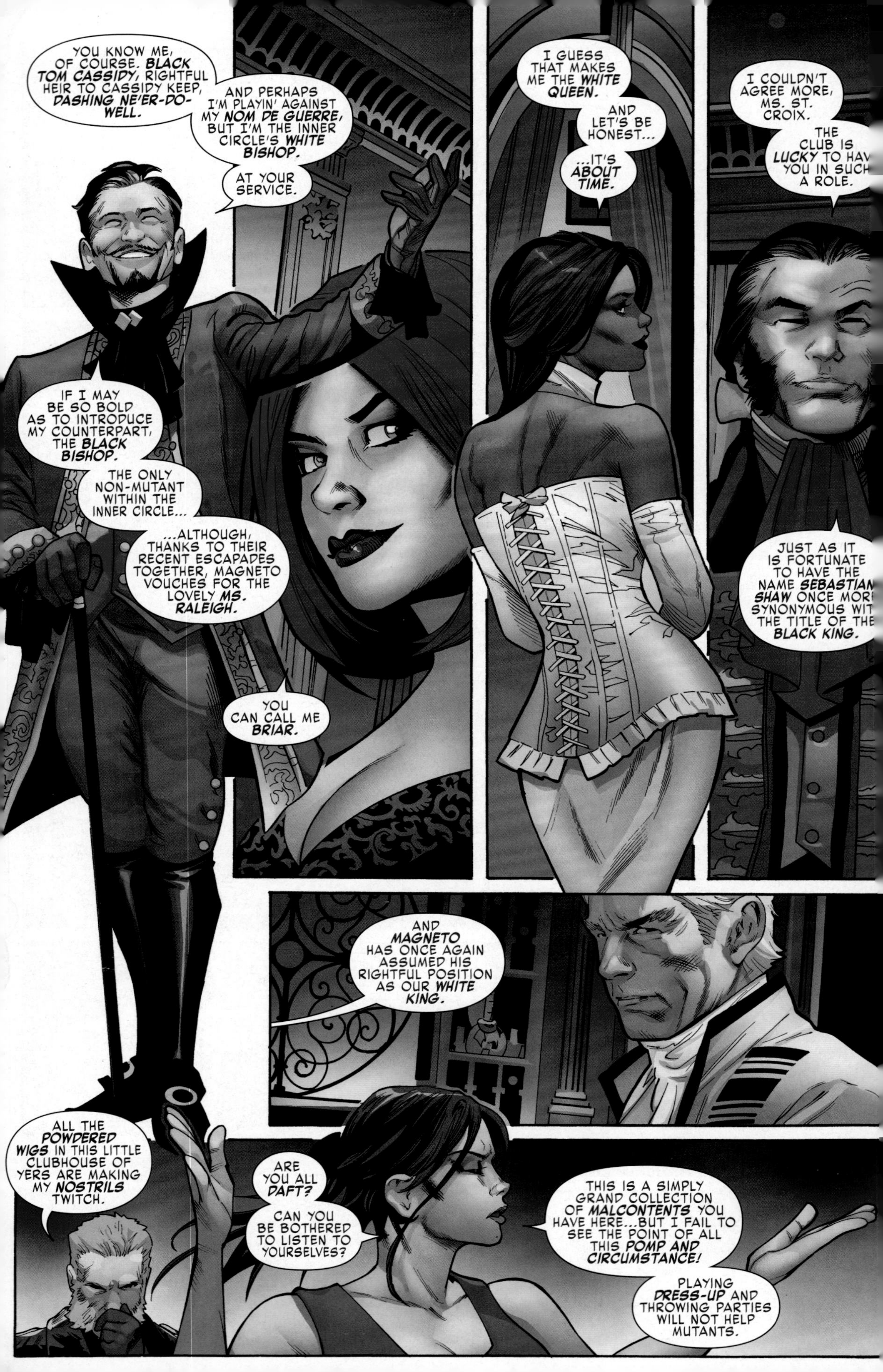

YOU KNOW ME, OF COURSE. BLACK TOM CASSIDY, RIGHTFUL HEIR TO CASSIDY KEEP, DASHING NE'ER-DO-WELL.
AND PERHAPS I'M PLAYIN' AGAINST MY NOM DE GUERRE, BUT I'M THE INNER CIRCLE'S WHITE BISHOP.
AT YOUR SERVICE.
IF I MAY BE SO BOLD AS TO INTRODUCE MY COUNTERPART, THE BLACK BISHOP.
THE ONLY NON-MUTANT WITHIN THE INNER CIRCLE...
...ALTHOUGH, THANKS TO THEIR RECENT ESCAPADES TOGETHER, MAGNETO VOUCHES FOR THE LOVELY MS. RALEIGH.
YOU CAN CALL ME BRIAR.
I GUESS THAT MAKES ME THE WHITE QUEEN.
AND LET'S BE HONEST...
...IT'S ABOUT TIME.
I COULDN'T AGREE MORE, MS. ST. CROIX.
THE CLUB IS LUCKY TO HAV YOU IN SUCH A ROLE.
JUST AS IT IS FORTUNATE TO HAVE THE NAME SEBASTIAN SHAW ONCE MORE SYNONYMOUS WIT THE TITLE OF THE BLACK KING.
AND MAGNETO HAS ONCE AGAIN ASSUMED HIS RIGHTFUL POSITION AS OUR WHITE KING.
ALL THE POWDERED WIGS IN THIS LITTLE CLUBHOUSE OF YERS ARE MAKING MY NOSTRILS TWITCH.
ARE YOU ALL DAFT?
CAN YOU BE BOTHERED TO LISTEN TO YOURSELVES?
THIS IS A SIMPLY GRAND COLLECTION OF MALCONTENTS YOU HAVE HERE...BUT I FAIL TO SEE THE POINT OF ALL THIS POMP AND CIRCUMSTANCE!
PLAYING DRESS-UP AND THROWING PARTIES WILL NOT HELP MUTANTS.

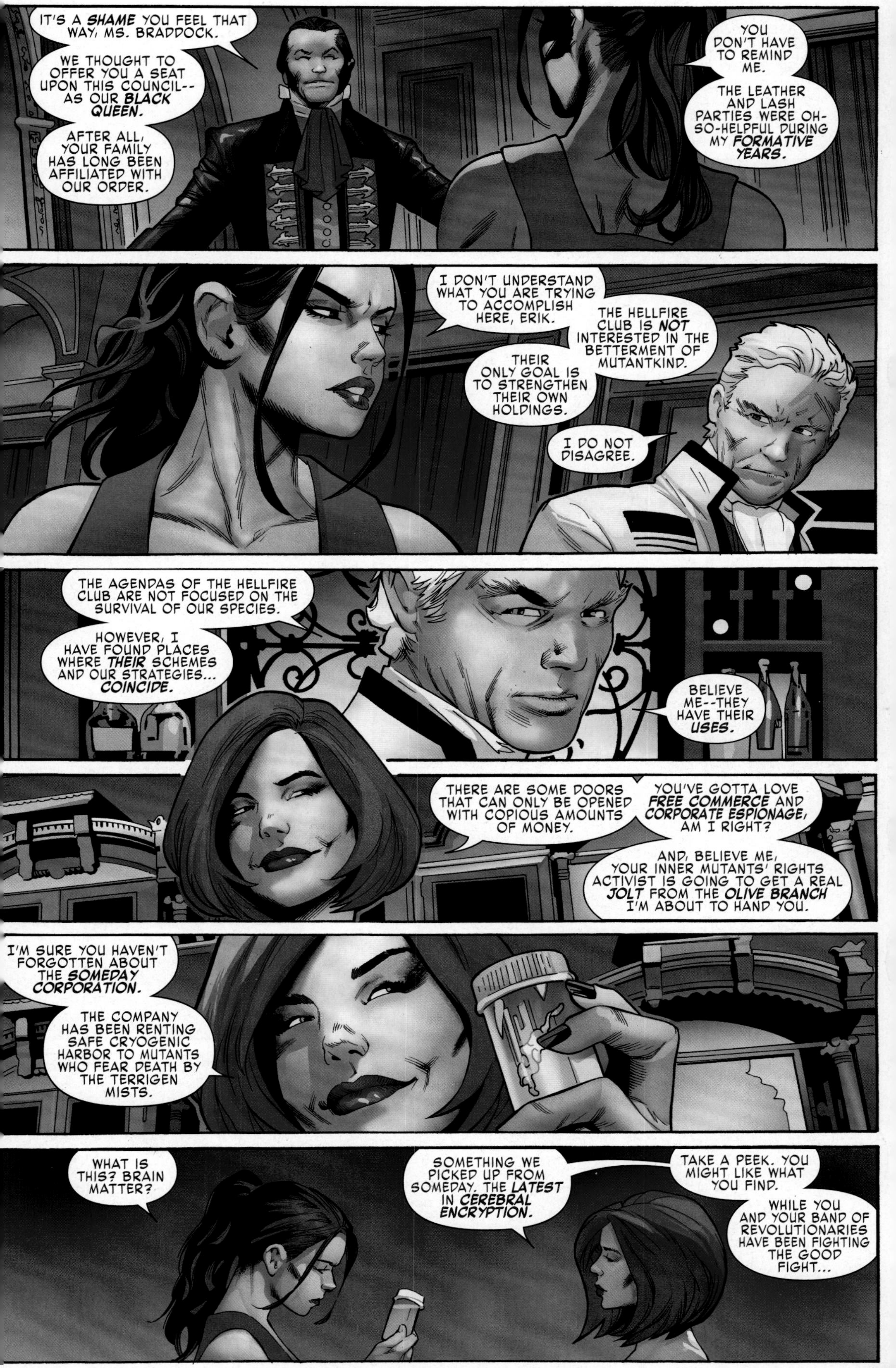
IT'S A SHAME YOU FEEL THAT WAY, MS. BRADDOCK.
WE THOUGHT TO OFFER YOU A SEAT UPON THIS COUNCIL-- AS OUR BLACK QUEEN.
AFTER ALL, YOUR FAMILY HAS LONG BEEN AFFILIATED WITH OUR ORDER.
YOU DON'T HAVE TO REMIND ME.
THE LEATHER AND LASH PARTIES WERE OH-SO-HELPFUL DURING MY FORMATIVE YEARS.
I DON'T UNDERSTAND WHAT YOU ARE TRYING TO ACCOMPLISH HERE, ERIK.
THE HELLFIRE CLUB IS NOT INTERESTED IN THE BETTERMENT OF MUTANTKIND.
THEIR ONLY GOAL IS TO STRENGTHEN THEIR OWN HOLDINGS.
I DO NOT DISAGREE.
THE AGENDAS OF THE HELLFIRE CLUB ARE NOT FOCUSED ON THE SURVIVAL OF OUR SPECIES.
HOWEVER, I HAVE FOUND PLACES WHERE THEIR SCHEMES AND OUR STRATEGIES... COINCIDE.
BELIEVE ME--THEY HAVE THEIR USES.
THERE ARE SOME DOORS THAT CAN ONLY BE OPENED WITH COPIOUS AMOUNTS OF MONEY.
YOU'VE GOTTA LOVE FREE COMMERCE AND CORPORATE ESPIONAGE, AM I RIGHT?
AND, BELIEVE ME, YOUR INNER MUTANTS' RIGHTS ACTIVIST IS GOING TO GET A REAL JOLT FROM THE OLIVE BRANCH I'M ABOUT TO HAND YOU.
I'M SURE YOU HAVEN'T FORGOTTEN ABOUT THE SOMEDAY CORPORATION.
THE COMPANY HAS BEEN RENTING SAFE CRYOGENIC HARBOR TO MUTANTS WHO FEAR DEATH BY THE TERRIGEN MISTS.
WHAT IS THIS? BRAIN MATTER?
SOMETHING WE PICKED UP FROM SOMEDAY. THE LATEST IN CEREBRAL ENCRYPTION.
TAKE A PEEK. YOU MIGHT LIKE WHAT YOU FIND.
WHILE YOU AND YOUR BAND OF REVOLUTIONARIES HAVE BEEN FIGHTING THE GOOD FIGHT...

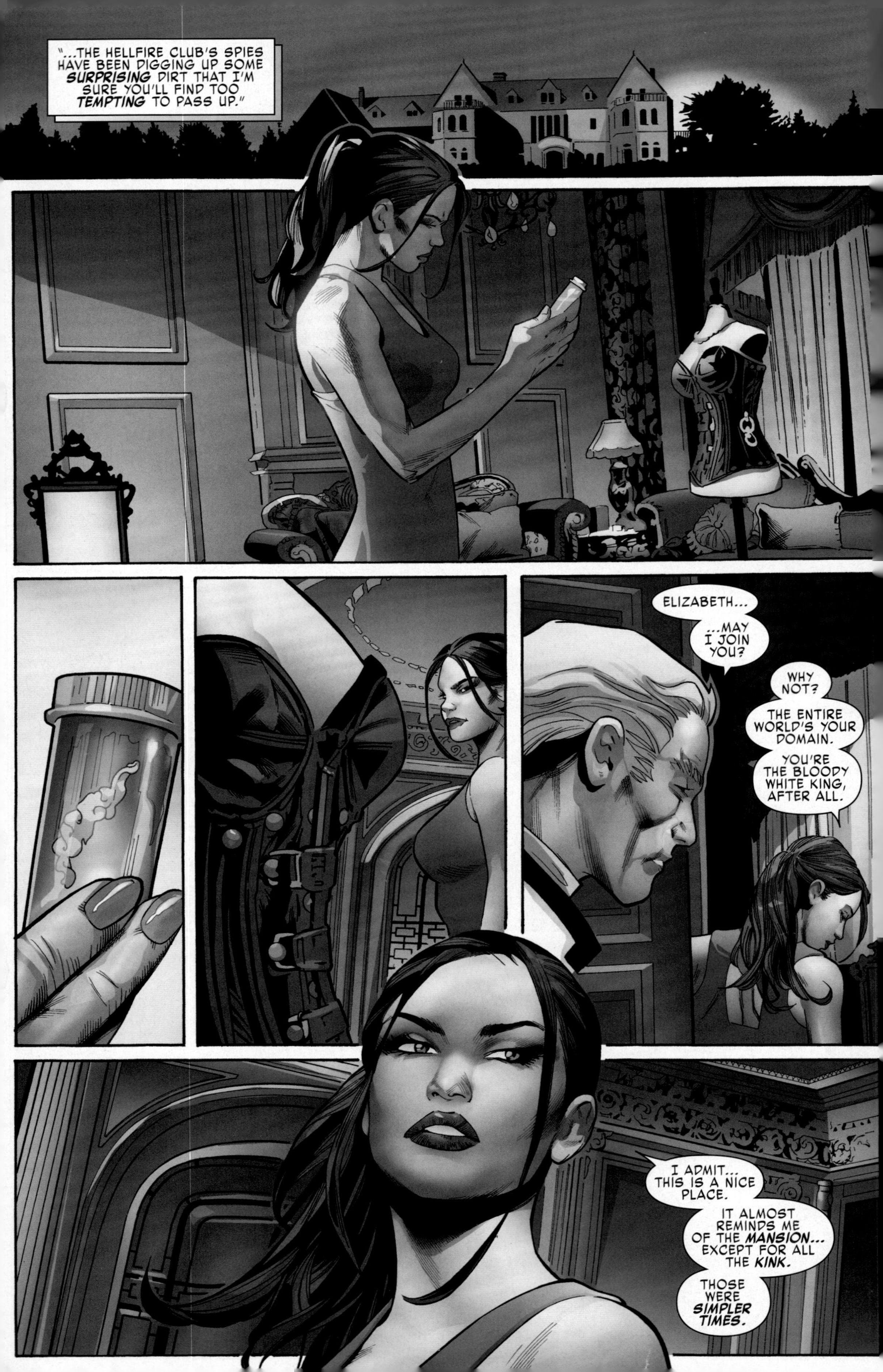
"...THE HELLFIRE CLUB'S SPIES HAVE BEEN DIGGING UP SOME SURPRISING DIRT THAT I'M SURE YOU'LL FIND TOO TEMPTING TO PASS UP."
ELIZABETH...
...MAY I JOIN YOU?
WHY NOT?
THE ENTIRE WORLD'S YOUR DOMAIN.
YOU'RE THE BLOODY WHITE KING, AFTER ALL.
I ADMIT... THIS IS A NICE PLACE.
IT ALMOST REMINDS ME OF THE MANSION... EXCEPT FOR ALL THE KINK.
THOSE WERE SIMPLER TIMES.

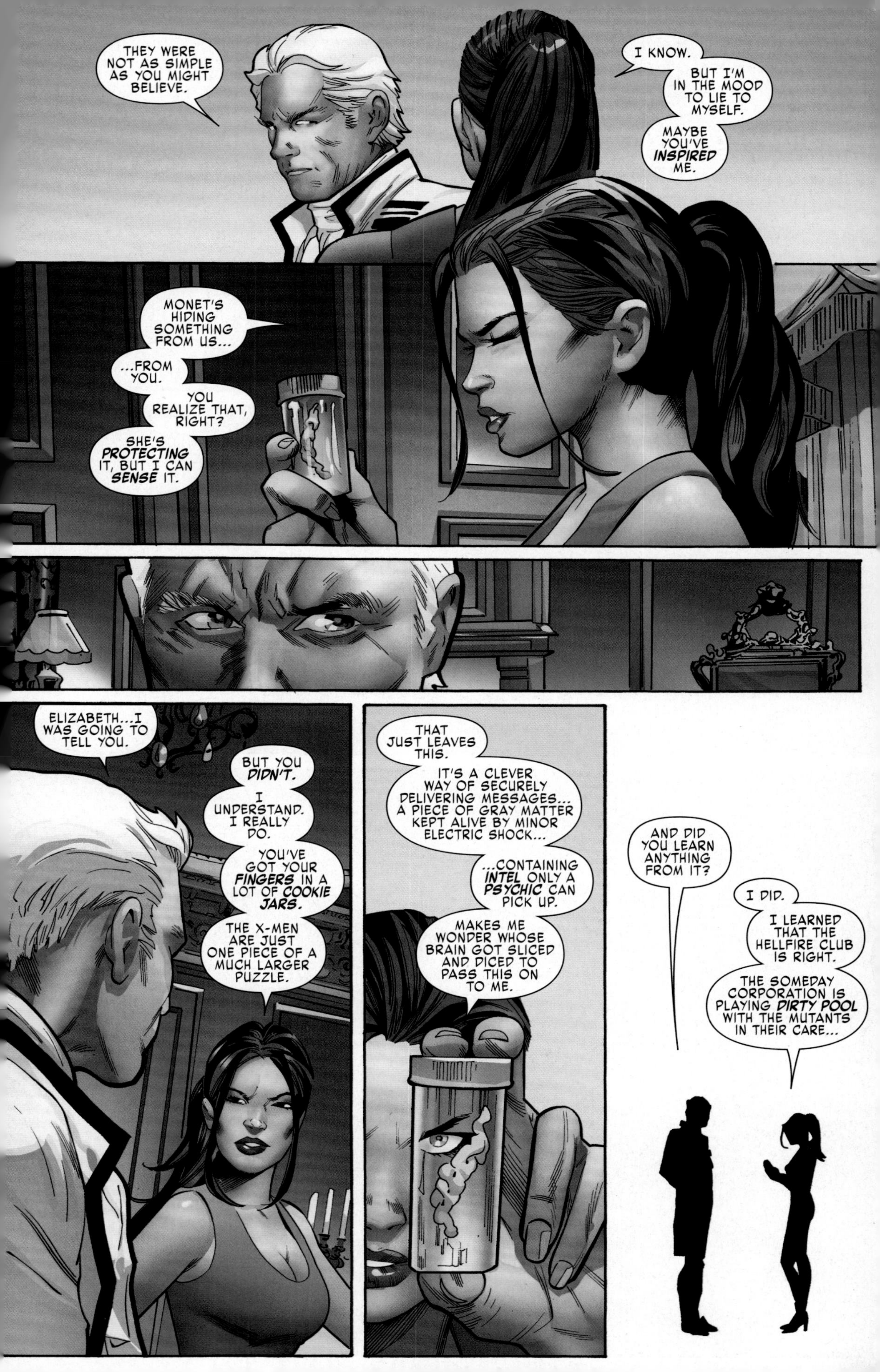
THEY WERE NOT AS SIMPLE AS YOU MIGHT BELIEVE.
I KNOW.
BUT I'M IN THE MOOD TO LIE TO MYSELF.
MAYBE YOU'VE INSPIRED ME.
MONET'S HIDING SOMETHING FROM US...
...FROM YOU.
YOU REALIZE THAT, RIGHT?
SHE'S PROTECTING IT, BUT I CAN SENSE IT.
ELIZABETH...I WAS GOING TO TELL YOU.
BUT YOU DIDN'T.
I UNDERSTAND. I REALLY DO.
YOU'VE GOT YOUR FINGERS IN A LOT OF COOKIE JARS.
THE X-MEN ARE JUST ONE PIECE OF A MUCH LARGER PUZZLE.
THAT JUST LEAVES THIS.
IT'S A CLEVER WAY OF SECURELY DELIVERING MESSAGES... A PIECE OF GRAY MATTER KEPT ALIVE BY MINOR ELECTRIC SHOCK...
...CONTAINING INTEL ONLY A PSYCHIC CAN PICK UP.
MAKES ME WONDER WHOSE BRAIN GOT SLICED AND DICED TO PASS THIS ON TO ME.
AND DID YOU LEARN ANYTHING FROM IT?
I DID.
I LEARNED THAT THE HELLFIRE CLUB IS RIGHT.
THE SOMEDAY CORPORATION IS PLAYING DIRTY POOL WITH THE MUTANTS IN THEIR CARE...

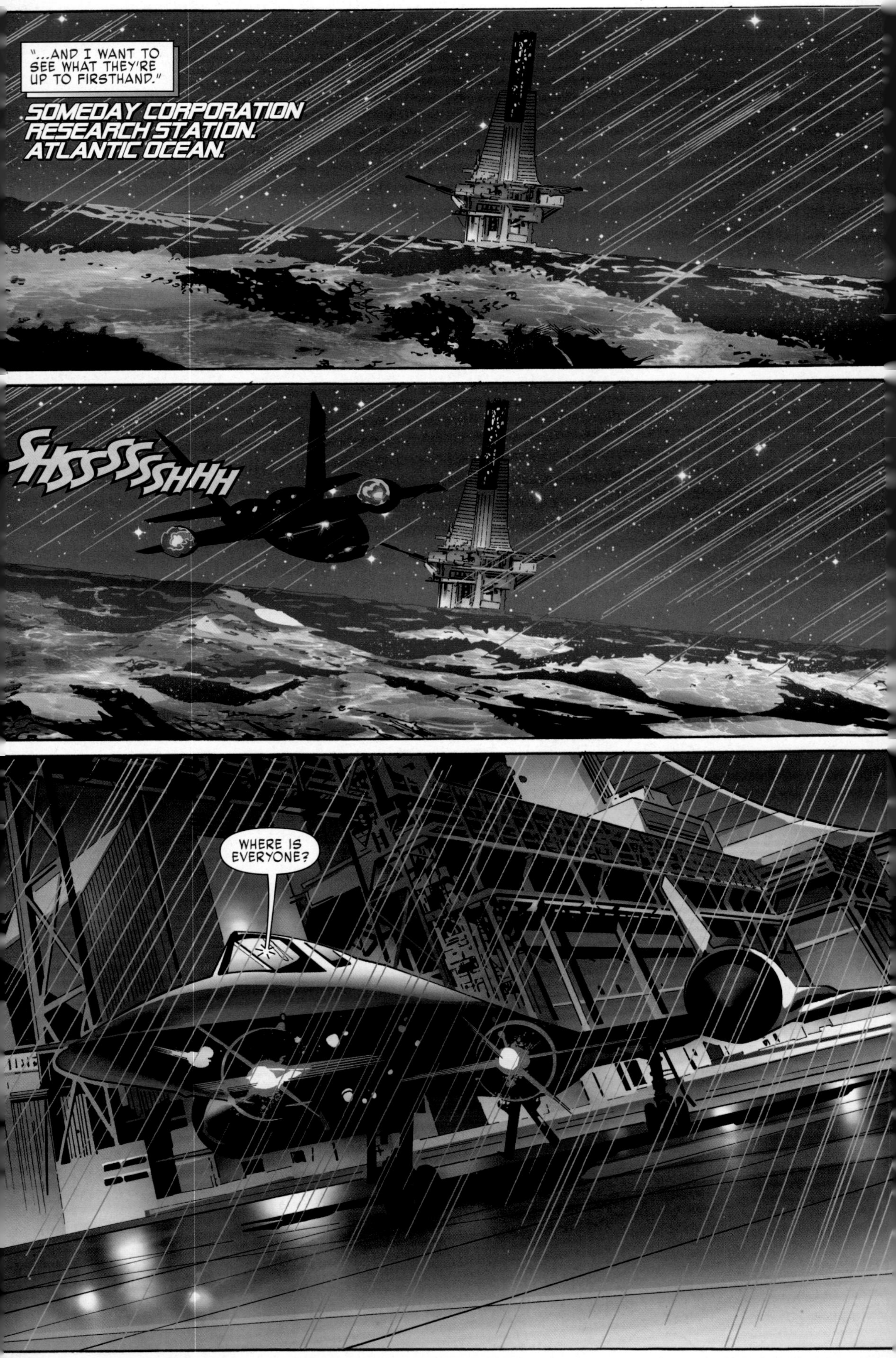
"...AND I WANT TO SEE WHAT THEY'RE UP TO FIRSTHAND."
SOMEDAY CORPORATION RESEARCH STATION. ATLANTIC OCEAN.
SHSSSSSSHHH
WHERE IS EVERYONE?

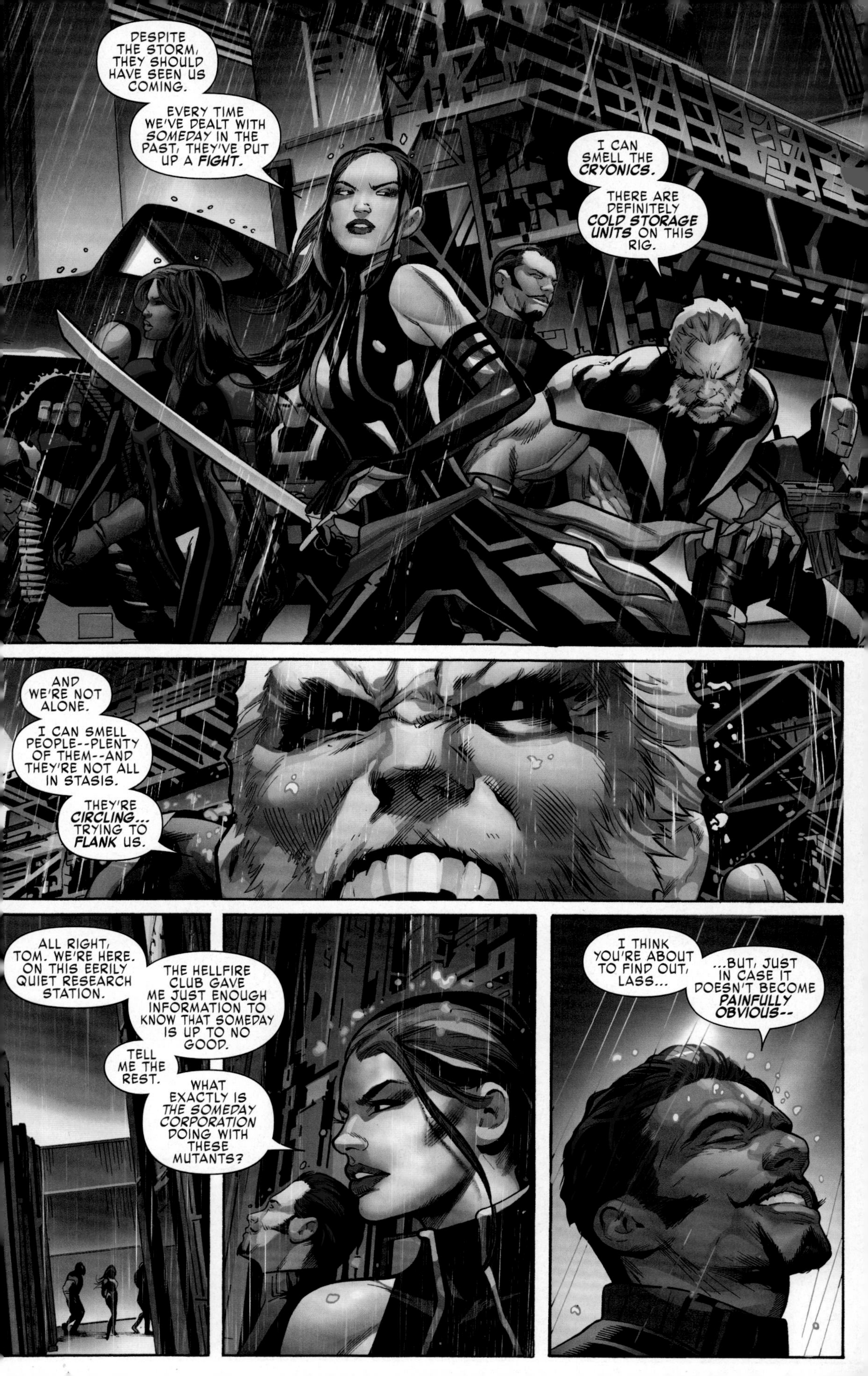
DESPITE THE STORM, THEY SHOULD HAVE SEEN US COMING.
EVERY TIME WE'VE DEALT WITH SOMEDAY IN THE PAST, THEY'VE PUT UP A FIGHT.
I CAN SMELL THE CRYONICS.
THERE ARE DEFINITELY COLD STORAGE UNITS ON THIS RIG.
AND WE'RE NOT ALONE.
I CAN SMELL PEOPLE--PLENTY OF THEM--AND THEY'RE NOT ALL IN STASIS.
THEY'RE CIRCLING... TRYING TO FLANK US.
ALL RIGHT, TOM. WE'RE HERE. ON THIS EERILY QUIET RESEARCH STATION.
THE HELLFIRE CLUB GAVE ME JUST ENOUGH INFORMATION TO KNOW THAT SOMEDAY IS UP TO NO GOOD.
TELL ME THE REST.
WHAT EXACTLY IS THE SOMEDAY CORPORATION DOING WITH THESE MUTANTS?
I THINK YOU'RE ABOUT TO FIND OUT, LASS...
...BUT, JUST IN CASE IT DOESN'T BECOME PAINFULLY OBVIOUS--

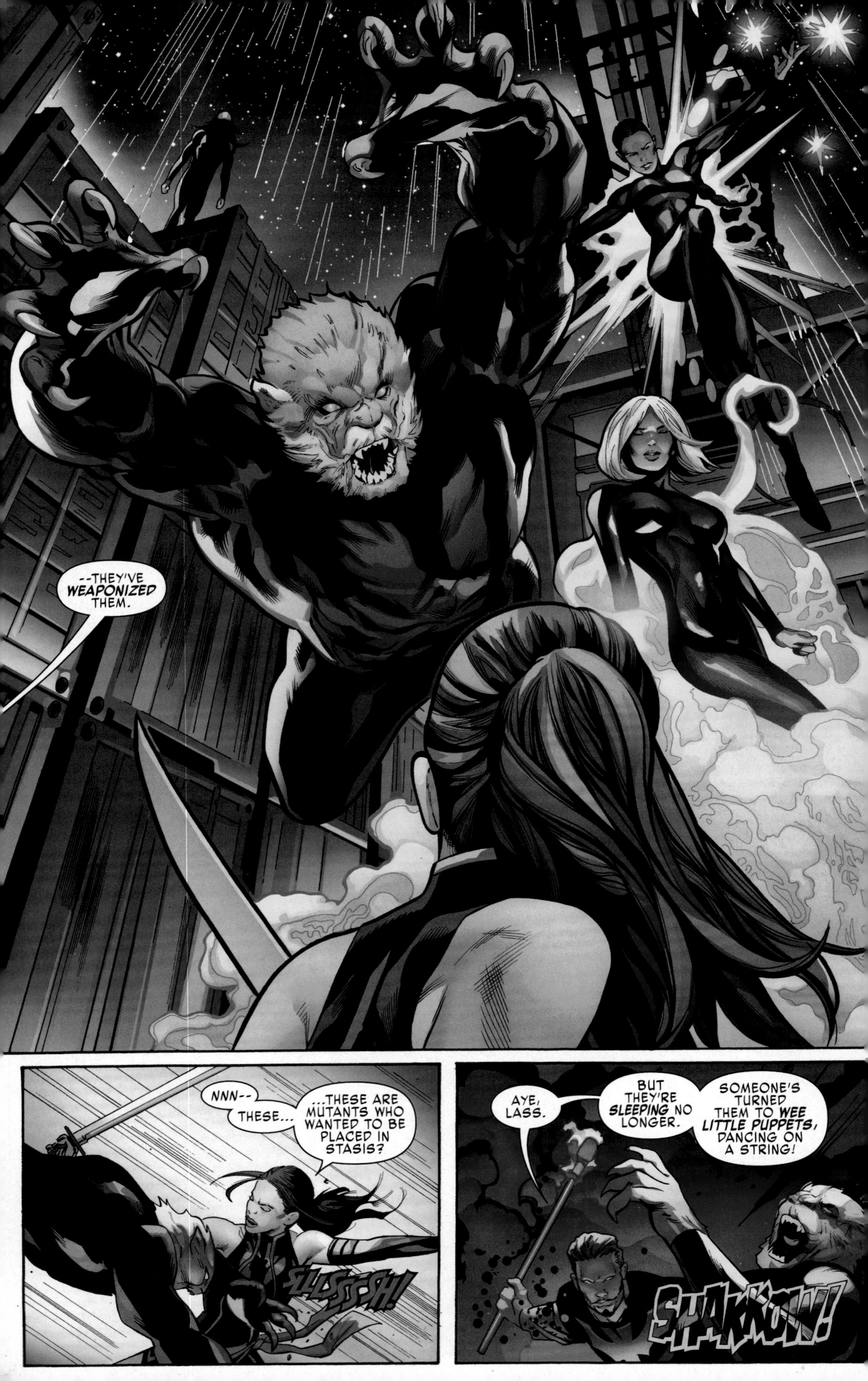
--THEY'VE WEAPONIZED THEM.
NNN--
THESE...
...THESE ARE MUTANTS WHO WANTED TO BE PLACED IN STASIS?
SHLLSSSH!
AYE, LASS.
BUT THEY'RE SLEEPING NO LONGER.
SOMEONE'S TURNED THEM TO WEE LITTLE PUPPETS, DANCING ON A STRING!

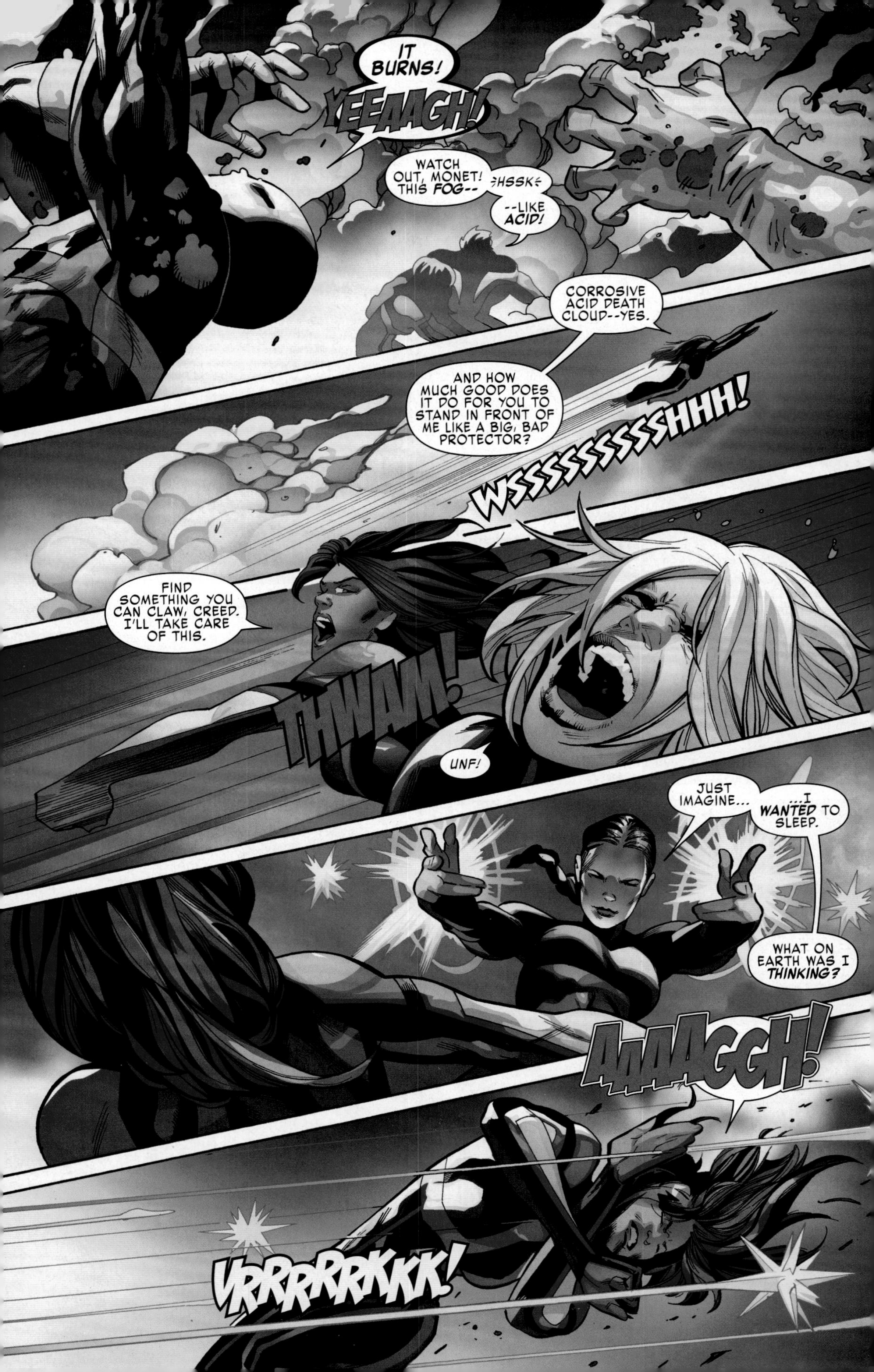
IT BURNS!
YEEAAGH!
WATCH OUT, MONET! THIS FOG--
HSSK
--LIKE ACID!
CORROSIVE ACID DEATH CLOUD--YES.
AND HOW MUCH GOOD DOES IT DO FOR YOU TO STAND IN FRONT OF ME LIKE A BIG, BAD PROTECTOR?
WSSSSSSSSSHHH!
FIND SOMETHING YOU CAN CLAW, CREED. I'LL TAKE CARE OF THIS.
THWAM!
UNF!
JUST IMAGINE...
...I WANTED TO SLEEP.
WHAT ON EARTH WAS I THINKING?
AAAAGGH!
VRRRRRKKK!

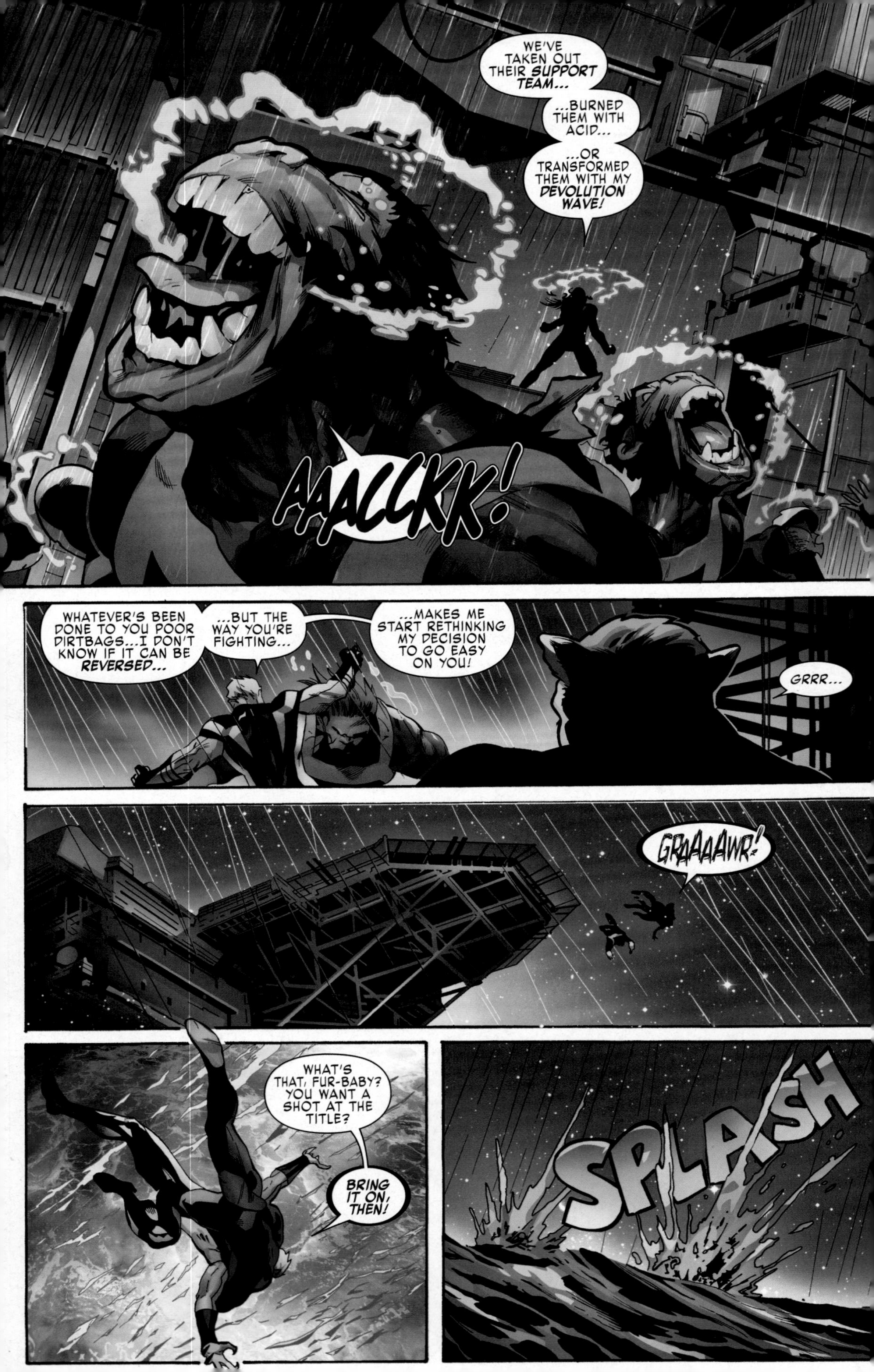

WE'VE TAKEN OUT THEIR SUPPORT TEAM...
...BURNED THEM WITH ACID...
...OR TRANSFORMED THEM WITH MY DEVOLUTION WAVE!
AAACCKK!
WHATEVER'S BEEN DONE TO YOU POOR DIRTBAGS...I DON'T KNOW IF IT CAN BE REVERSED...
...BUT THE WAY YOU'RE FIGHTING...
...MAKES ME START RETHINKING MY DECISION TO GO EASY ON YOU!
GRRR...
GRAAAAWR!
WHAT'S THAT, FUR-BABY? YOU WANT A SHOT AT THE TITLE?
BRING IT ON, THEN!
SPLASH

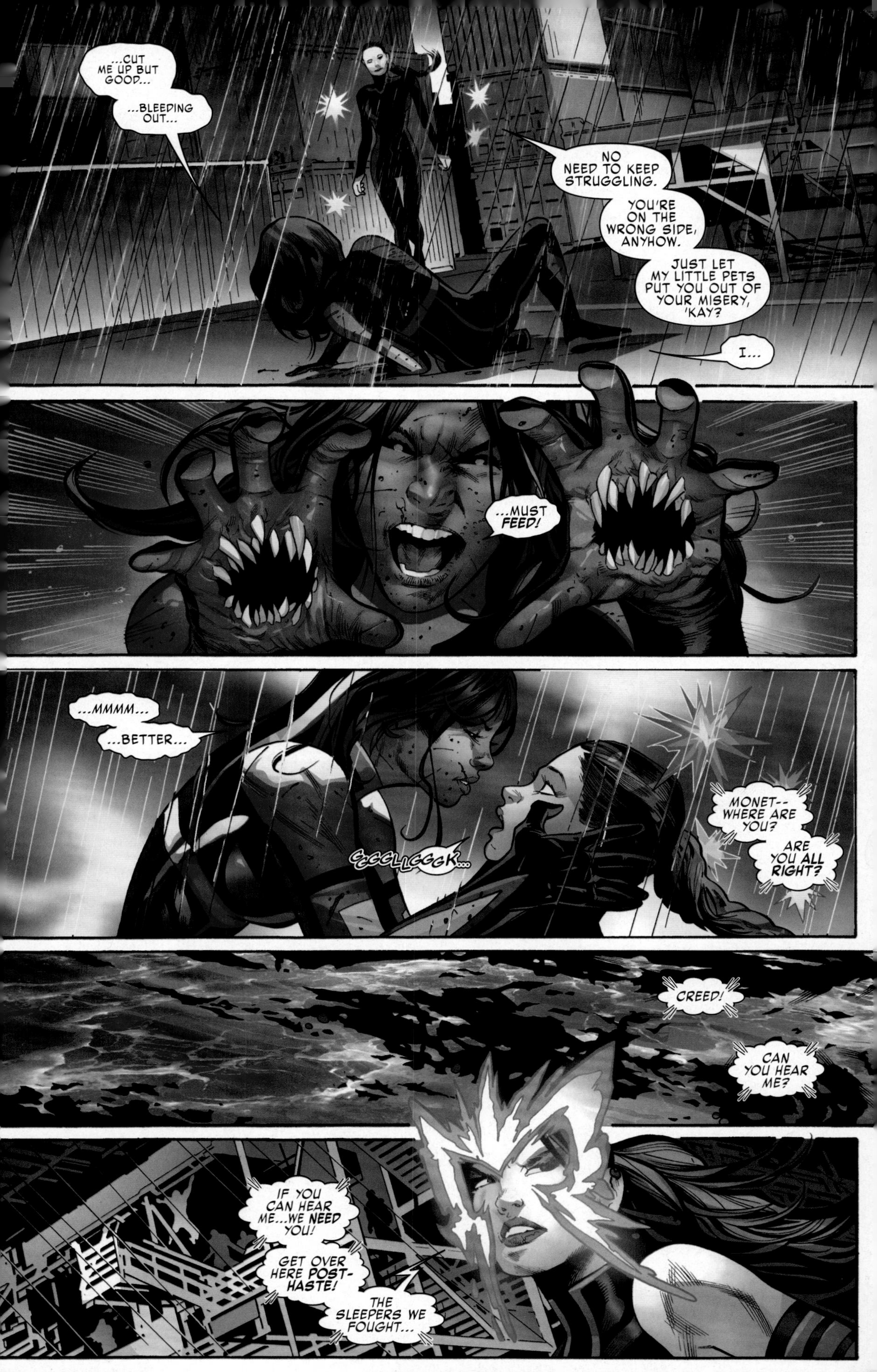

...CUT ME UP BUT GOOD...
...BLEEDING OUT...
NO NEED TO KEEP STRUGGLING.
YOU'RE ON THE WRONG SIDE, ANYHOW.
JUST LET MY LITTLE PETS PUT YOU OUT OF YOUR MISERY, 'KAY?
I...
...MUST FEED!
...MMMM...
...BETTER...
MONET-- WHERE ARE YOU?
ARE YOU ALL RIGHT?
GGGLLGGGK...
CREED!
CAN YOU HEAR ME?
IF YOU CAN HEAR ME...WE NEED YOU!
GET OVER HERE POST-HASTE!
THE SLEEPERS WE FOUGHT...

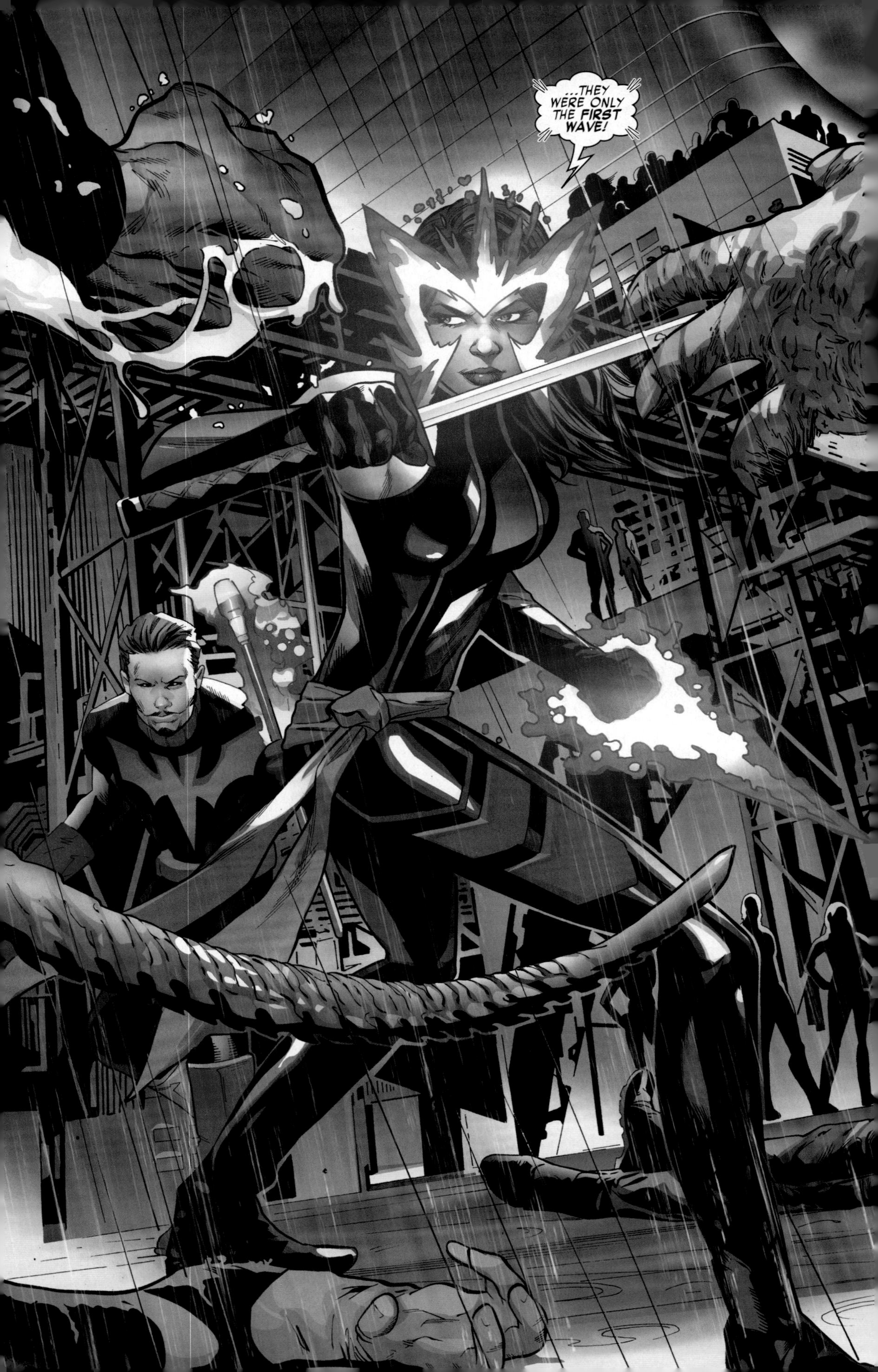
...THEY WERE ONLY THE FIRST WAVE!

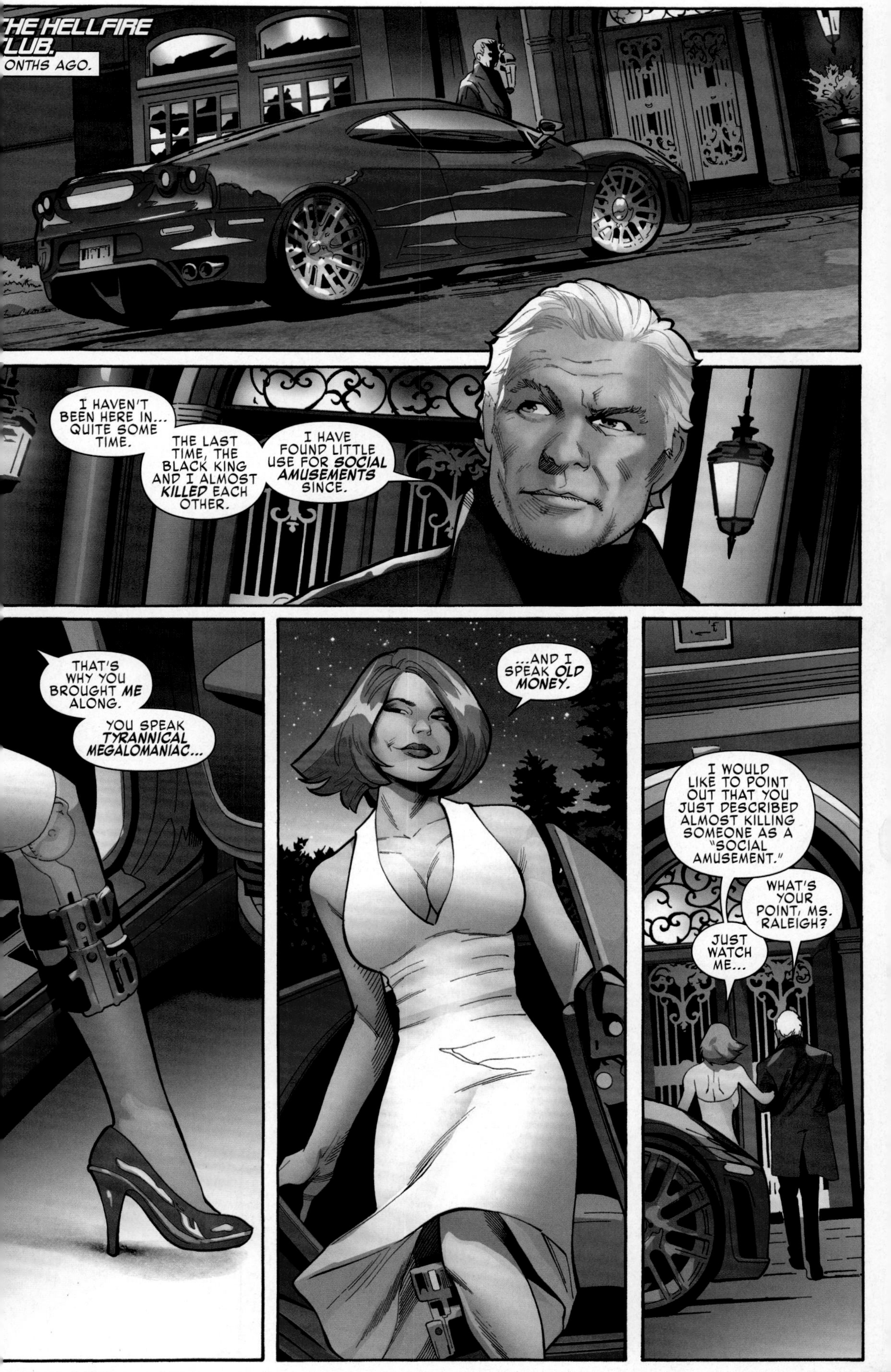
THE HELLFIRE CLUB.
ONTHS AGO.
I HAVEN'T BEEN HERE IN... QUITE SOME TIME.
THE LAST TIME, THE BLACK KING AND I ALMOST KILLED EACH OTHER.
I HAVE FOUND LITTLE USE FOR SOCIAL AMUSEMENTS SINCE.
THAT'S WHY YOU BROUGHT ME ALONG.
YOU SPEAK TYRANNICAL MEGALOMANIAC...
...AND I SPEAK OLD MONEY.
I WOULD LIKE TO POINT OUT THAT YOU JUST DESCRIBED ALMOST KILLING SOMEONE AS A "SOCIAL AMUSEMENT."
WHAT'S YOUR POINT, MS. RALEIGH?
JUST WATCH ME...

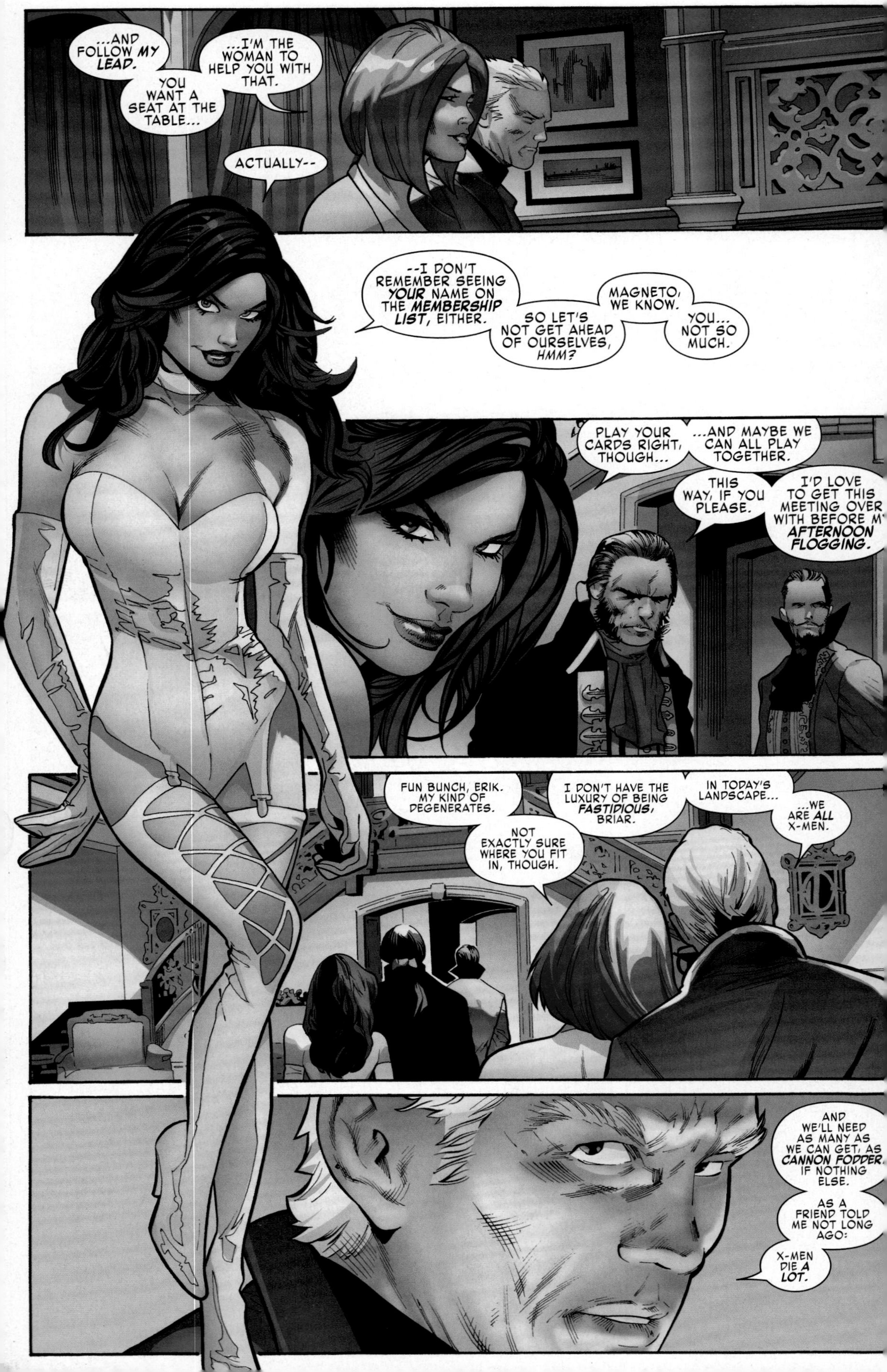
...AND FOLLOW MY LEAD.
YOU WANT A SEAT AT THE TABLE...
...I'M THE WOMAN TO HELP YOU WITH THAT.
ACTUALLY--
--I DON'T REMEMBER SEEING YOUR NAME ON THE MEMBERSHIP LIST, EITHER.
SO LET'S NOT GET AHEAD OF OURSELVES, HMM?
MAGNETO, WE KNOW.
YOU... NOT SO MUCH.
PLAY YOUR CARDS RIGHT, THOUGH...
...AND MAYBE WE CAN ALL PLAY TOGETHER.
THIS WAY, IF YOU PLEASE.
I'D LOVE TO GET THIS MEETING OVER WITH BEFORE MY AFTERNOON FLOGGING.
FUN BUNCH, ERIK. MY KIND OF DEGENERATES.
NOT EXACTLY SURE WHERE YOU FIT IN, THOUGH.
I DON'T HAVE THE LUXURY OF BEING FASTIDIOUS, BRIAR.
IN TODAY'S LANDSCAPE...
...WE ARE ALL X-MEN.
AND WE'LL NEED AS MANY AS WE CAN GET, AS CANNON FODDER IF NOTHING ELSE.
AS A FRIEND TOLD ME NOT LONG AGO:
X-MEN DIE A LOT.

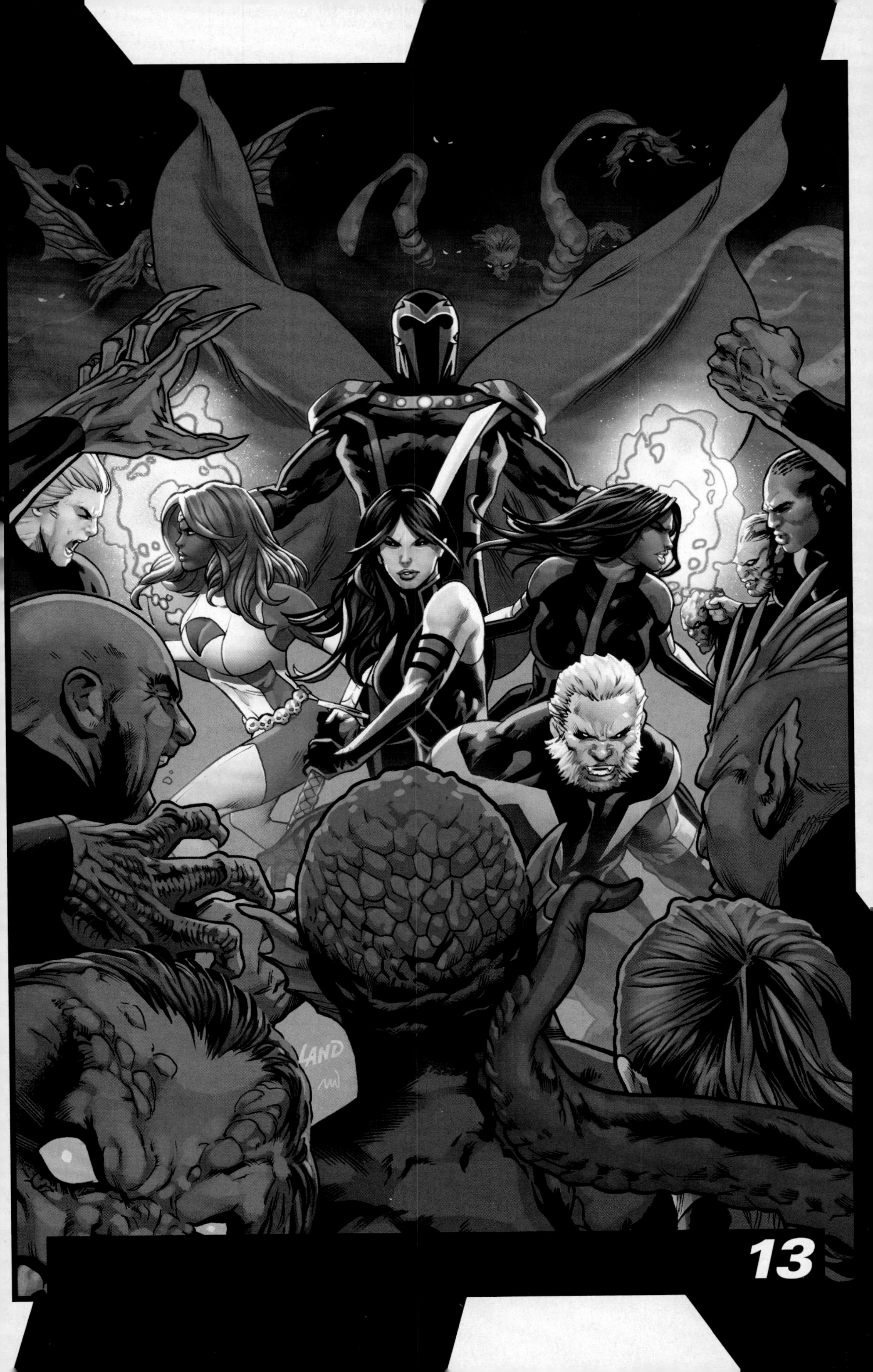
13

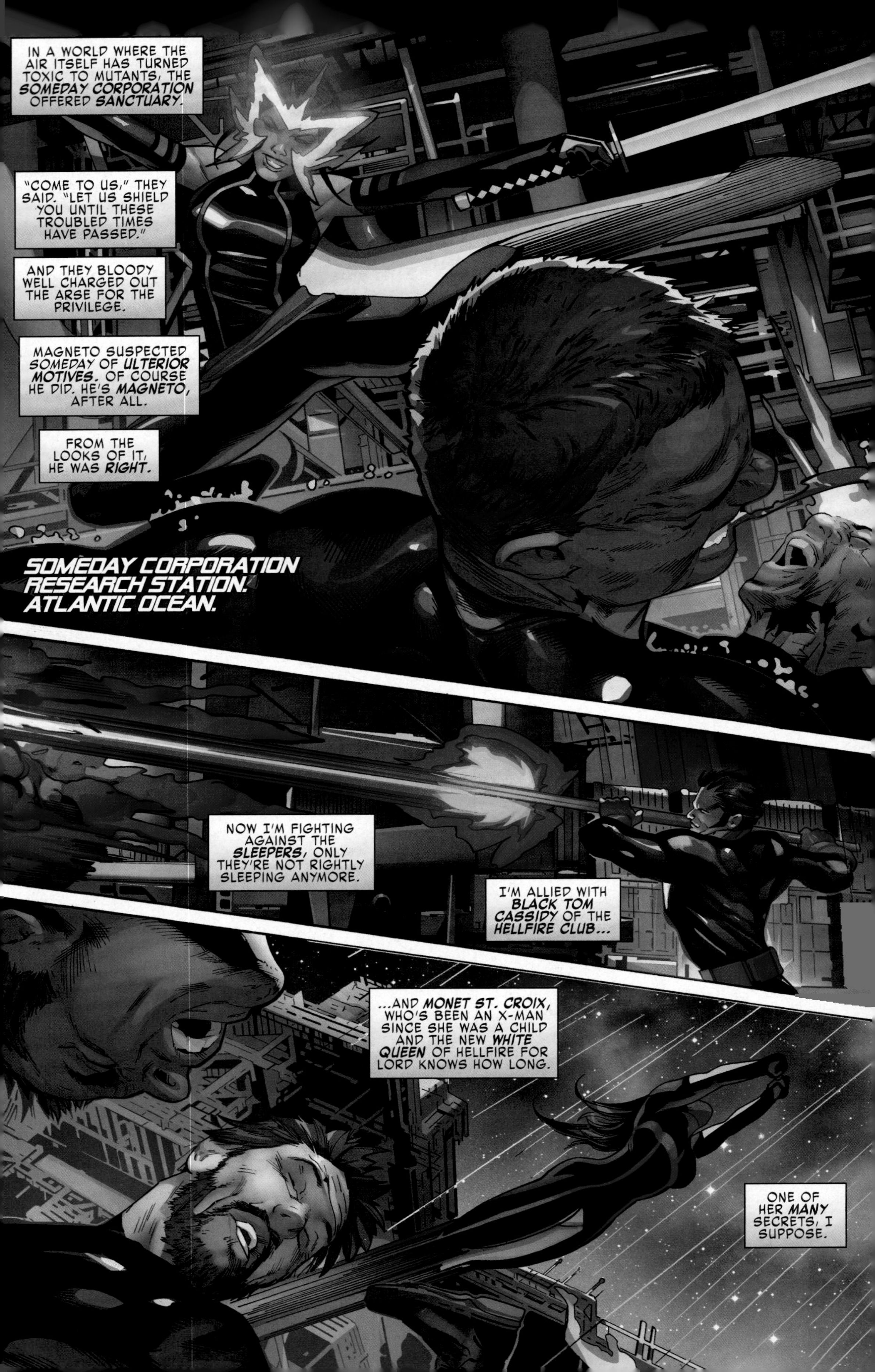
IN A WORLD WHERE THE AIR ITSELF HAS TURNED TOXIC TO MUTANTS, THE SOMEDAY CORPORATION OFFERED SANCTUARY.
"COME TO US," THEY SAID. "LET US SHIELD YOU UNTIL THESE TROUBLED TIMES HAVE PASSED."
AND THEY BLOODY WELL CHARGED OUT THE ARSE FOR THE PRIVILEGE.
MAGNETO SUSPECTED SOMEDAY OF ULTERIOR MOTIVES. OF COURSE HE DID. HE'S MAGNETO, AFTER ALL.
FROM THE LOOKS OF IT, HE WAS RIGHT.
SOMEDAY CORPORATION RESEARCH STATION. ATLANTIC OCEAN.
NOW I'M FIGHTING AGAINST THE SLEEPERS, ONLY THEY'RE NOT RIGHTLY SLEEPING ANYMORE.
I'M ALLIED WITH BLACK TOM CASSIDY OF THE HELLFIRE CLUB...
...AND MONET ST. CROIX, WHO'S BEEN AN X-MAN SINCE SHE WAS A CHILD AND THE NEW WHITE QUEEN OF HELLFIRE FOR LORD KNOWS HOW LONG.
ONE OF HER MANY SECRETS, I SUPPOSE.

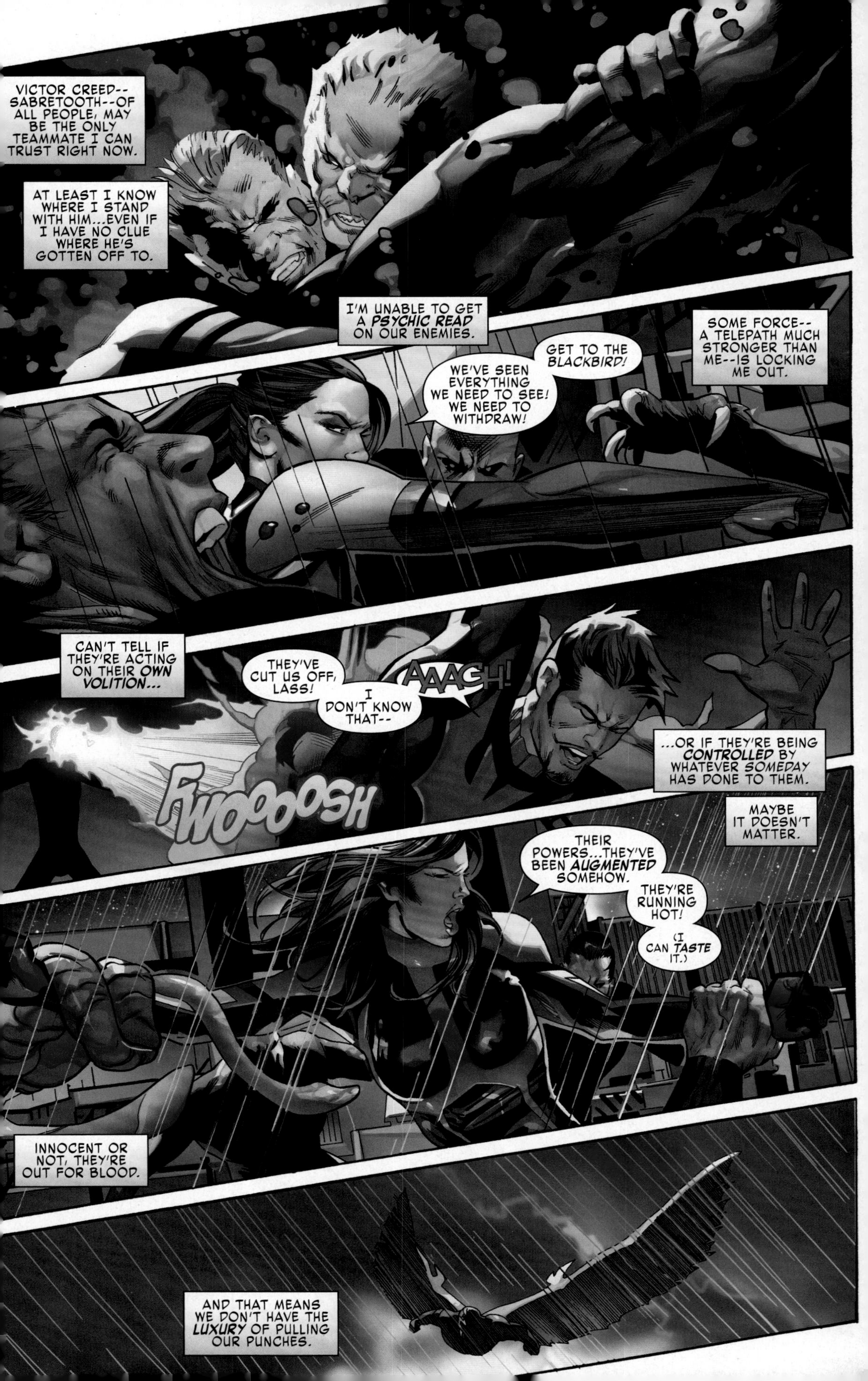

VICTOR CREED--SABRETOOTH--OF ALL PEOPLE, MAY BE THE ONLY TEAMMATE I CAN TRUST RIGHT NOW.
AT LEAST I KNOW WHERE I STAND WITH HIM...EVEN IF I HAVE NO CLUE WHERE HE'S GOTTEN OFF TO.
I'M UNABLE TO GET A *PSYCHIC READ* ON OUR ENEMIES.
SOME FORCE--A TELEPATH MUCH STRONGER THAN ME--IS LOCKING ME OUT.
WE'VE SEEN EVERYTHING WE NEED TO SEE! WE NEED TO WITHDRAW!
GET TO THE *BLACKBIRD!*
CAN'T TELL IF THEY'RE ACTING ON THEIR *OWN VOLITION...*
THEY'VE CUT US OFF, LASS!
I DON'T KNOW THAT--
AAAGH!
...OR IF THEY'RE BEING *CONTROLLED* BY WHATEVER *SOMEDAY* HAS DONE TO THEM.
FWOOOOOSH
MAYBE IT DOESN'T MATTER.
THEIR POWERS...THEY'VE BEEN *AUGMENTED* SOMEHOW.
THEY'RE RUNNING HOT!
(I CAN *TASTE* IT.)
INNOCENT OR NOT, THEY'RE OUT FOR BLOOD.
AND THAT MEANS WE DON'T HAVE THE *LUXURY* OF PULLING OUR PUNCHES.

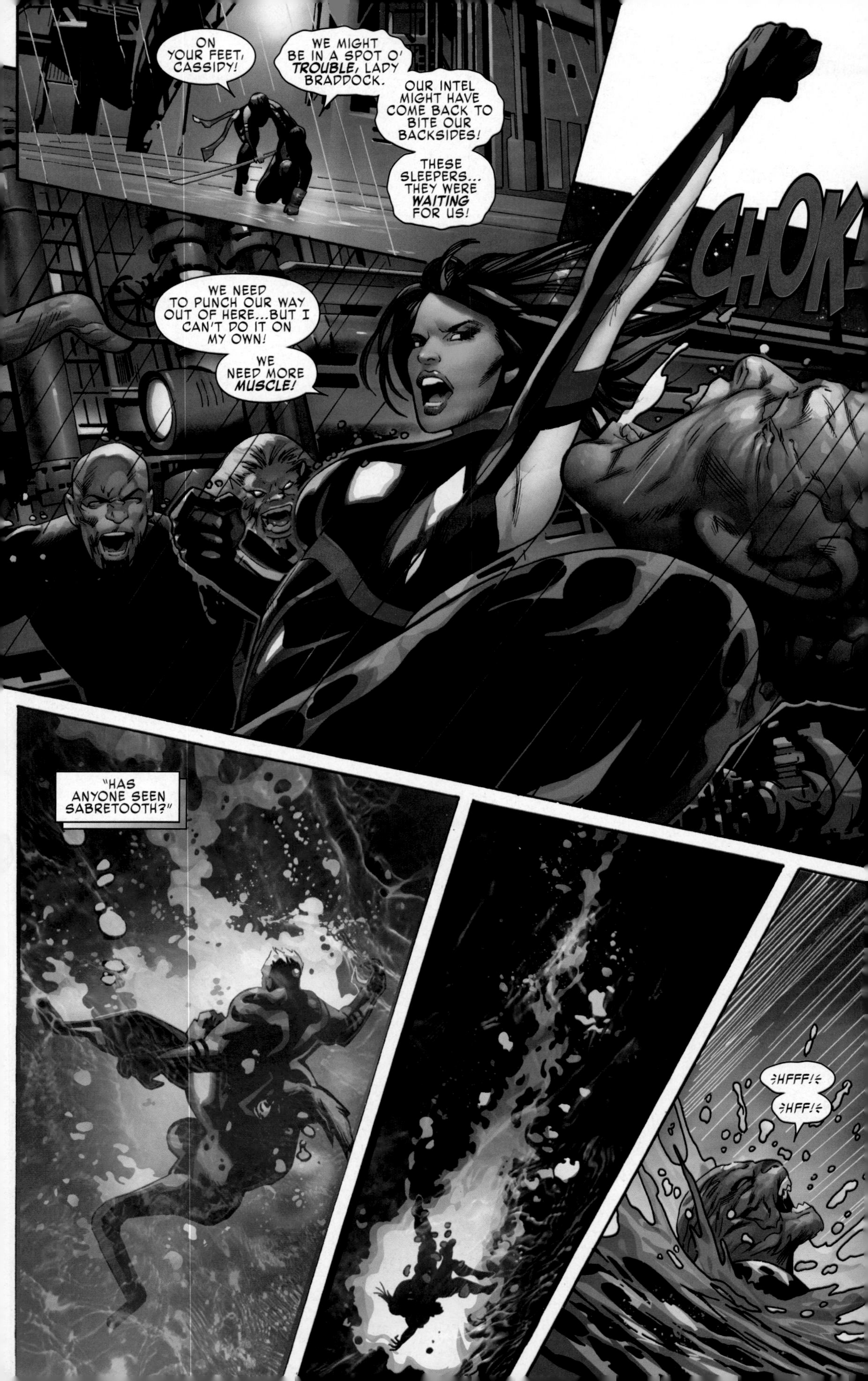
ON YOUR FEET, CASSIDY!
WE MIGHT BE IN A SPOT O' TROUBLE, LADY BRADDOCK.
OUR INTEL MIGHT HAVE COME BACK TO BITE OUR BACKSIDES!
THESE SLEEPERS... THEY WERE WAITING FOR US!
CHOK
WE NEED TO PUNCH OUR WAY OUT OF HERE...BUT I CAN'T DO IT ON MY OWN!
WE NEED MORE MUSCLE!
"HAS ANYONE SEEN SABRETOOTH?"
HFFF!
HFF!

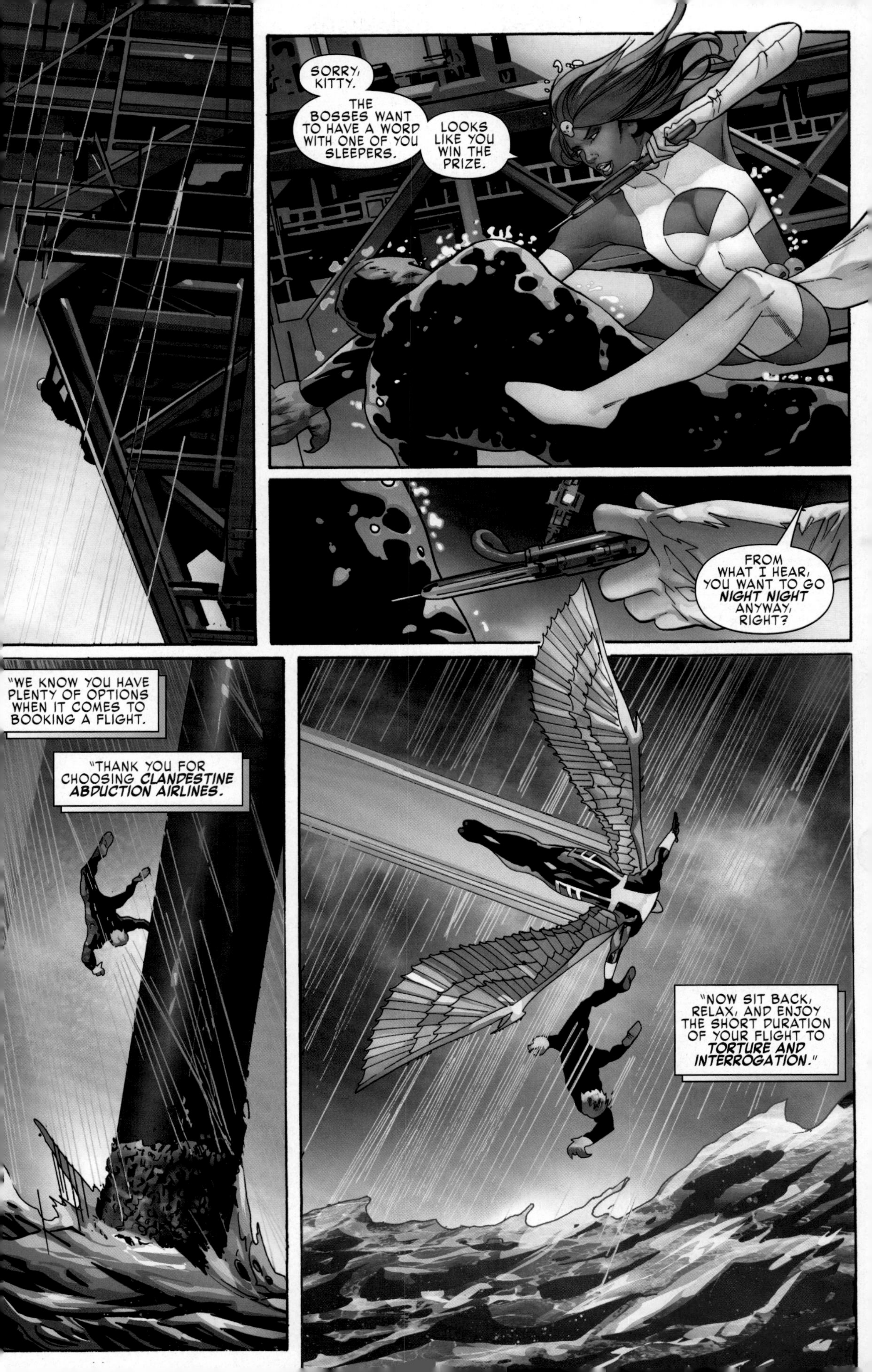
SORRY, KITTY.
THE BOSSES WANT TO HAVE A WORD WITH ONE OF YOU SLEEPERS.
LOOKS LIKE YOU WIN THE PRIZE.
FROM WHAT I HEAR, YOU WANT TO GO NIGHT NIGHT ANYWAY, RIGHT?
"WE KNOW YOU HAVE PLENTY OF OPTIONS WHEN IT COMES TO BOOKING A FLIGHT.
"THANK YOU FOR CHOOSING CLANDESTINE ABDUCTION AIRLINES.
"NOW SIT BACK, RELAX, AND ENJOY THE SHORT DURATION OF YOUR FLIGHT TO TORTURE AND INTERROGATION."

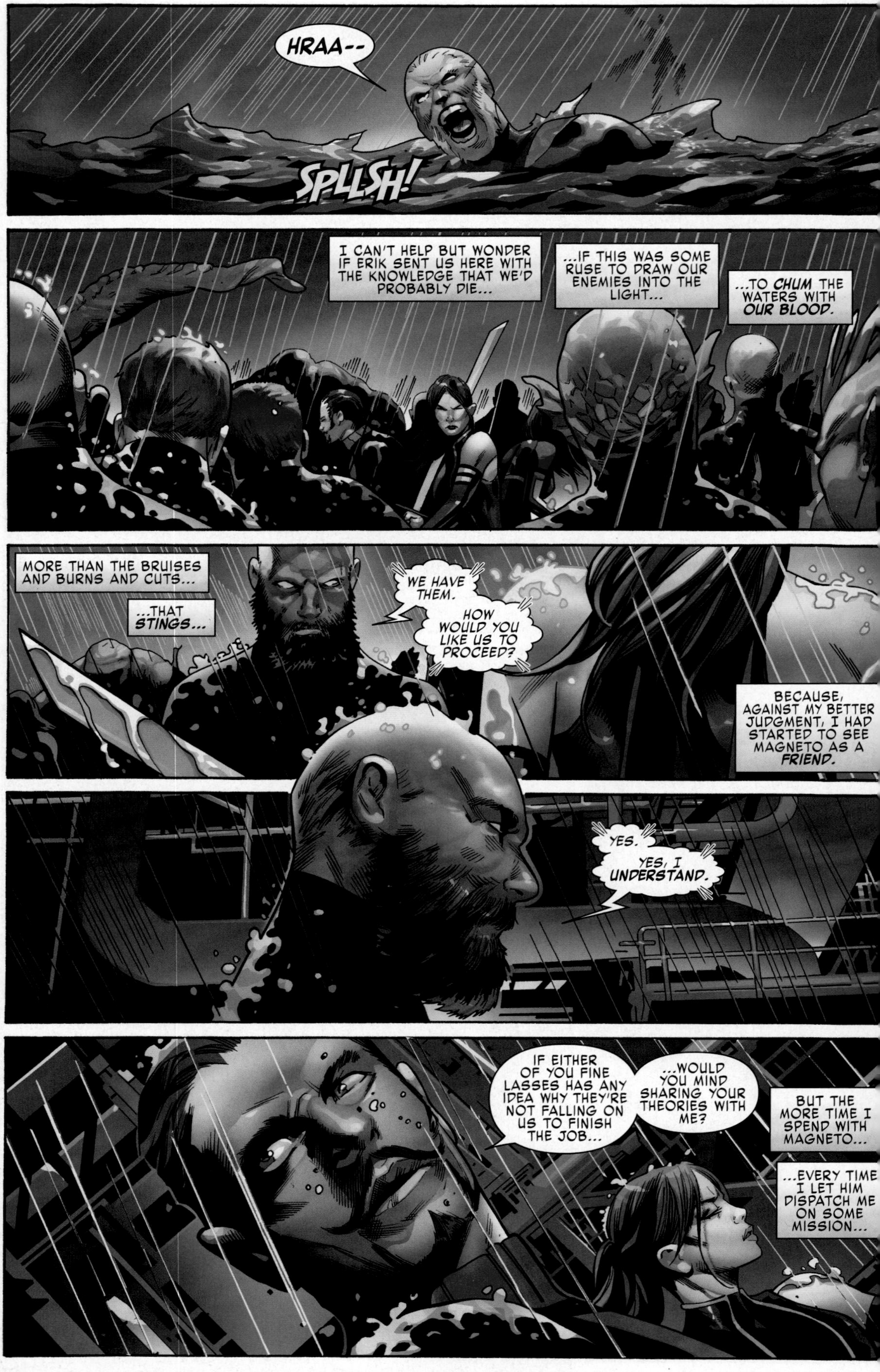
HRAA--
SPLLSH!
I CAN'T HELP BUT WONDER IF ERIK SENT US HERE WITH THE KNOWLEDGE THAT WE'D PROBABLY DIE...
...IF THIS WAS SOME RUSE TO DRAW OUR ENEMIES INTO THE LIGHT...
...TO CHUM THE WATERS WITH OUR BLOOD.
MORE THAN THE BRUISES AND BURNS AND CUTS...
...THAT STINGS...
WE HAVE THEM.
HOW WOULD YOU LIKE US TO PROCEED?
BECAUSE, AGAINST MY BETTER JUDGMENT, I HAD STARTED TO SEE MAGNETO AS A FRIEND.
YES.
YES, I UNDERSTAND.
IF EITHER OF YOU FINE LASSES HAS ANY IDEA WHY THEY'RE NOT FALLING ON US TO FINISH THE JOB...
...WOULD YOU MIND SHARING YOUR THEORIES WITH ME?
BUT THE MORE TIME I SPEND WITH MAGNETO...
...EVERY TIME I LET HIM DISPATCH ME ON SOME MISSION...

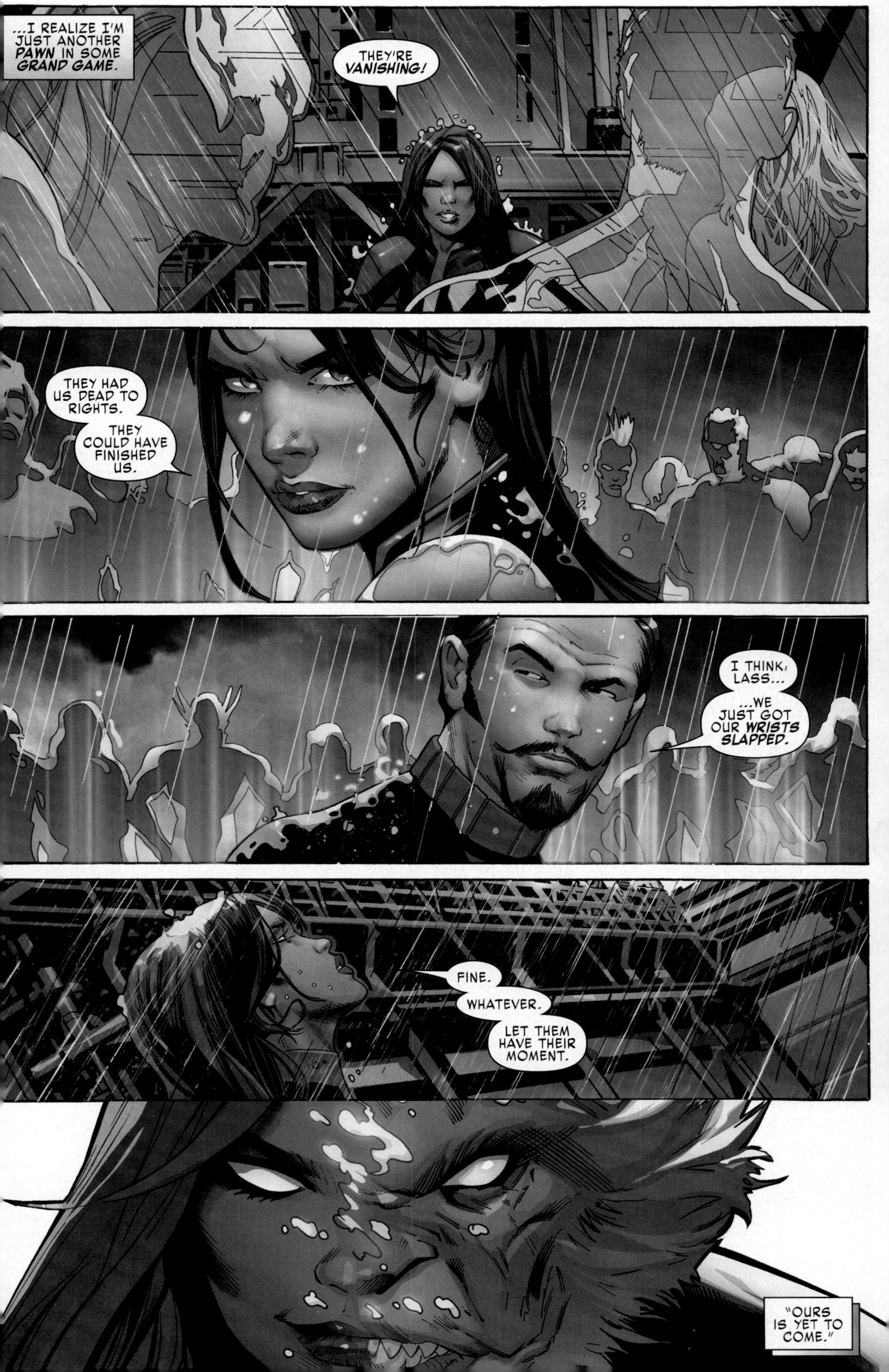

...I REALIZE I'M JUST ANOTHER PAWN IN SOME GRAND GAME.
THEY'RE VANISHING!
THEY HAD US DEAD TO RIGHTS.
THEY COULD HAVE FINISHED US.
I THINK, LASS...
...WE JUST GOT OUR WRISTS SLAPPED.
FINE.
WHATEVER.
LET THEM HAVE THEIR MOMENT.
"OURS IS YET TO COME."

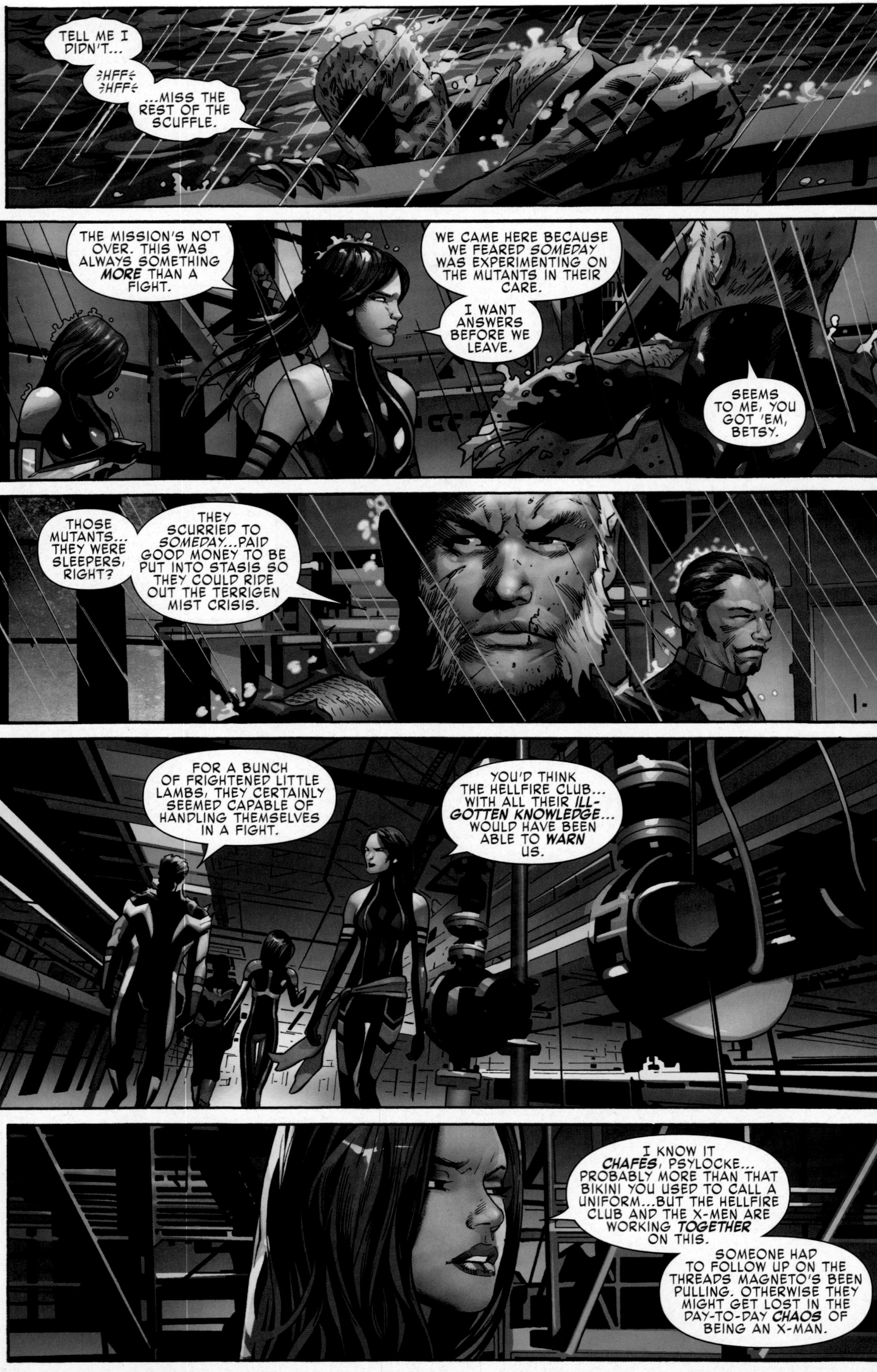
TELL ME I DIDN'T...
⋽HFF⋼ ⋽HFF⋼
...MISS THE REST OF THE SCUFFLE.
THE MISSION'S NOT OVER. THIS WAS ALWAYS SOMETHING *MORE* THAN A FIGHT.
WE CAME HERE BECAUSE WE FEARED *SOMEDAY* WAS EXPERIMENTING ON THE MUTANTS IN THEIR CARE.
I WANT ANSWERS BEFORE WE LEAVE.
SEEMS TO ME, YOU GOT 'EM, BETSY.
THOSE MUTANTS... THEY WERE SLEEPERS, RIGHT?
THEY SCURRIED TO *SOMEDAY*...PAID GOOD MONEY TO BE PUT INTO STASIS SO THEY COULD RIDE OUT THE TERRIGEN MIST CRISIS.
FOR A BUNCH OF FRIGHTENED LITTLE LAMBS, THEY CERTAINLY SEEMED CAPABLE OF HANDLING THEMSELVES IN A FIGHT.
YOU'D THINK THE HELLFIRE CLUB... WITH ALL THEIR *ILL-GOTTEN KNOWLEDGE*... WOULD HAVE BEEN ABLE TO *WARN* US.
I KNOW IT *CHAFES*, PSYLOCKE... PROBABLY MORE THAN THAT BIKINI YOU USED TO CALL A UNIFORM...BUT THE HELLFIRE CLUB AND THE X-MEN ARE WORKING *TOGETHER* ON THIS.
SOMEONE HAD TO FOLLOW UP ON THE THREADS MAGNETO'S BEEN PULLING. OTHERWISE THEY MIGHT GET LOST IN THE DAY-TO-DAY *CHAOS* OF BEING AN X-MAN.

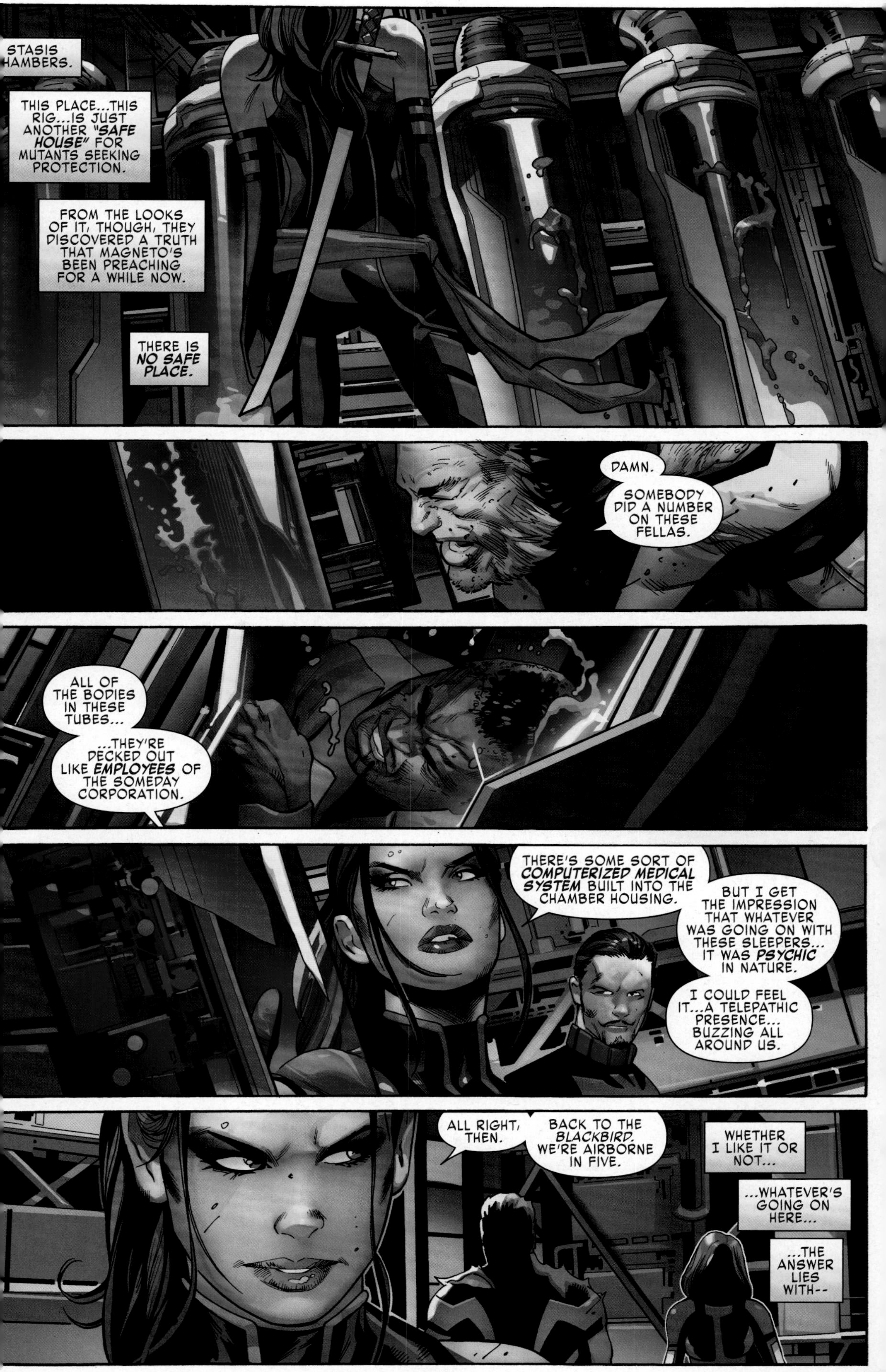
STASIS CHAMBERS.
THIS PLACE...THIS RIG...IS JUST ANOTHER "SAFE HOUSE" FOR MUTANTS SEEKING PROTECTION.
FROM THE LOOKS OF IT, THOUGH, THEY DISCOVERED A TRUTH THAT MAGNETO'S BEEN PREACHING FOR A WHILE NOW.
THERE IS NO SAFE PLACE.
DAMN.
SOMEBODY DID A NUMBER ON THESE FELLAS.
ALL OF THE BODIES IN THESE TUBES...
...THEY'RE DECKED OUT LIKE EMPLOYEES OF THE SOMEDAY CORPORATION.
THERE'S SOME SORT OF COMPUTERIZED MEDICAL SYSTEM BUILT INTO THE CHAMBER HOUSING.
BUT I GET THE IMPRESSION THAT WHATEVER WAS GOING ON WITH THESE SLEEPERS... IT WAS PSYCHIC IN NATURE.
I COULD FEEL IT...A TELEPATHIC PRESENCE... BUZZING ALL AROUND US.
ALL RIGHT, THEN.
BACK TO THE BLACKBIRD. WE'RE AIRBORNE IN FIVE.
WHETHER I LIKE IT OR NOT...
...WHATEVER'S GOING ON HERE...
...THE ANSWER LIES WITH--

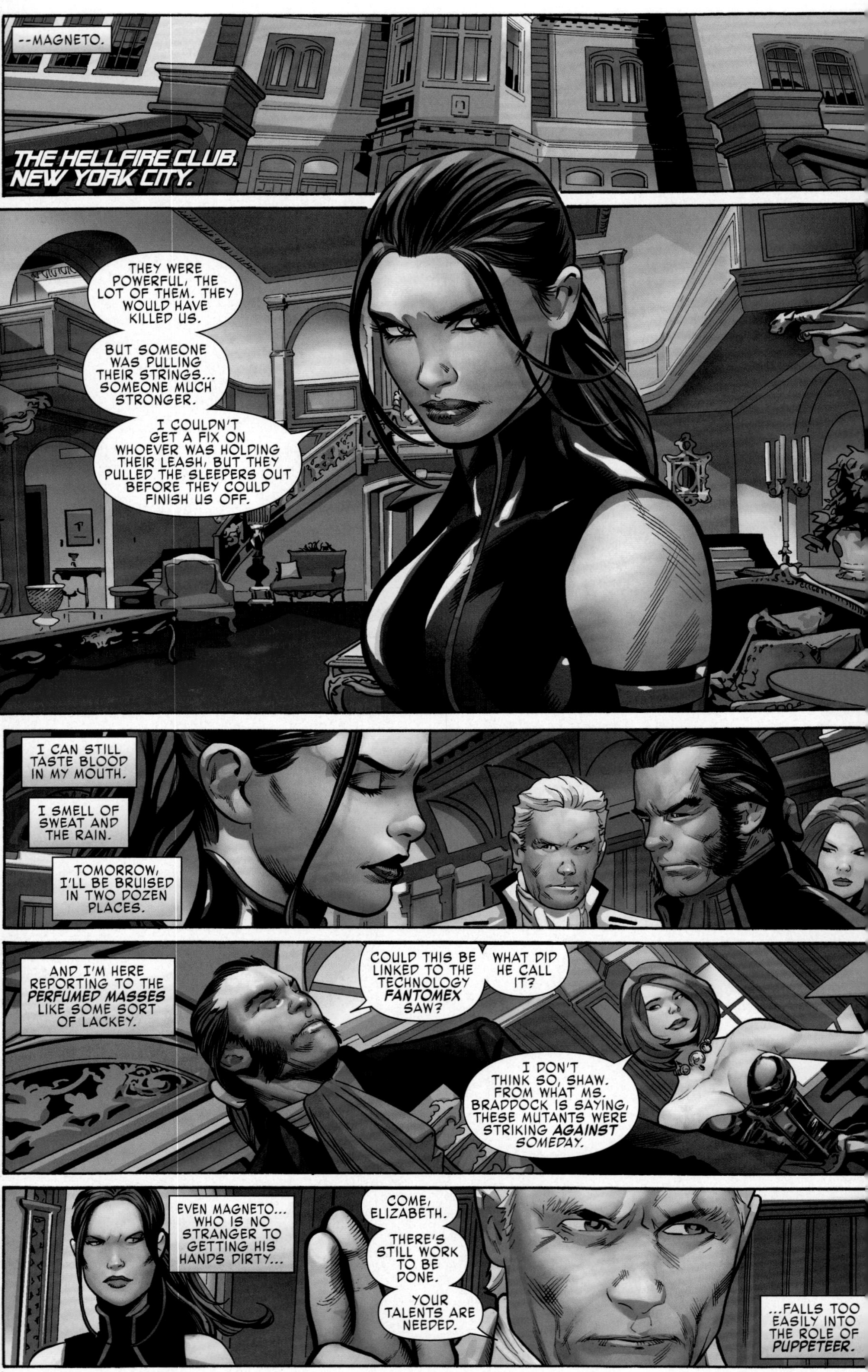
--MAGNETO.
THE HELLFIRE CLUB. NEW YORK CITY.
THEY WERE POWERFUL, THE LOT OF THEM. THEY WOULD HAVE KILLED US.
BUT SOMEONE WAS PULLING THEIR STRINGS... SOMEONE MUCH STRONGER.
I COULDN'T GET A FIX ON WHOEVER WAS HOLDING THEIR LEASH, BUT THEY PULLED THE SLEEPERS OUT BEFORE THEY COULD FINISH US OFF.
I CAN STILL TASTE BLOOD IN MY MOUTH.
I SMELL OF SWEAT AND THE RAIN.
TOMORROW, I'LL BE BRUISED IN TWO DOZEN PLACES.
AND I'M HERE REPORTING TO THE PERFUMED MASSES LIKE SOME SORT OF LACKEY.
COULD THIS BE LINKED TO THE TECHNOLOGY FANTOMEX SAW?
WHAT DID HE CALL IT?
I DON'T THINK SO, SHAW. FROM WHAT MS. BRADDOCK IS SAYING, THESE MUTANTS WERE STRIKING AGAINST SOMEDAY.
EVEN MAGNETO... WHO IS NO STRANGER TO GETTING HIS HANDS DIRTY...
COME, ELIZABETH.
THERE'S STILL WORK TO BE DONE.
YOUR TALENTS ARE NEEDED.
...FALLS TOO EASILY INTO THE ROLE OF PUPPETEER.

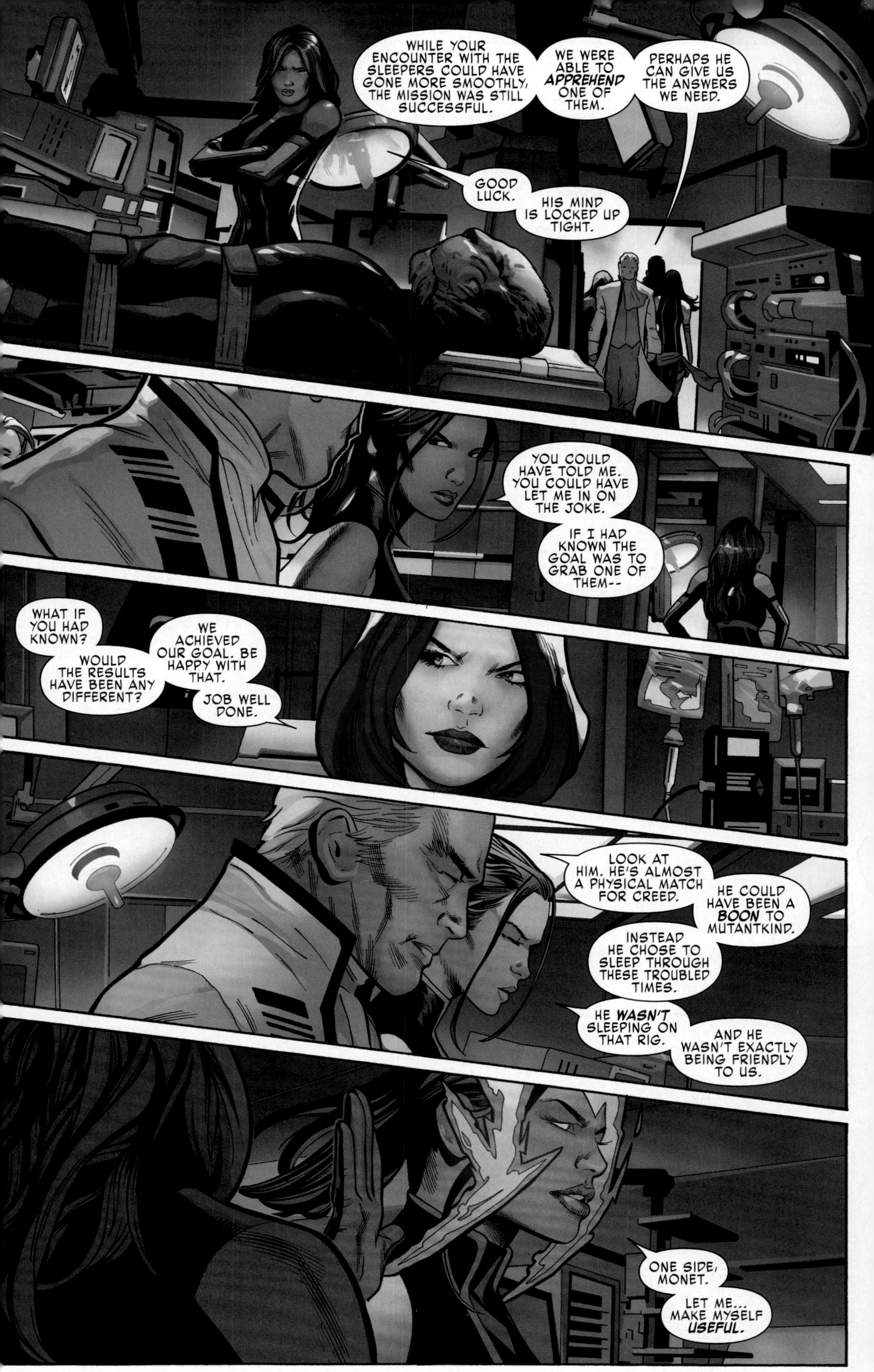
WHILE YOUR ENCOUNTER WITH THE SLEEPERS COULD HAVE GONE MORE SMOOTHLY, THE MISSION WAS STILL SUCCESSFUL.
WE WERE ABLE TO APPREHEND ONE OF THEM.
PERHAPS HE CAN GIVE US THE ANSWERS WE NEED.
GOOD LUCK.
HIS MIND IS LOCKED UP TIGHT.
YOU COULD HAVE TOLD ME. YOU COULD HAVE LET ME IN ON THE JOKE.
IF I HAD KNOWN THE GOAL WAS TO GRAB ONE OF THEM--
WHAT IF YOU HAD KNOWN?
WOULD THE RESULTS HAVE BEEN ANY DIFFERENT?
WE ACHIEVED OUR GOAL. BE HAPPY WITH THAT.
JOB WELL DONE.
LOOK AT HIM. HE'S ALMOST A PHYSICAL MATCH FOR CREED.
HE COULD HAVE BEEN A BOON TO MUTANTKIND.
INSTEAD HE CHOSE TO SLEEP THROUGH THESE TROUBLED TIMES.
HE WASN'T SLEEPING ON THAT RIG.
AND HE WASN'T EXACTLY BEING FRIENDLY TO US.
ONE SIDE, MONET.
LET ME... MAKE MYSELF USEFUL.

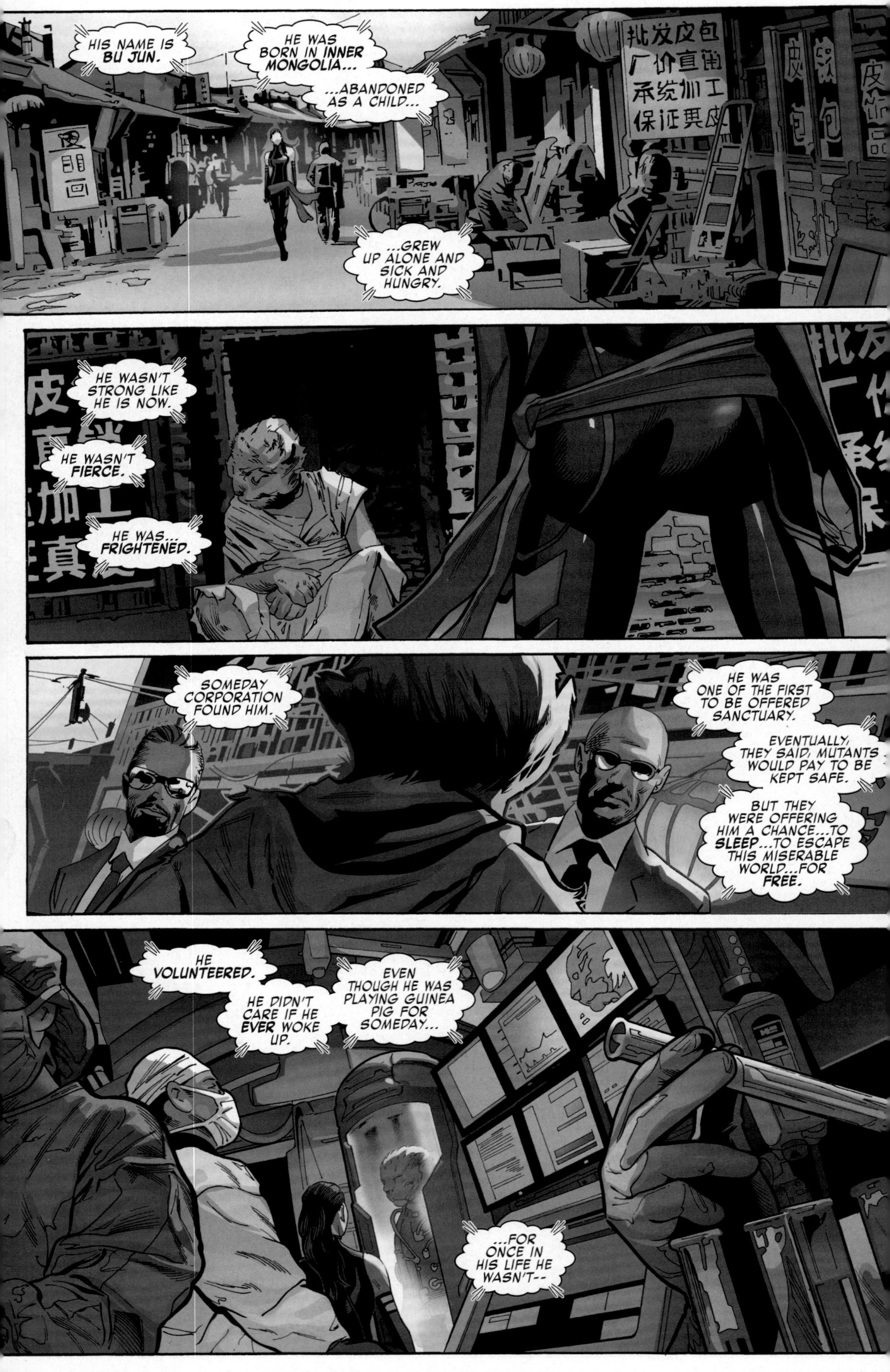

HIS NAME IS **BU JUN.**
HE WAS BORN IN **INNER MONGOLIA...**
...ABANDONED AS A CHILD...
...GREW UP ALONE AND SICK AND HUNGRY.
批发皮包
HE WASN'T STRONG LIKE HE IS NOW.
HE WASN'T **FIERCE.**
HE WAS... **FRIGHTENED.**
SOMEDAY CORPORATION FOUND HIM.
HE WAS ONE OF THE FIRST TO BE OFFERED SANCTUARY.
EVENTUALLY, THEY SAID, MUTANTS WOULD PAY TO BE KEPT SAFE.
BUT THEY WERE OFFERING HIM A CHANCE...TO **SLEEP**...TO ESCAPE THIS MISERABLE WORLD...FOR **FREE.**
HE **VOLUNTEERED.**
HE DIDN'T CARE IF HE **EVER** WOKE UP.
EVEN THOUGH HE WAS PLAYING GUINEA PIG FOR SOMEDAY...
...FOR ONCE IN HIS LIFE HE WASN'T--

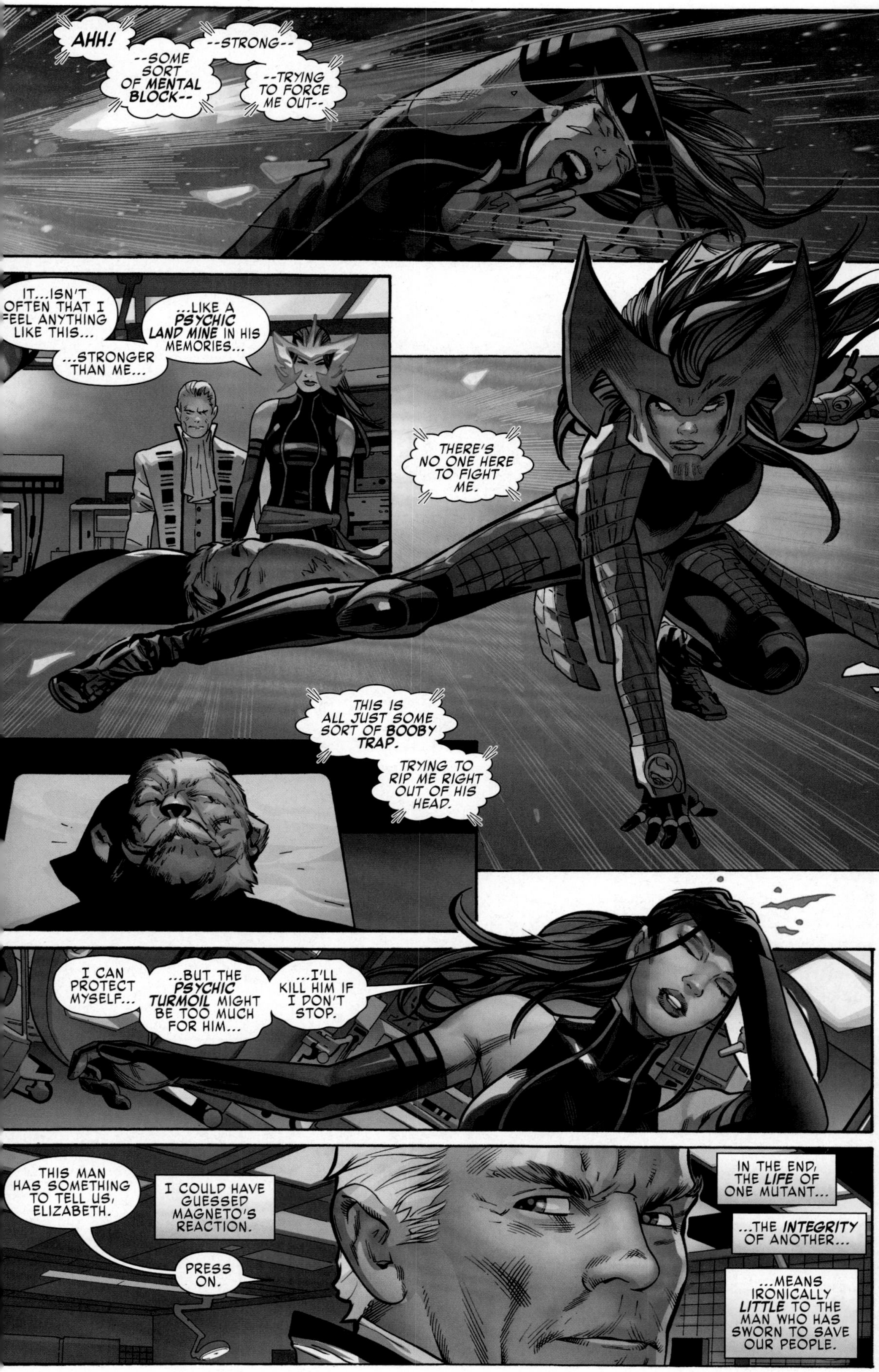
AHH!
--SOME SORT OF MENTAL BLOCK--
--STRONG--
--TRYING TO FORCE ME OUT--
IT...ISN'T OFTEN THAT I FEEL ANYTHING LIKE THIS...
...STRONGER THAN ME...
...LIKE A PSYCHIC LAND MINE IN HIS MEMORIES...
THERE'S NO ONE HERE TO FIGHT ME.
THIS IS ALL JUST SOME SORT OF BOOBY TRAP.
TRYING TO RIP ME RIGHT OUT OF HIS HEAD.
I CAN PROTECT MYSELF...
...BUT THE PSYCHIC TURMOIL MIGHT BE TOO MUCH FOR HIM...
...I'LL KILL HIM IF I DON'T STOP.
THIS MAN HAS SOMETHING TO TELL US, ELIZABETH.
I COULD HAVE GUESSED MAGNETO'S REACTION.
PRESS ON.
IN THE END, THE LIFE OF ONE MUTANT...
...THE INTEGRITY OF ANOTHER...
...MEANS IRONICALLY LITTLE TO THE MAN WHO HAS SWORN TO SAVE OUR PEOPLE.

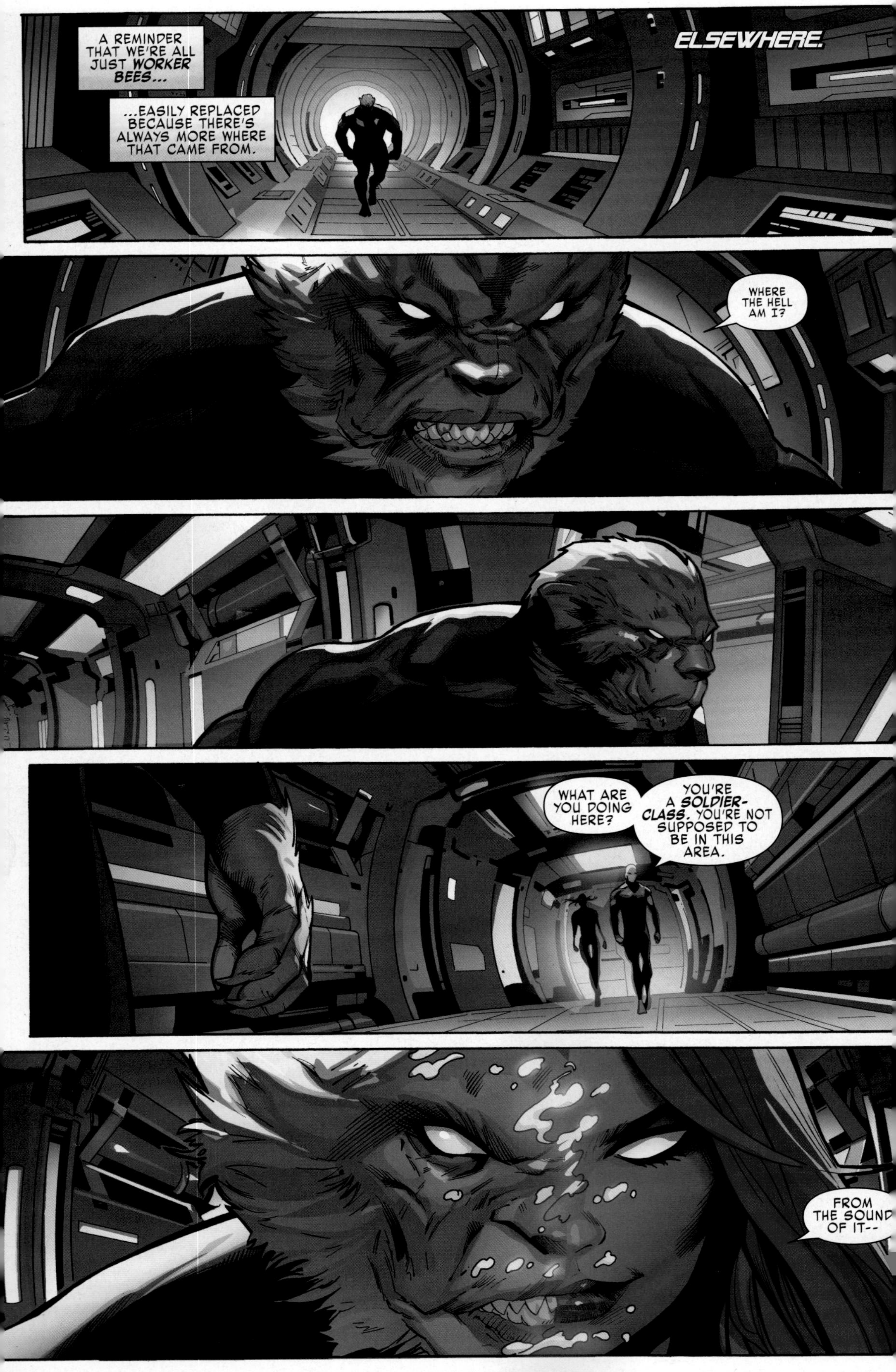
A REMINDER THAT WE'RE ALL JUST WORKER BEES...
...EASILY REPLACED BECAUSE THERE'S ALWAYS MORE WHERE THAT CAME FROM.
ELSEWHERE.
WHERE THE HELL AM I?
WHAT ARE YOU DOING HERE?
YOU'RE A SOLDIER-CLASS. YOU'RE NOT SUPPOSED TO BE IN THIS AREA.
FROM THE SOUND OF IT--

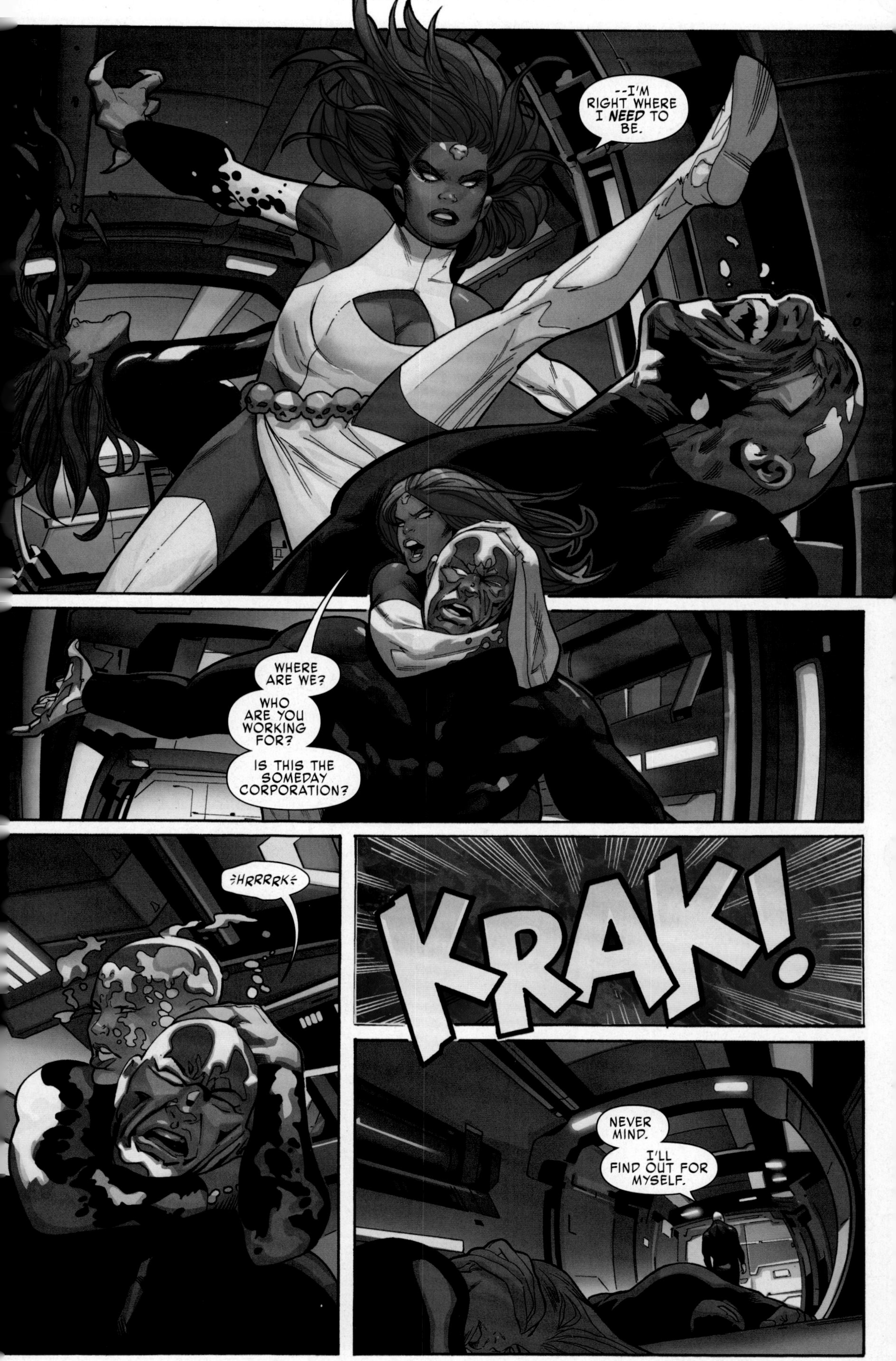
--I'M RIGHT WHERE I *NEED* TO BE.
WHERE ARE WE?
WHO ARE YOU WORKING FOR?
IS THIS THE SOMEDAY CORPORATION?
HRRRRK
KRAK!
NEVER MIND.
I'LL FIND OUT FOR MYSELF.

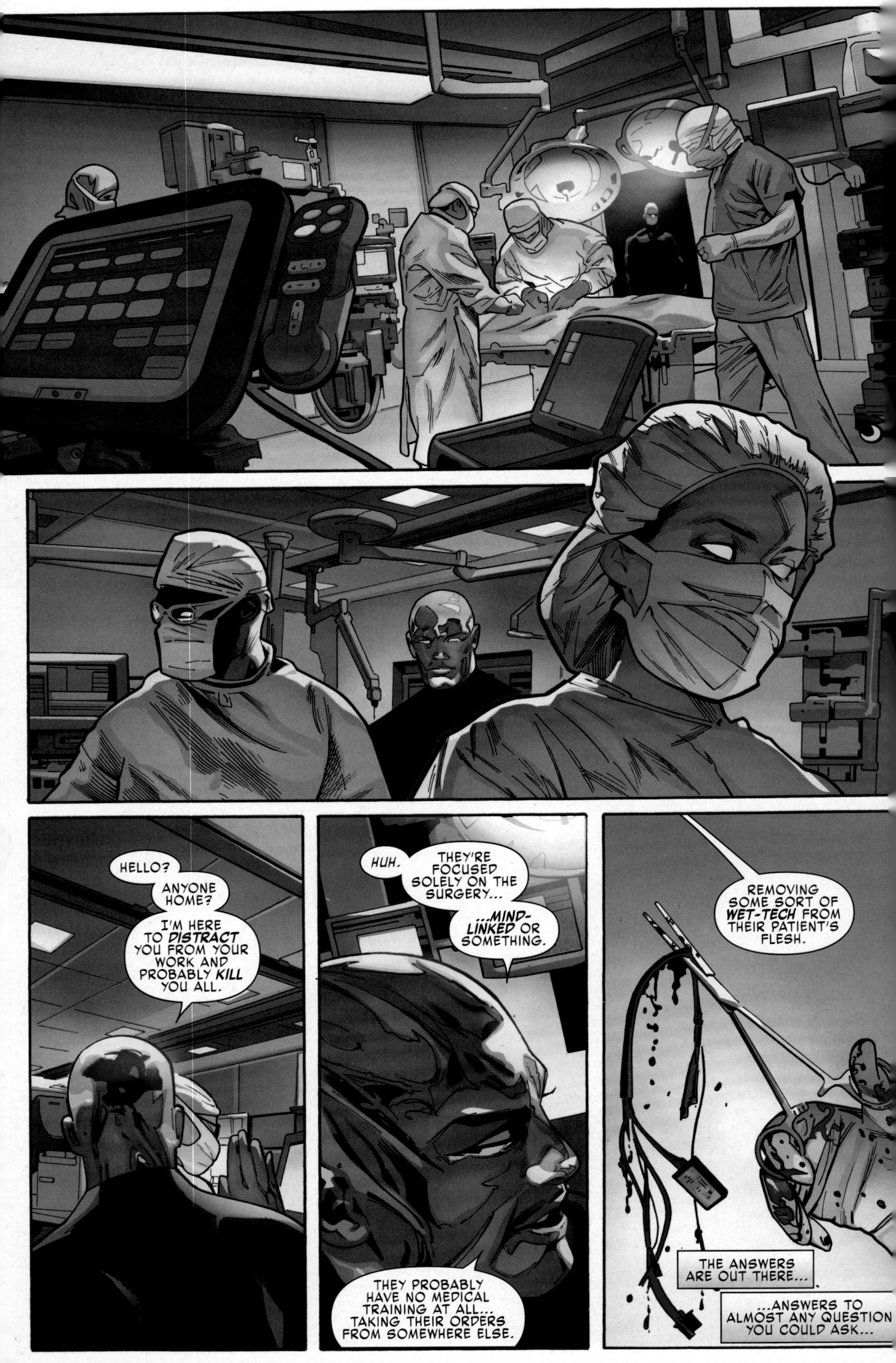
HELLO?
ANYONE HOME?
I'M HERE TO DISTRACT YOU FROM YOUR WORK AND PROBABLY KILL YOU ALL.
HUH.
THEY'RE FOCUSED SOLELY ON THE SURGERY...
...MIND-LINKED OR SOMETHING.
THEY PROBABLY HAVE NO MEDICAL TRAINING AT ALL... TAKING THEIR ORDERS FROM SOMEWHERE ELSE.
REMOVING SOME SORT OF WET-TECH FROM THEIR PATIENT'S FLESH.
THE ANSWERS ARE OUT THERE...
...ANSWERS TO ALMOST ANY QUESTION YOU COULD ASK...

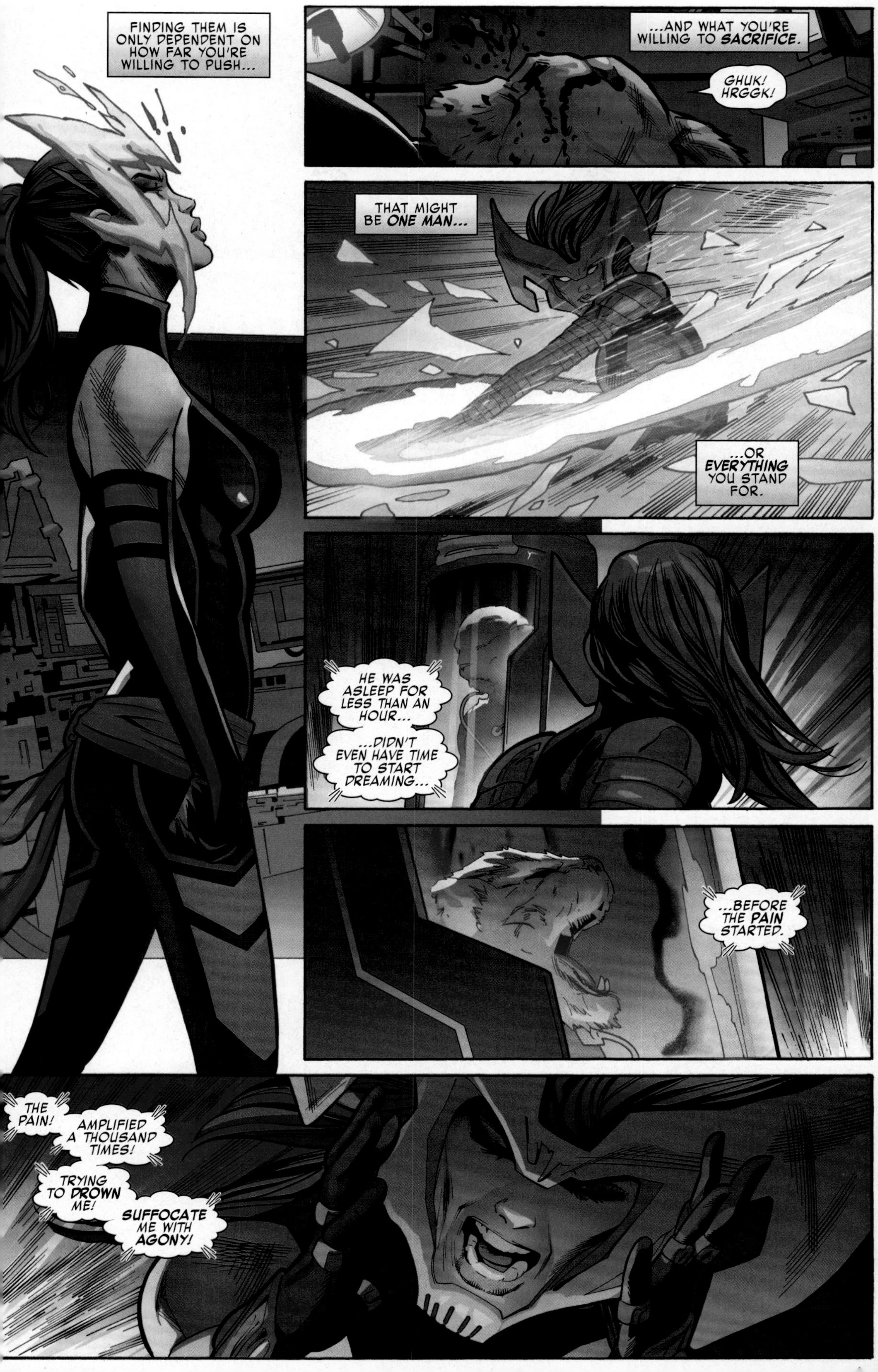
FINDING THEM IS ONLY DEPENDENT ON HOW FAR YOU'RE WILLING TO PUSH...
...AND WHAT YOU'RE WILLING TO SACRIFICE.
GHUK! HRGGK!
THAT MIGHT BE ONE MAN...
...OR EVERYTHING YOU STAND FOR.
HE WAS ASLEEP FOR LESS THAN AN HOUR...
...DIDN'T EVEN HAVE TIME TO START DREAMING...
...BEFORE THE PAIN STARTED.
THE PAIN!
AMPLIFIED A THOUSAND TIMES!
TRYING TO DROWN ME!
SUFFOCATE ME WITH AGONY!

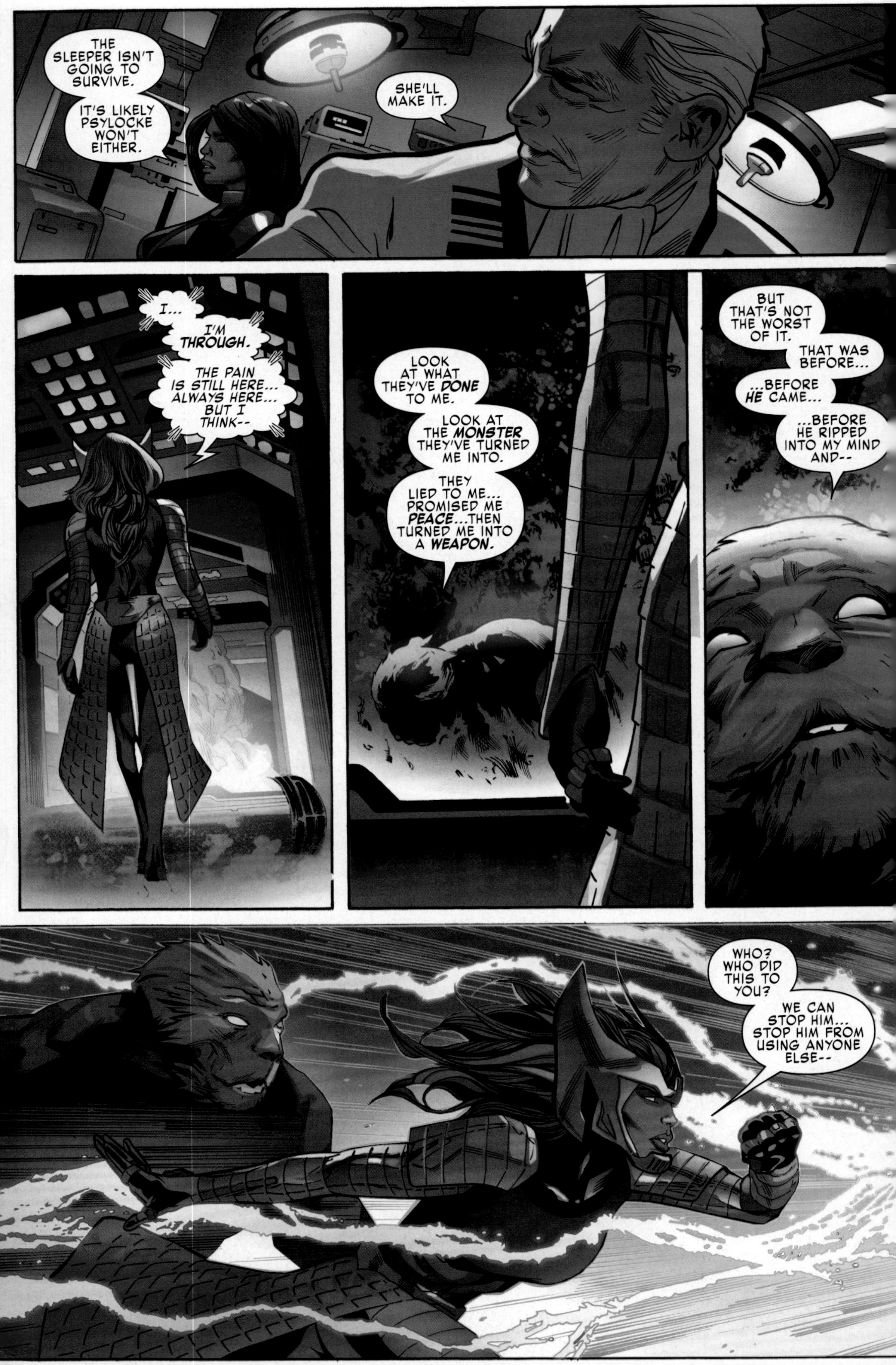
THE SLEEPER ISN'T GOING TO SURVIVE.
IT'S LIKELY PSYLOCKE WON'T EITHER.
SHE'LL MAKE IT.
I...
I'M THROUGH.
THE PAIN IS STILL HERE... ALWAYS HERE... BUT I THINK--
LOOK AT WHAT THEY'VE DONE TO ME.
LOOK AT THE MONSTER THEY'VE TURNED ME INTO.
THEY LIED TO ME... PROMISED ME PEACE...THEN TURNED ME INTO A WEAPON.
BUT THAT'S NOT THE WORST OF IT.
THAT WAS BEFORE...
...BEFORE HE CAME...
...BEFORE HE RIPPED INTO MY MIND AND--
WHO? WHO DID THIS TO YOU?
WE CAN STOP HIM... STOP HIM FROM USING ANYONE ELSE--

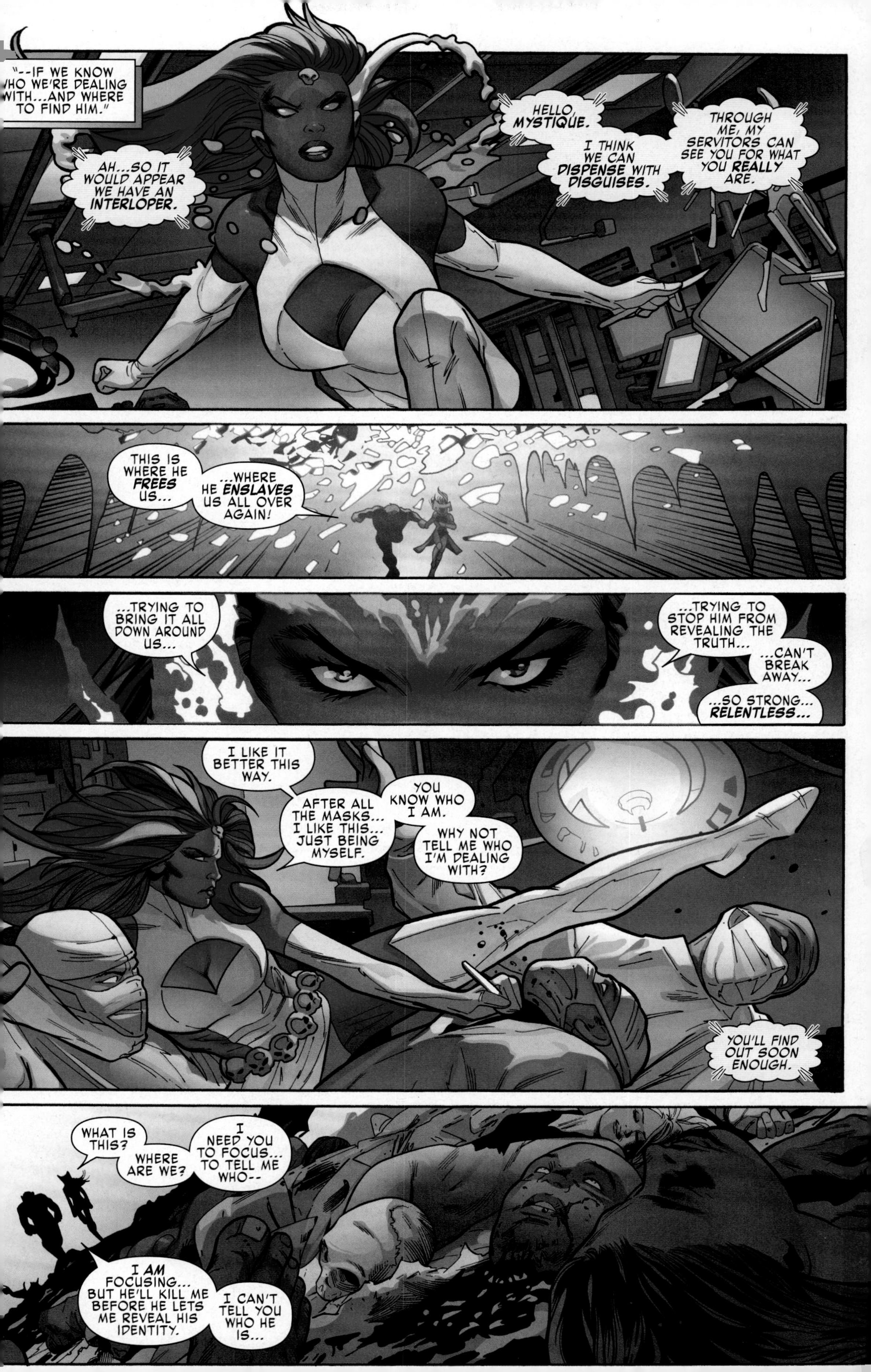

"--IF WE KNOW WHO WE'RE DEALING WITH...AND WHERE TO FIND HIM."
AH...SO IT WOULD APPEAR WE HAVE AN INTERLOPER.
HELLO, MYSTIQUE.
I THINK WE CAN DISPENSE WITH DISGUISES.
THROUGH ME, MY SERVITORS CAN SEE YOU FOR WHAT YOU REALLY ARE.
THIS IS WHERE HE FREES US...
...WHERE HE ENSLAVES US ALL OVER AGAIN!
...TRYING TO BRING IT ALL DOWN AROUND US...
...TRYING TO STOP HIM FROM REVEALING THE TRUTH...
...CAN'T BREAK AWAY...
...SO STRONG... RELENTLESS...
I LIKE IT BETTER THIS WAY.
AFTER ALL THE MASKS... I LIKE THIS... JUST BEING MYSELF.
YOU KNOW WHO I AM.
WHY NOT TELL ME WHO I'M DEALING WITH?
YOU'LL FIND OUT SOON ENOUGH.
WHAT IS THIS?
WHERE ARE WE?
I NEED YOU TO FOCUS... TO TELL ME WHO--
I AM FOCUSING... BUT HE'LL KILL ME BEFORE HE LETS ME REVEAL HIS IDENTITY.
I CAN'T TELL YOU WHO HE IS...

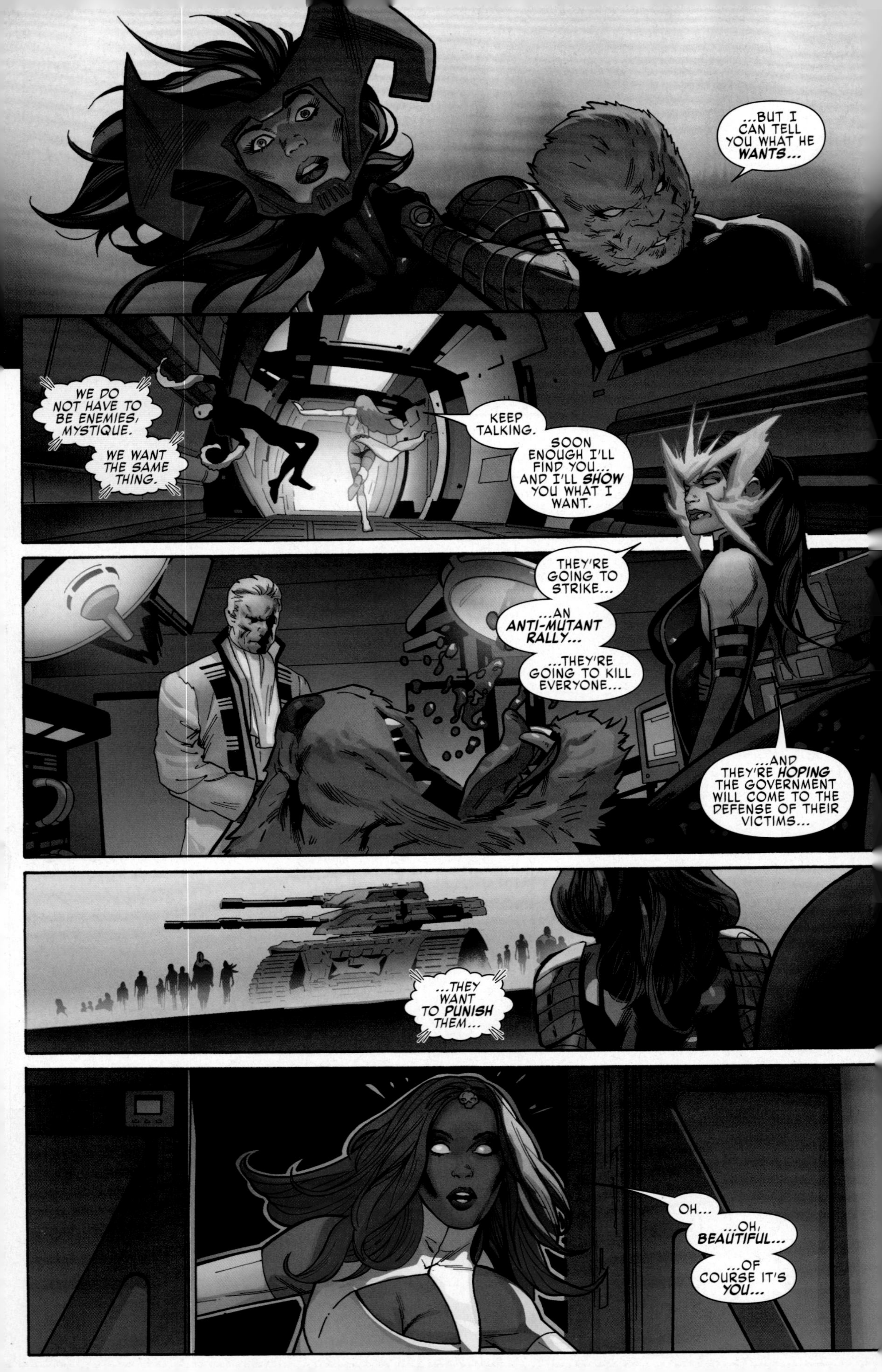
...BUT I CAN TELL YOU WHAT HE WANTS...
WE DO NOT HAVE TO BE ENEMIES, MYSTIQUE.
WE WANT THE SAME THING.
KEEP TALKING.
SOON ENOUGH I'LL FIND YOU... AND I'LL SHOW YOU WHAT I WANT.
THEY'RE GOING TO STRIKE...
...AN ANTI-MUTANT RALLY...
...THEY'RE GOING TO KILL EVERYONE...
...AND THEY'RE HOPING THE GOVERNMENT WILL COME TO THE DEFENSE OF THEIR VICTIMS...
...THEY WANT TO PUNISH THEM...
OH...
...OH, BEAUTIFUL...
...OF COURSE IT'S YOU...

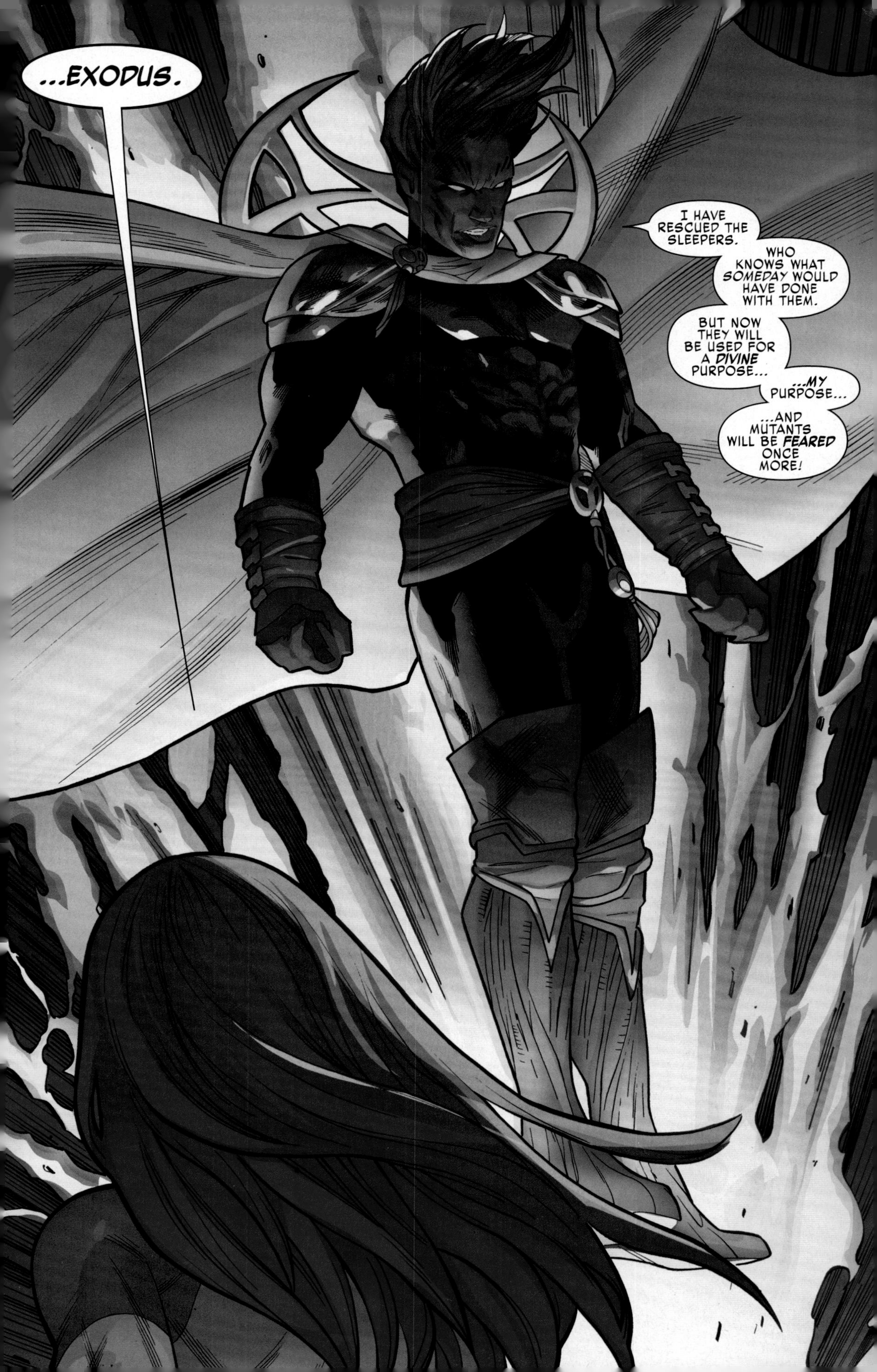
...EXODUS.
I HAVE RESCUED THE SLEEPERS.
WHO KNOWS WHAT SOMEDAY WOULD HAVE DONE WITH THEM.
BUT NOW THEY WILL BE USED FOR A DIVINE PURPOSE...
...MY PURPOSE...
...AND MUTANTS WILL BE FEARED ONCE MORE!

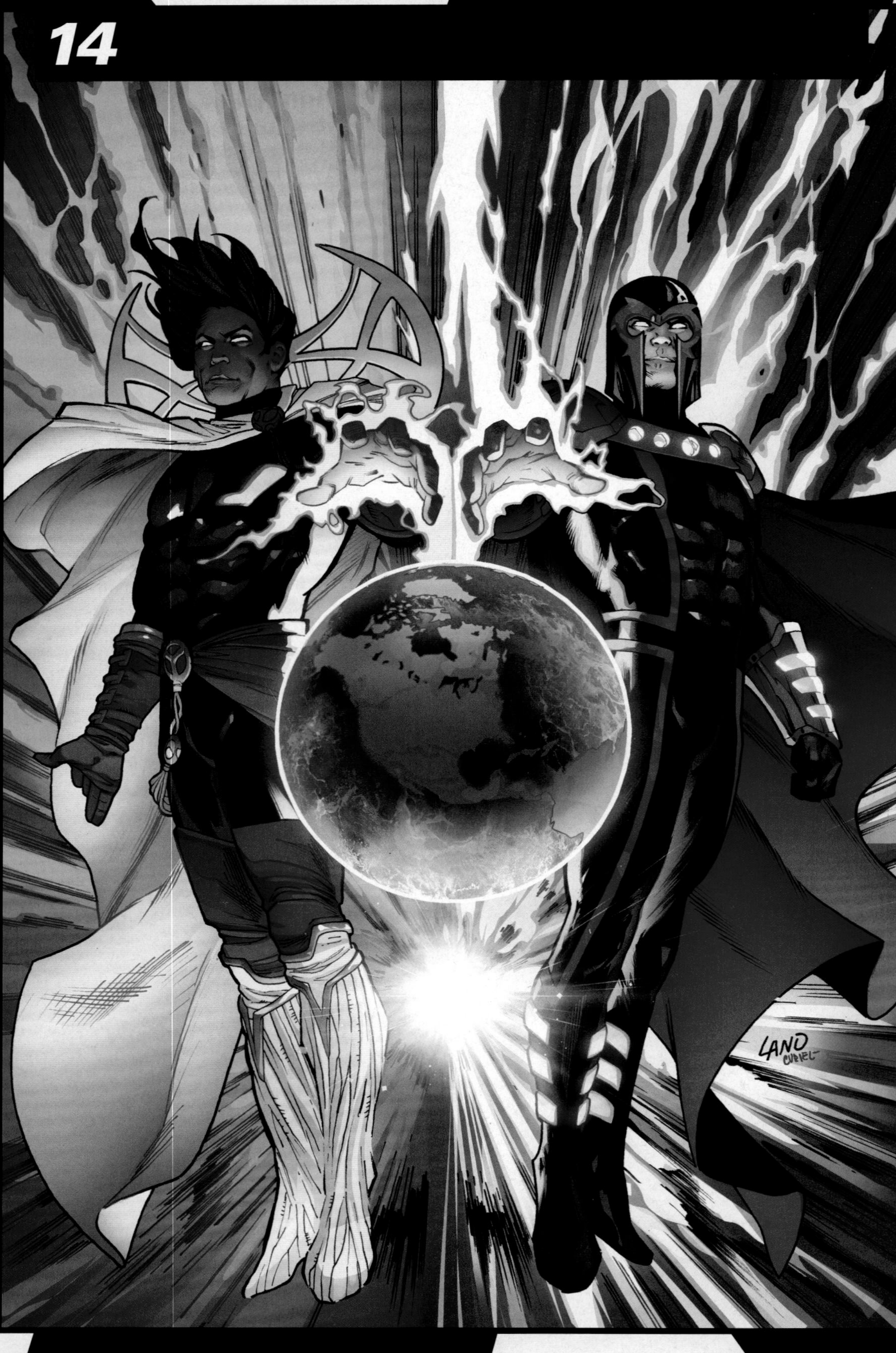
14

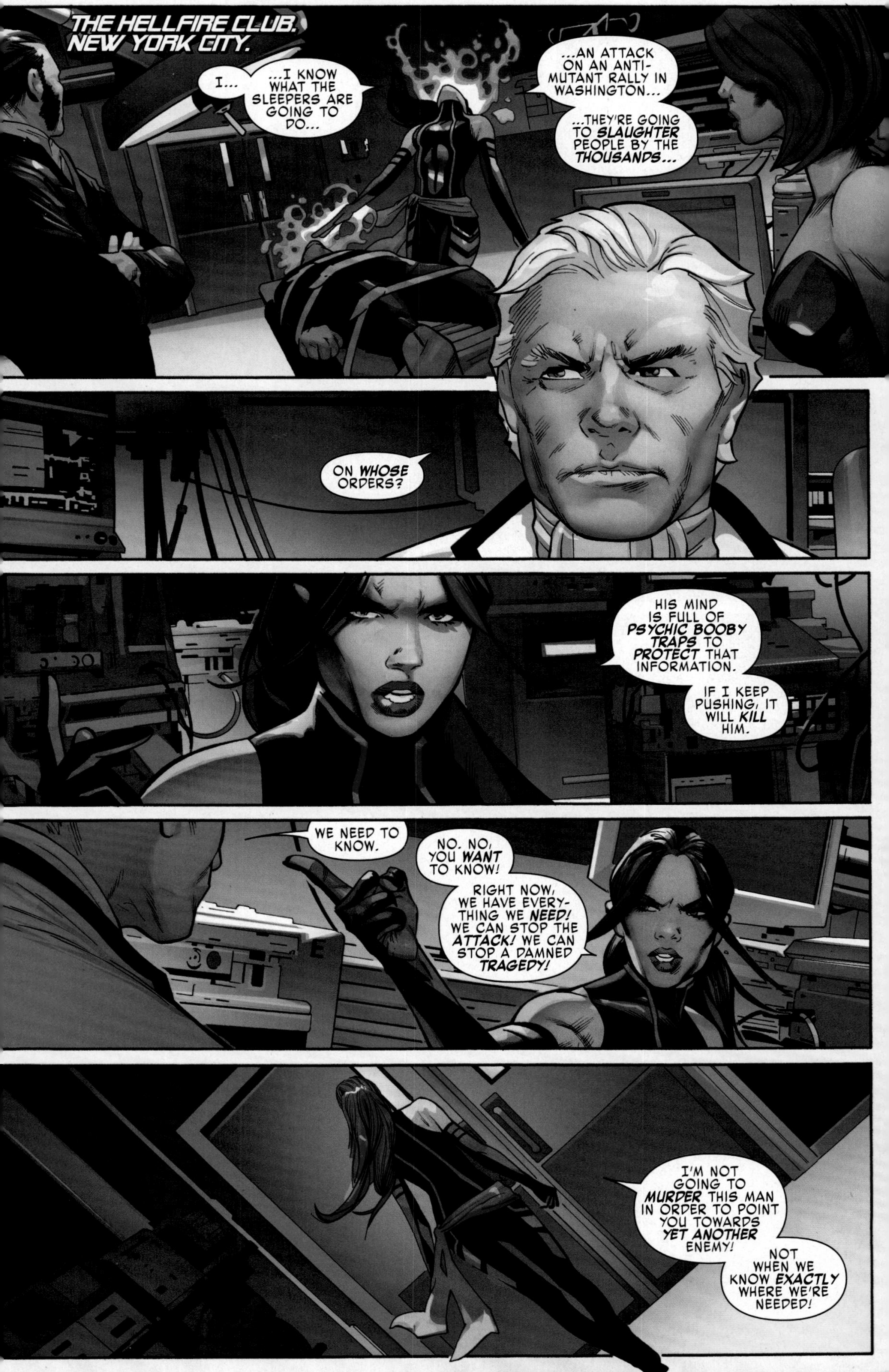
THE HELLFIRE CLUB. NEW YORK CITY.
I...
...I KNOW WHAT THE SLEEPERS ARE GOING TO DO...
...AN ATTACK ON AN ANTI-MUTANT RALLY IN WASHINGTON...
...THEY'RE GOING TO SLAUGHTER PEOPLE BY THE THOUSANDS...
ON WHOSE ORDERS?
HIS MIND IS FULL OF PSYCHIC BOOBY TRAPS TO PROTECT THAT INFORMATION.
IF I KEEP PUSHING, IT WILL KILL HIM.
WE NEED TO KNOW.
NO. NO, YOU WANT TO KNOW!
RIGHT NOW, WE HAVE EVERY-THING WE NEED! WE CAN STOP THE ATTACK! WE CAN STOP A DAMNED TRAGEDY!
I'M NOT GOING TO MURDER THIS MAN IN ORDER TO POINT YOU TOWARDS YET ANOTHER ENEMY!
NOT WHEN WE KNOW EXACTLY WHERE WE'RE NEEDED!

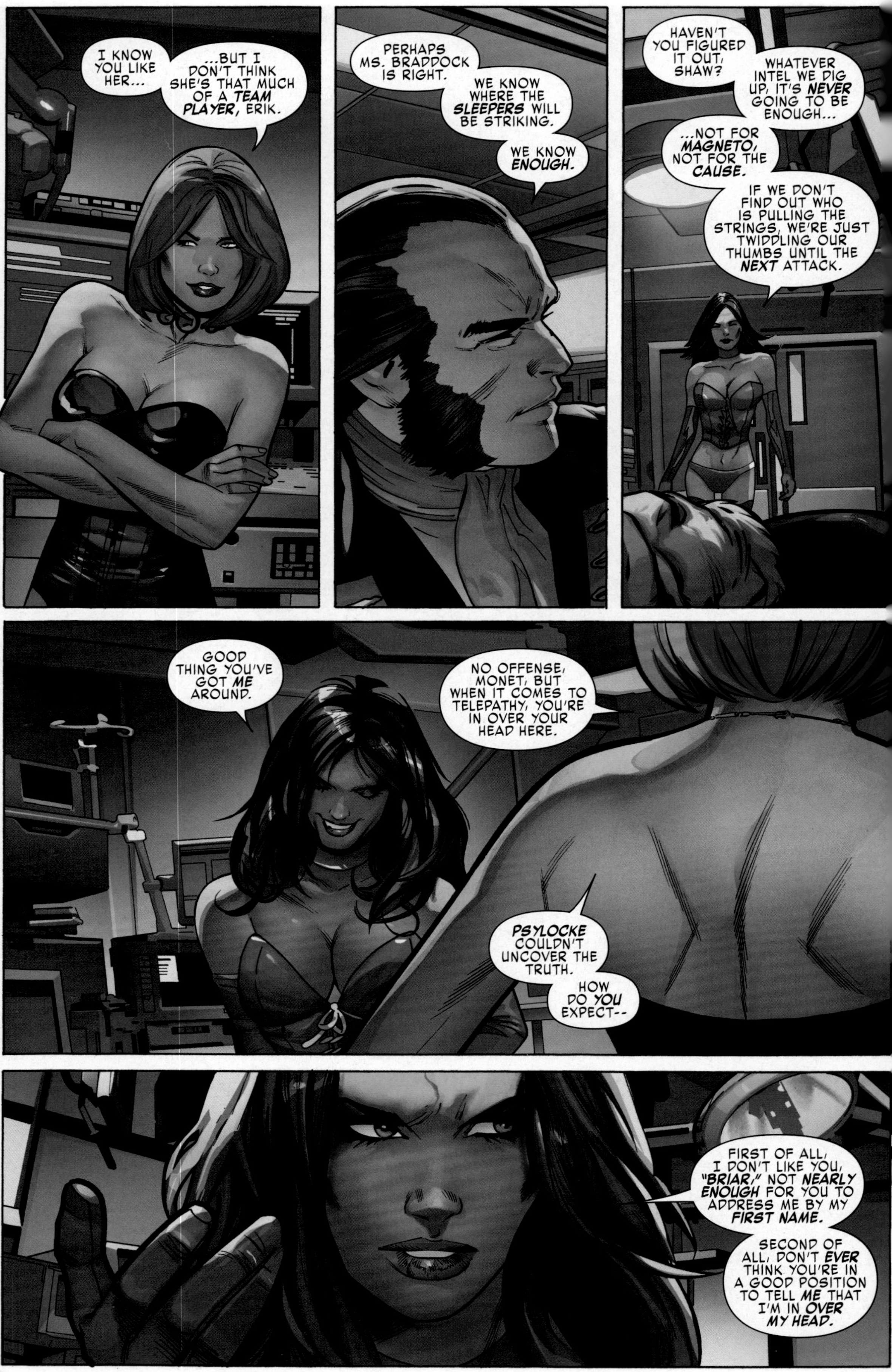
I KNOW YOU LIKE HER...
...BUT I DON'T THINK SHE'S THAT MUCH OF A TEAM PLAYER, ERIK.
PERHAPS MS. BRADDOCK IS RIGHT.
WE KNOW WHERE THE SLEEPERS WILL BE STRIKING.
WE KNOW ENOUGH.
HAVEN'T YOU FIGURED IT OUT, SHAW?
WHATEVER INTEL WE DIG UP, IT'S NEVER GOING TO BE ENOUGH...
...NOT FOR MAGNETO, NOT FOR THE CAUSE.
IF WE DON'T FIND OUT WHO IS PULLING THE STRINGS, WE'RE JUST TWIDDLING OUR THUMBS UNTIL THE NEXT ATTACK.
GOOD THING YOU'VE GOT ME AROUND.
NO OFFENSE, MONET, BUT WHEN IT COMES TO TELEPATHY, YOU'RE IN OVER YOUR HEAD HERE.
PSYLOCKE COULDN'T UNCOVER THE TRUTH.
HOW DO YOU EXPECT--
FIRST OF ALL, I DON'T LIKE YOU, "BRIAR," NOT NEARLY ENOUGH FOR YOU TO ADDRESS ME BY MY FIRST NAME.
SECOND OF ALL, DON'T EVER THINK YOU'RE IN A GOOD POSITION TO TELL ME THAT I'M IN OVER MY HEAD.

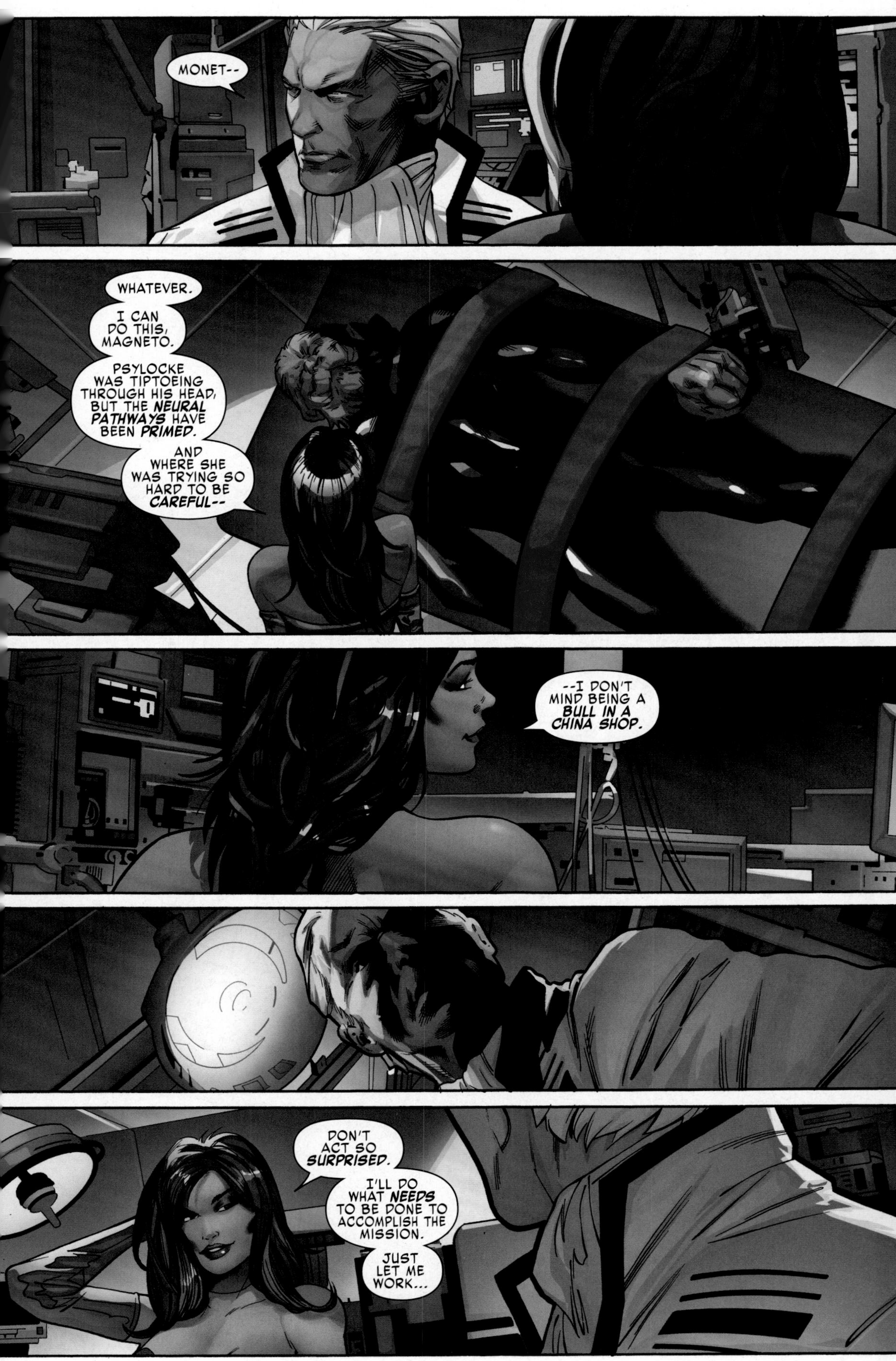
MONET--
WHATEVER.
I CAN DO THIS, MAGNETO.
PSYLOCKE WAS TIPTOEING THROUGH HIS HEAD, BUT THE NEURAL PATHWAYS HAVE BEEN PRIMED.
AND WHERE SHE WAS TRYING SO HARD TO BE CAREFUL--
--I DON'T MIND BEING A BULL IN A CHINA SHOP.
DON'T ACT SO SURPRISED.
I'LL DO WHAT NEEDS TO BE DONE TO ACCOMPLISH THE MISSION.
JUST LET ME WORK...

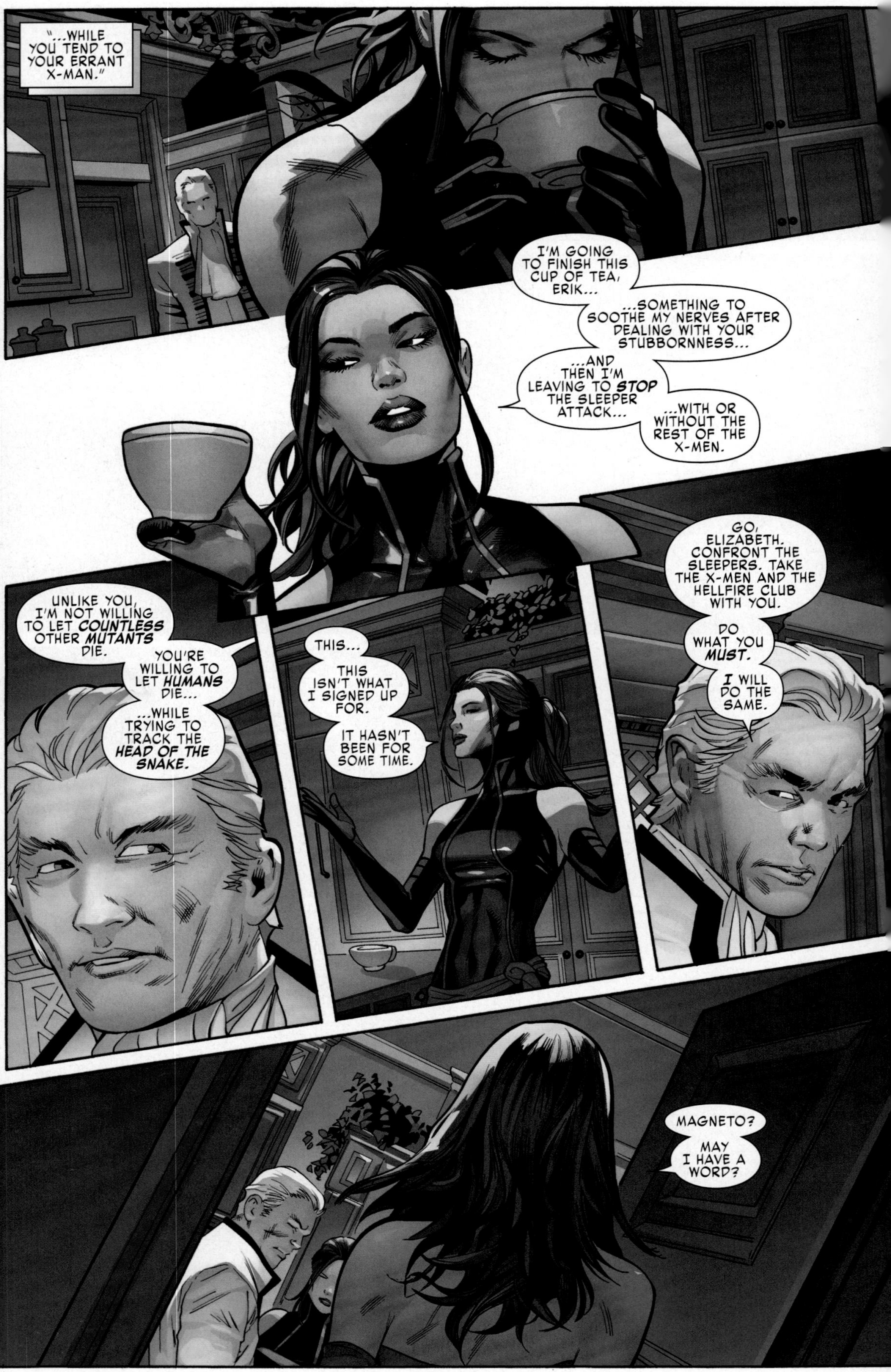
"...WHILE YOU TEND TO YOUR ERRANT X-MAN."
I'M GOING TO FINISH THIS CUP OF TEA, ERIK...
...SOMETHING TO SOOTHE MY NERVES AFTER DEALING WITH YOUR STUBBORNNESS...
...AND THEN I'M LEAVING TO STOP THE SLEEPER ATTACK...
...WITH OR WITHOUT THE REST OF THE X-MEN.
UNLIKE YOU, I'M NOT WILLING TO LET COUNTLESS OTHER MUTANTS DIE.
YOU'RE WILLING TO LET HUMANS DIE...
...WHILE TRYING TO TRACK THE HEAD OF THE SNAKE.
THIS...
THIS ISN'T WHAT I SIGNED UP FOR.
IT HASN'T BEEN FOR SOME TIME.
GO, ELIZABETH. CONFRONT THE SLEEPERS. TAKE THE X-MEN AND THE HELLFIRE CLUB WITH YOU.
DO WHAT YOU MUST.
I WILL DO THE SAME.
MAGNETO?
MAY I HAVE A WORD?

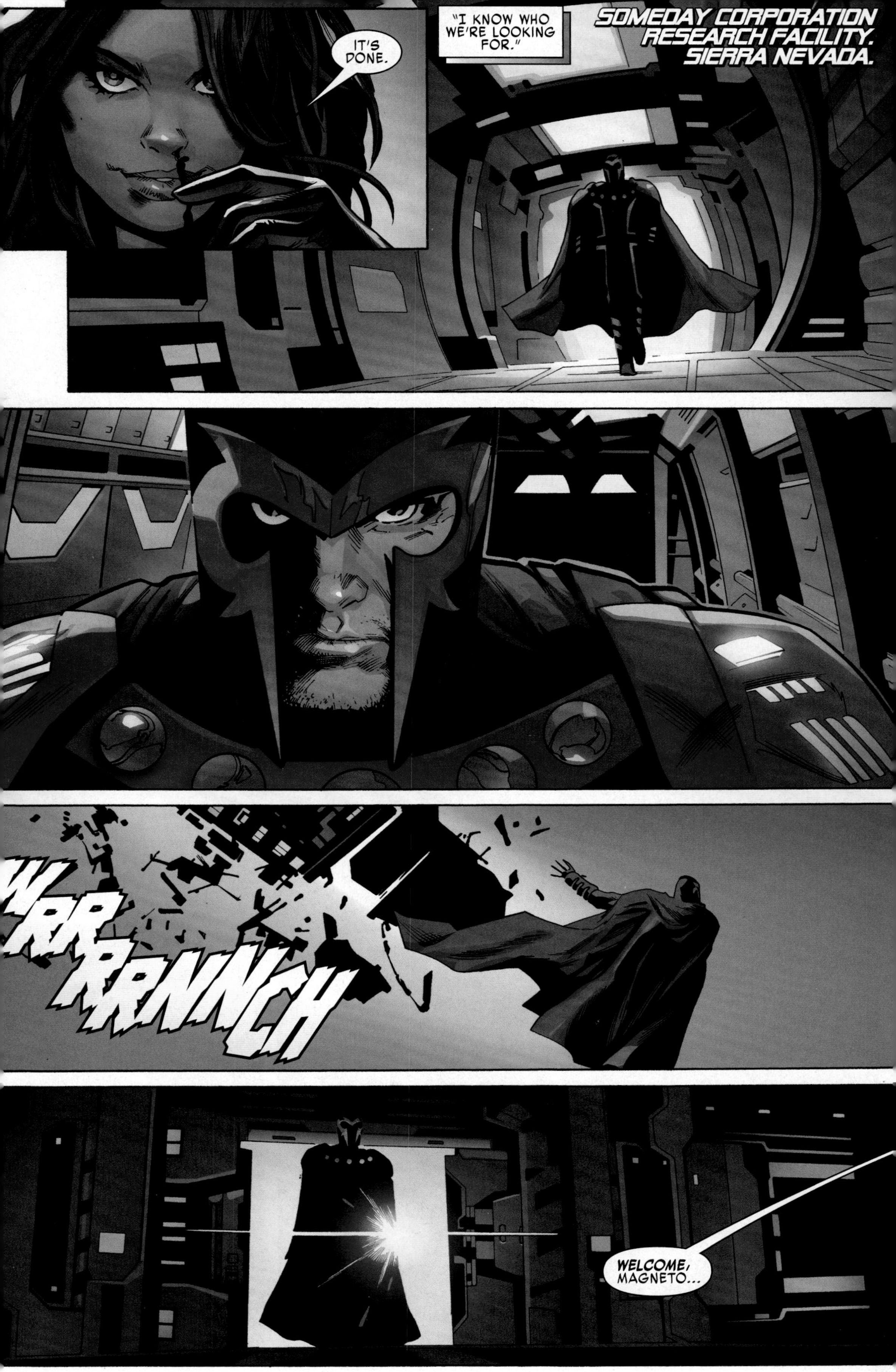
SOMEDAY CORPORATION RESEARCH FACILITY. SIERRA NEVADA.
IT'S DONE.
"I KNOW WHO WE'RE LOOKING FOR."
WRRRRRNNNCH
WELCOME, MAGNETO...

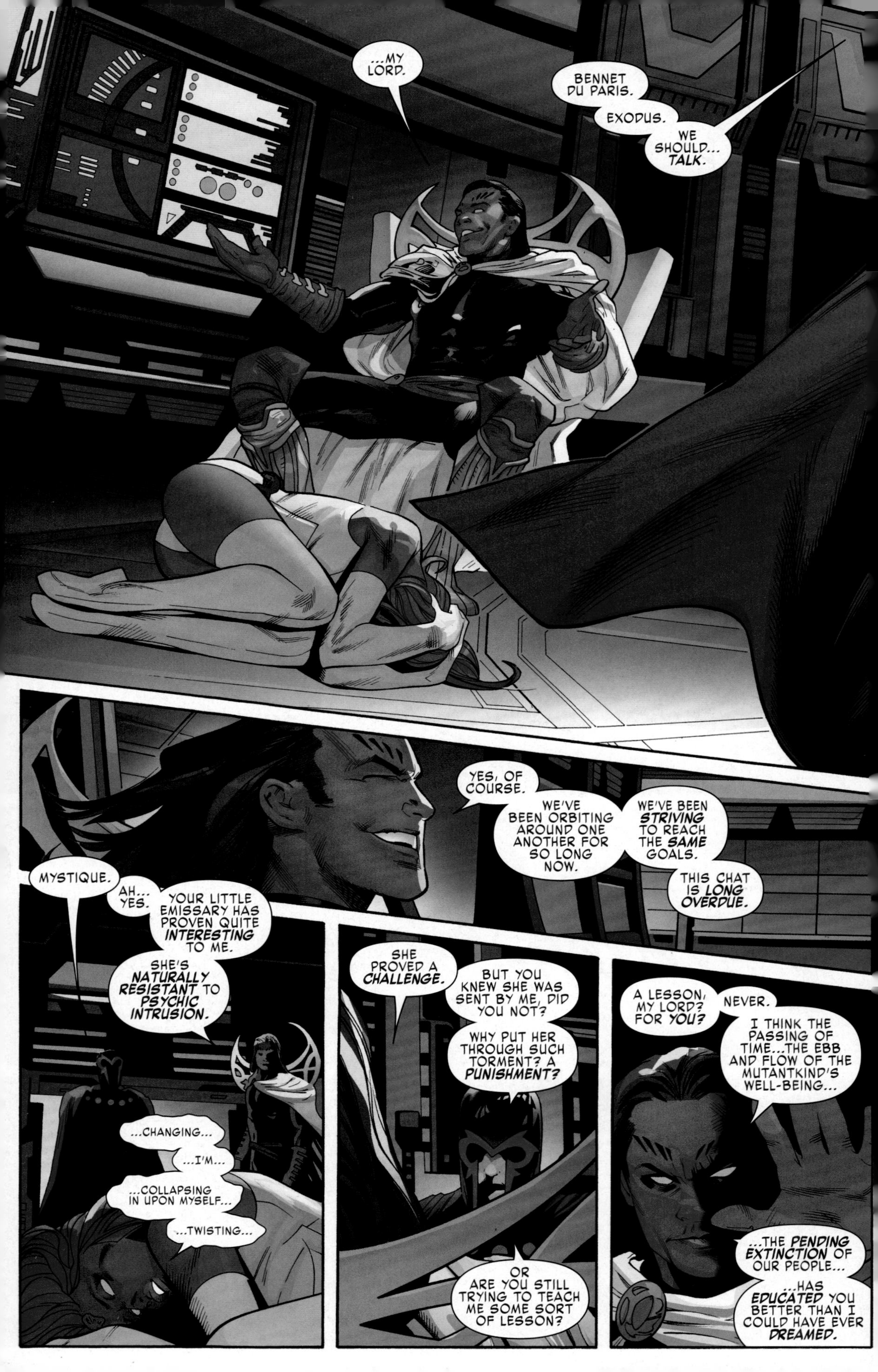
...MY LORD.
BENNET DU PARIS.
EXODUS.
WE SHOULD... TALK.
YES, OF COURSE.
WE'VE BEEN ORBITING AROUND ONE ANOTHER FOR SO LONG NOW.
WE'VE BEEN STRIVING TO REACH THE SAME GOALS.
THIS CHAT IS LONG OVERDUE.
MYSTIQUE.
AH... YES.
YOUR LITTLE EMISSARY HAS PROVEN QUITE INTERESTING TO ME.
SHE'S NATURALLY RESISTANT TO PSYCHIC INTRUSION.
...CHANGING...
...I'M...
...COLLAPSING IN UPON MYSELF...
...TWISTING...
SHE PROVED A CHALLENGE.
BUT YOU KNEW SHE WAS SENT BY ME, DID YOU NOT?
WHY PUT HER THROUGH SUCH TORMENT? A PUNISHMENT?
OR ARE YOU STILL TRYING TO TEACH ME SOME SORT OF LESSON?
A LESSON, MY LORD? FOR YOU?
NEVER.
I THINK THE PASSING OF TIME...THE EBB AND FLOW OF THE MUTANTKIND'S WELL-BEING...
...THE PENDING EXTINCTION OF OUR PEOPLE...
...HAS EDUCATED YOU BETTER THAN I COULD HAVE EVER DREAMED.

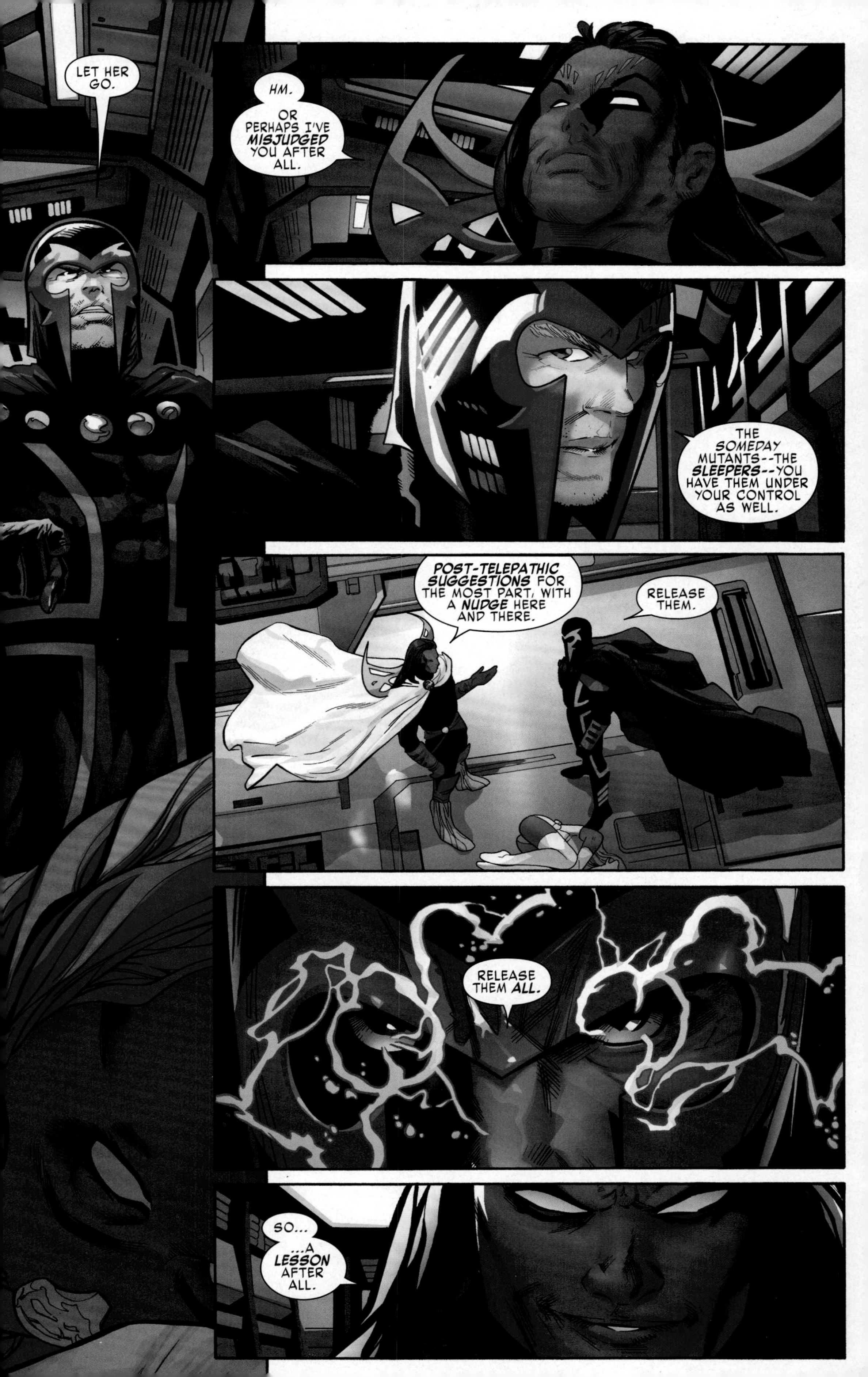
LET HER GO.
HM.
OR PERHAPS I'VE MISJUDGED YOU AFTER ALL.
THE SOMEDAY MUTANTS--THE SLEEPERS--YOU HAVE THEM UNDER YOUR CONTROL AS WELL.
POST-TELEPATHIC SUGGESTIONS FOR THE MOST PART, WITH A NUDGE HERE AND THERE.
RELEASE THEM.
RELEASE THEM ALL.
SO...
...A LESSON AFTER ALL.

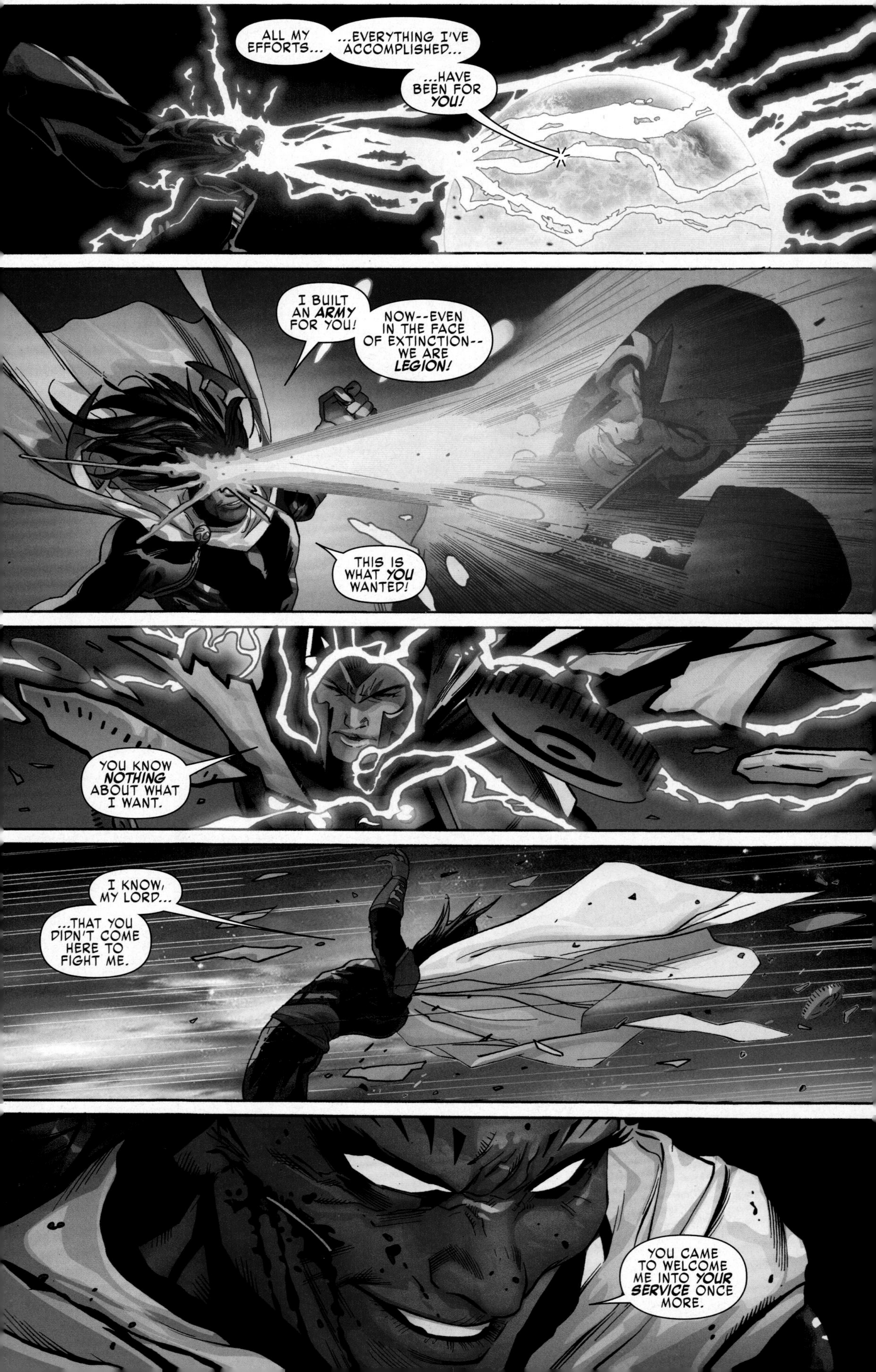
ALL MY EFFORTS...
...EVERYTHING I'VE ACCOMPLISHED...
...HAVE BEEN FOR YOU!
I BUILT AN ARMY FOR YOU!
NOW--EVEN IN THE FACE OF EXTINCTION--WE ARE LEGION!
THIS IS WHAT YOU WANTED!
YOU KNOW NOTHING ABOUT WHAT I WANT.
I KNOW, MY LORD...
...THAT YOU DIDN'T COME HERE TO FIGHT ME.
YOU CAME TO WELCOME ME INTO YOUR SERVICE ONCE MORE.

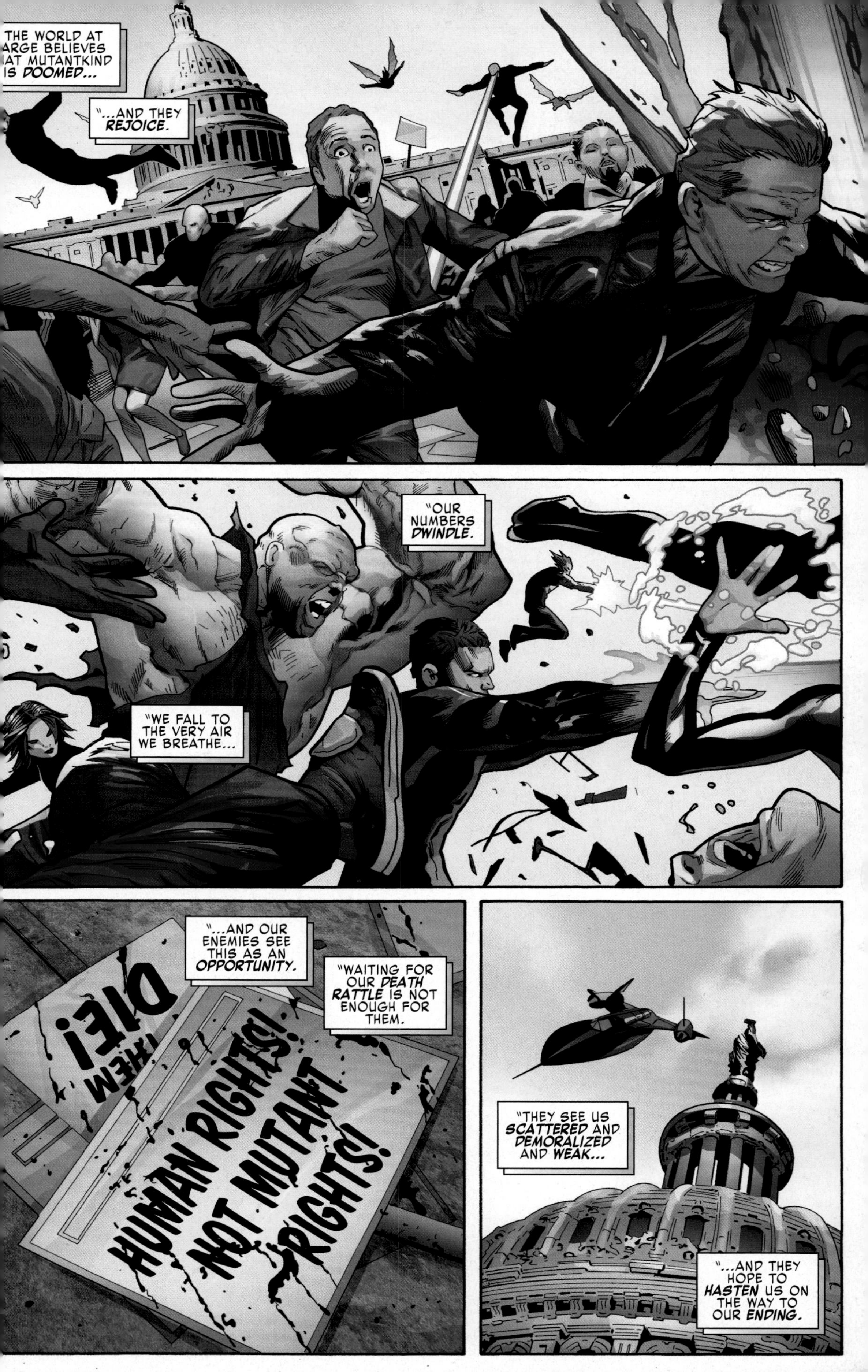
THE WORLD AT
ARGE BELIEVES
AT MUTANTKIND
IS DOOMED...
"...AND THEY
REJOICE.
"OUR
NUMBERS
DWINDLE.
"WE FALL TO
THE VERY AIR
WE BREATHE...
"...AND OUR
ENEMIES SEE
THIS AS AN
OPPORTUNITY.
"WAITING FOR
OUR DEATH
RATTLE IS NOT
ENOUGH FOR
THEM.
DIE!
THEM
HUMAN RIGHTS!
NOT MUTANT
RIGHTS!
"THEY SEE US
SCATTERED AND
DEMORALIZED
AND WEAK...
"...AND THEY
HOPE TO
HASTEN US ON
THE WAY TO
OUR ENDING.

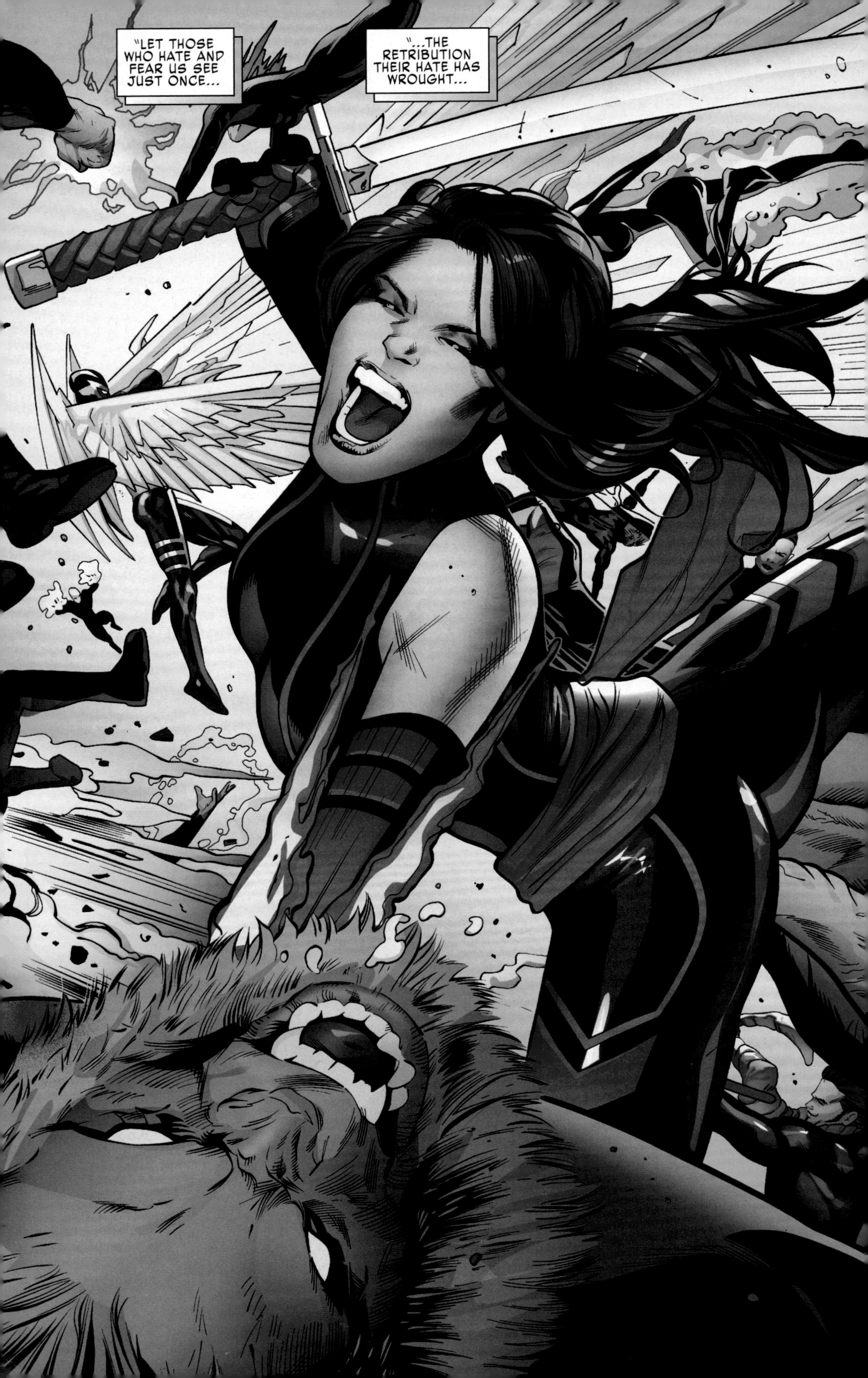
"LET THOSE WHO HATE AND FEAR US SEE JUST ONCE...
"...THE RETRIBUTION THEIR HATE HAS WROUGHT...

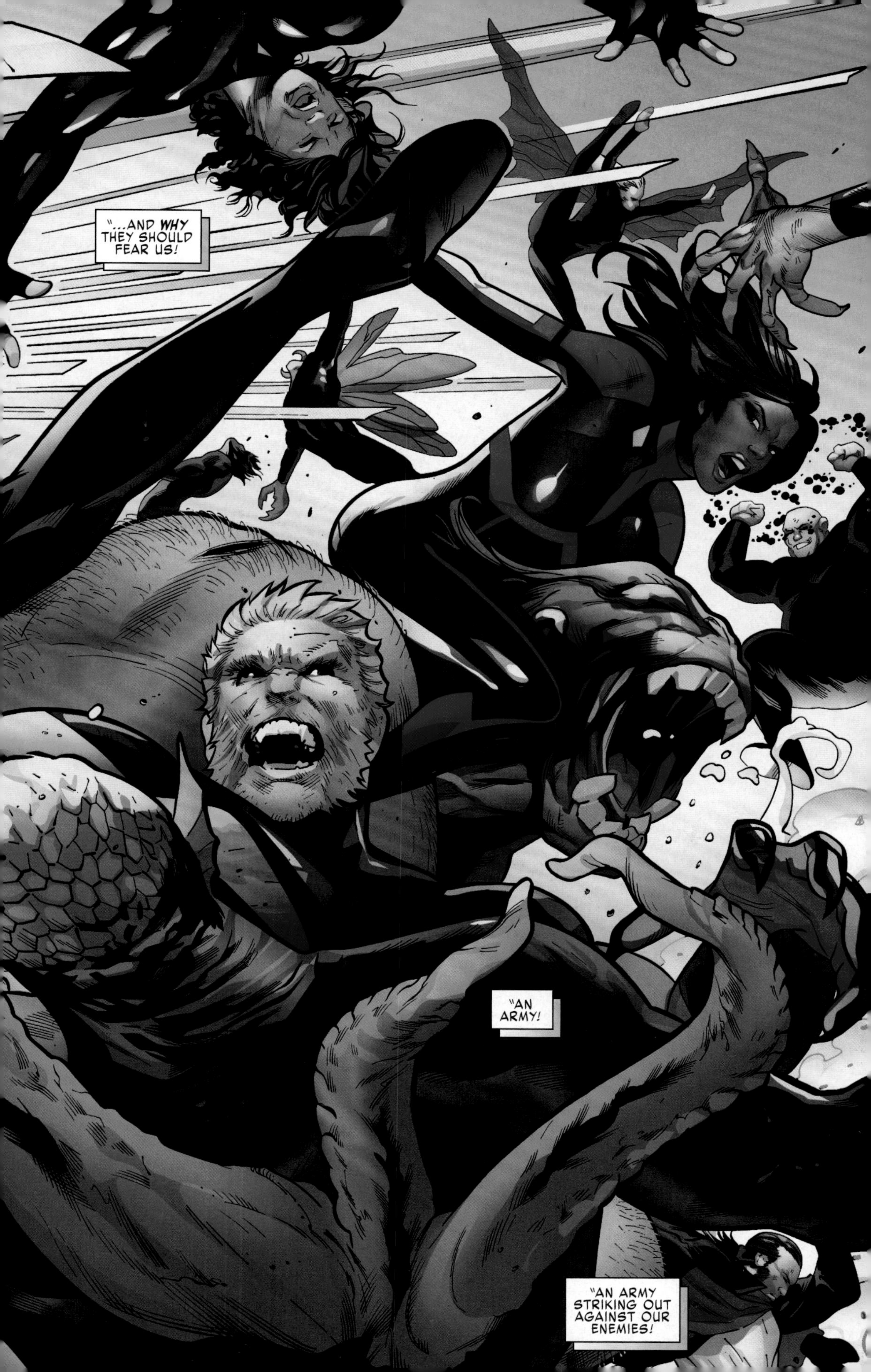
"...AND WHY THEY SHOULD FEAR US!
"AN ARMY!
"AN ARMY STRIKING OUT AGAINST OUR ENEMIES!

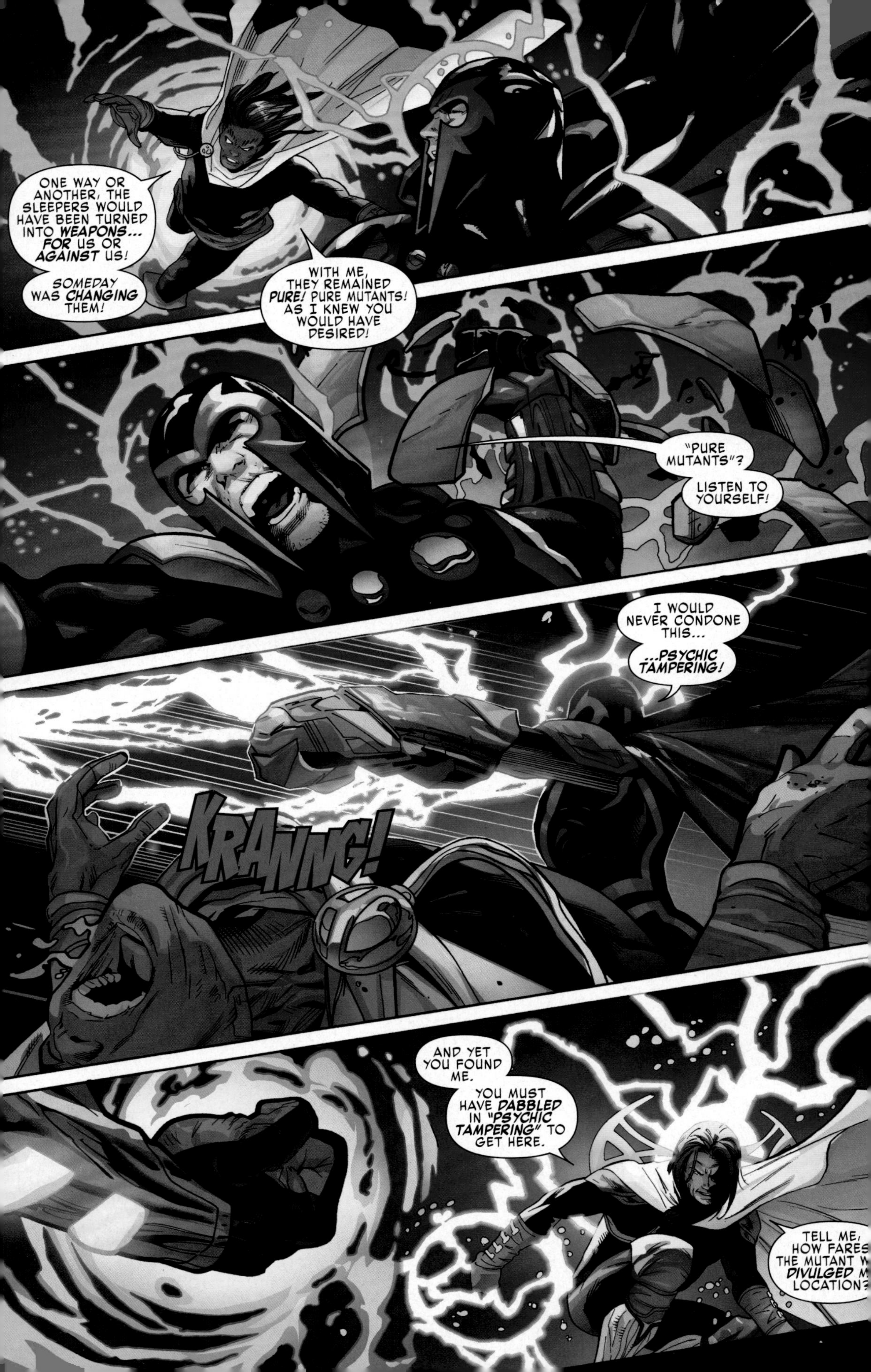
ONE WAY OR ANOTHER, THE SLEEPERS WOULD HAVE BEEN TURNED INTO WEAPONS... FOR US OR AGAINST US!
SOMEDAY WAS CHANGING THEM!
WITH ME, THEY REMAINED PURE! PURE MUTANTS! AS I KNEW YOU WOULD HAVE DESIRED!
"PURE MUTANTS"?
LISTEN TO YOURSELF!
I WOULD NEVER CONDONE THIS...
...PSYCHIC TAMPERING!
KRANNG!
AND YET YOU FOUND ME.
YOU MUST HAVE DABBLED IN "PSYCHIC TAMPERING" TO GET HERE.
TELL ME, HOW FARES THE MUTANT W DIVULGED M LOCATION?

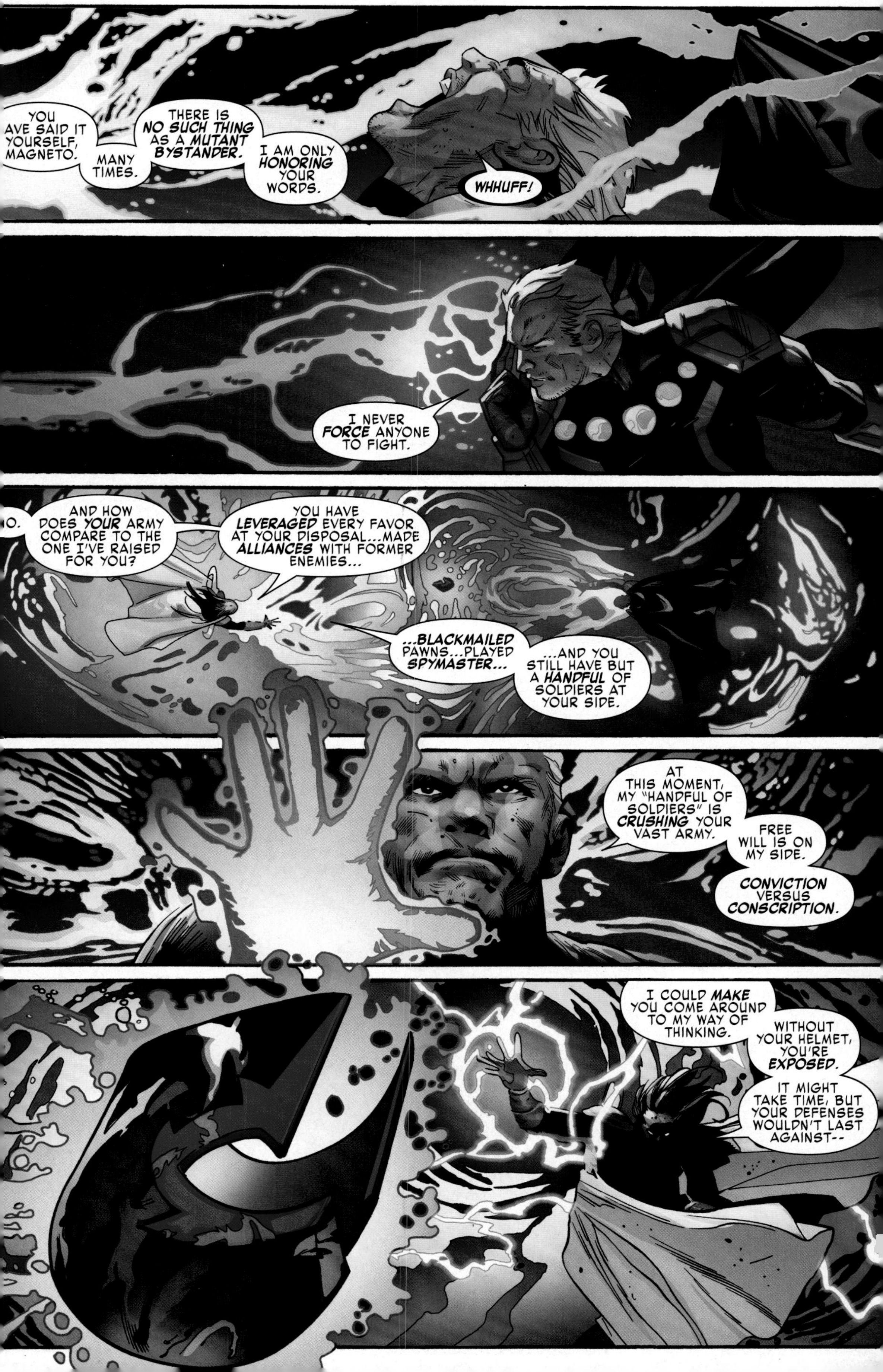

YOU AVE SAID IT YOURSELF, MAGNETO.
MANY TIMES.
THERE IS NO SUCH THING AS A MUTANT BYSTANDER.
I AM ONLY HONORING YOUR WORDS.
WHHUFF!
I NEVER FORCE ANYONE TO FIGHT.
O.
AND HOW DOES YOUR ARMY COMPARE TO THE ONE I'VE RAISED FOR YOU?
YOU HAVE LEVERAGED EVERY FAVOR AT YOUR DISPOSAL...MADE ALLIANCES WITH FORMER ENEMIES...
...BLACKMAILED PAWNS...PLAYED SPYMASTER...
...AND YOU STILL HAVE BUT A HANDFUL OF SOLDIERS AT YOUR SIDE.
AT THIS MOMENT, MY "HANDFUL OF SOLDIERS" IS CRUSHING YOUR VAST ARMY.
FREE WILL IS ON MY SIDE.
CONVICTION VERSUS CONSCRIPTION.
I COULD MAKE YOU COME AROUND TO MY WAY OF THINKING.
WITHOUT YOUR HELMET, YOU'RE EXPOSED.
IT MIGHT TAKE TIME, BUT YOUR DEFENSES WOULDN'T LAST AGAINST--

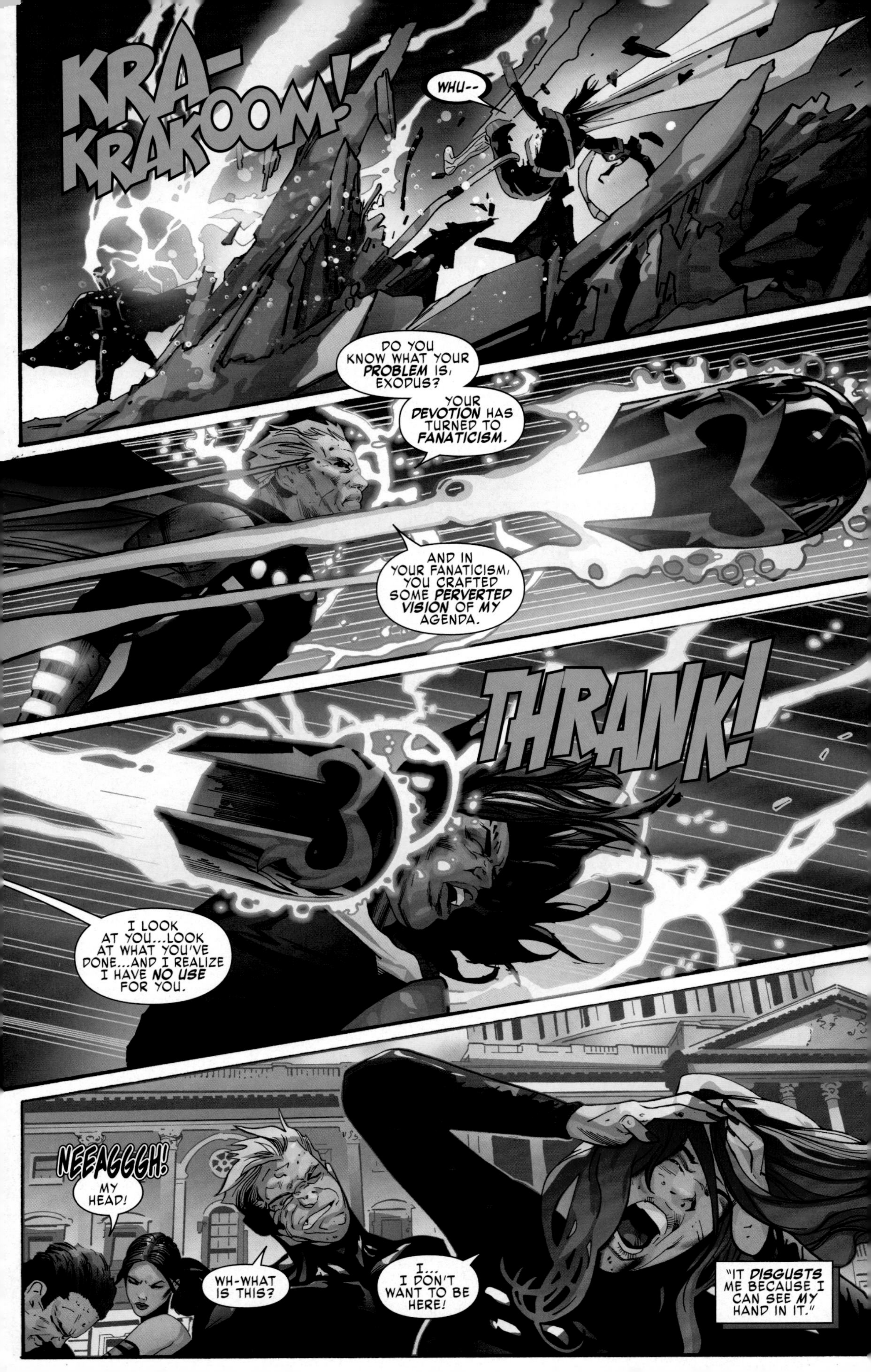

KRA-KRAKOOM!
WHU--
DO YOU KNOW WHAT YOUR PROBLEM IS, EXODUS?
YOUR DEVOTION HAS TURNED TO FANATICISM.
AND IN YOUR FANATICISM, YOU CRAFTED SOME PERVERTED VISION OF MY AGENDA.
THRANK!
I LOOK AT YOU...LOOK AT WHAT YOU'VE DONE...AND I REALIZE I HAVE NO USE FOR YOU.
NEEAGGGH!
MY HEAD!
WH-WHAT IS THIS?
I... I DON'T WANT TO BE HERE!
"IT DISGUSTS ME BECAUSE I CAN SEE MY HAND IN IT."

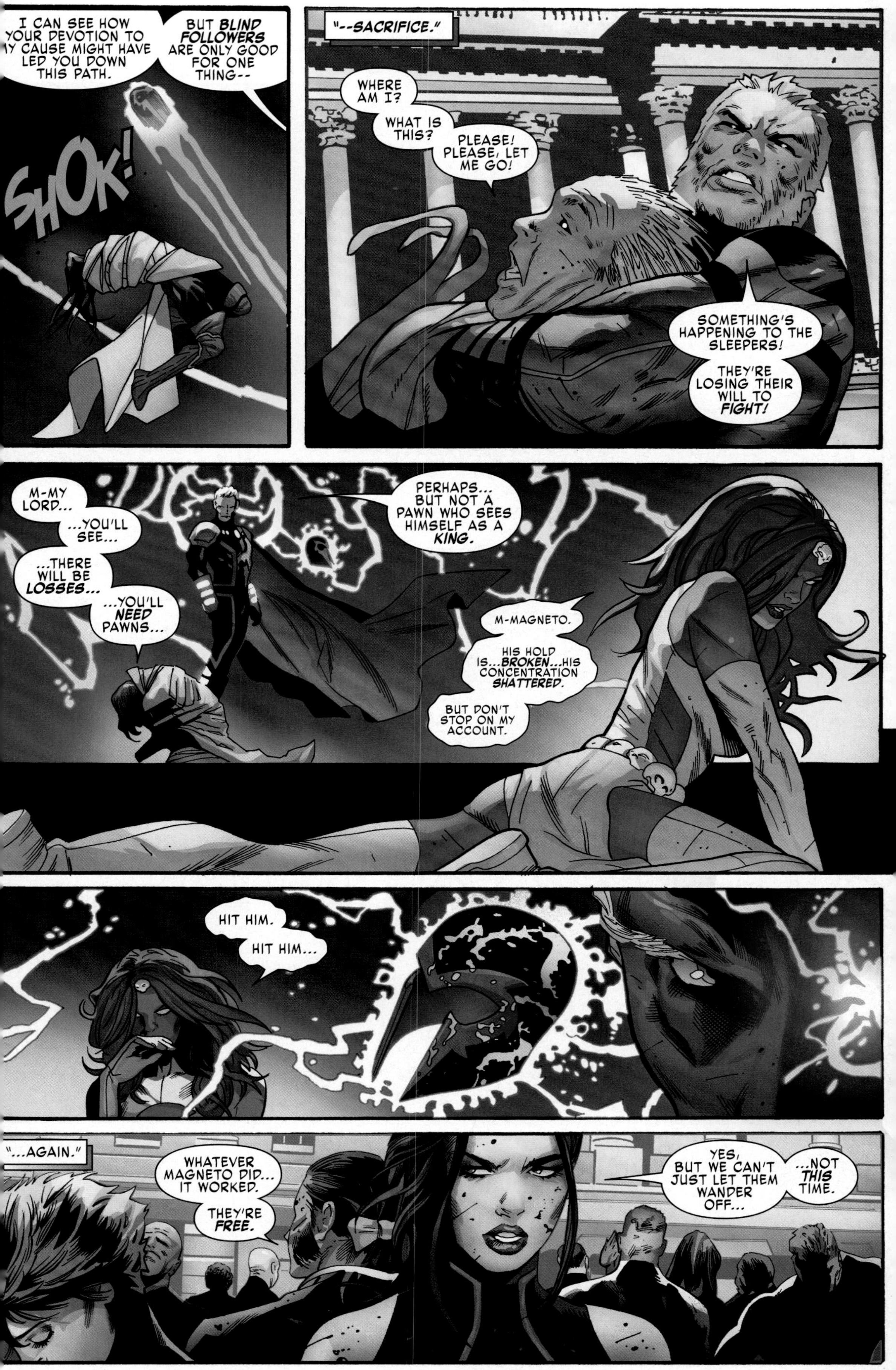
I CAN SEE HOW YOUR DEVOTION TO MY CAUSE MIGHT HAVE LED YOU DOWN THIS PATH.
BUT BLIND FOLLOWERS ARE ONLY GOOD FOR ONE THING--
SHOK!
"--SACRIFICE."
WHERE AM I?
WHAT IS THIS?
PLEASE! PLEASE, LET ME GO!
SOMETHING'S HAPPENING TO THE SLEEPERS!
THEY'RE LOSING THEIR WILL TO FIGHT!
M-MY LORD...
...YOU'LL SEE...
...THERE WILL BE LOSSES...
...YOU'LL NEED PAWNS...
PERHAPS... BUT NOT A PAWN WHO SEES HIMSELF AS A KING.
M-MAGNETO.
HIS HOLD IS...BROKEN...HIS CONCENTRATION SHATTERED.
BUT DON'T STOP ON MY ACCOUNT.
HIT HIM.
HIT HIM...
"...AGAIN."
WHATEVER MAGNETO DID... IT WORKED.
THEY'RE FREE.
YES, BUT WE CAN'T JUST LET THEM WANDER OFF...
...NOT THIS TIME.

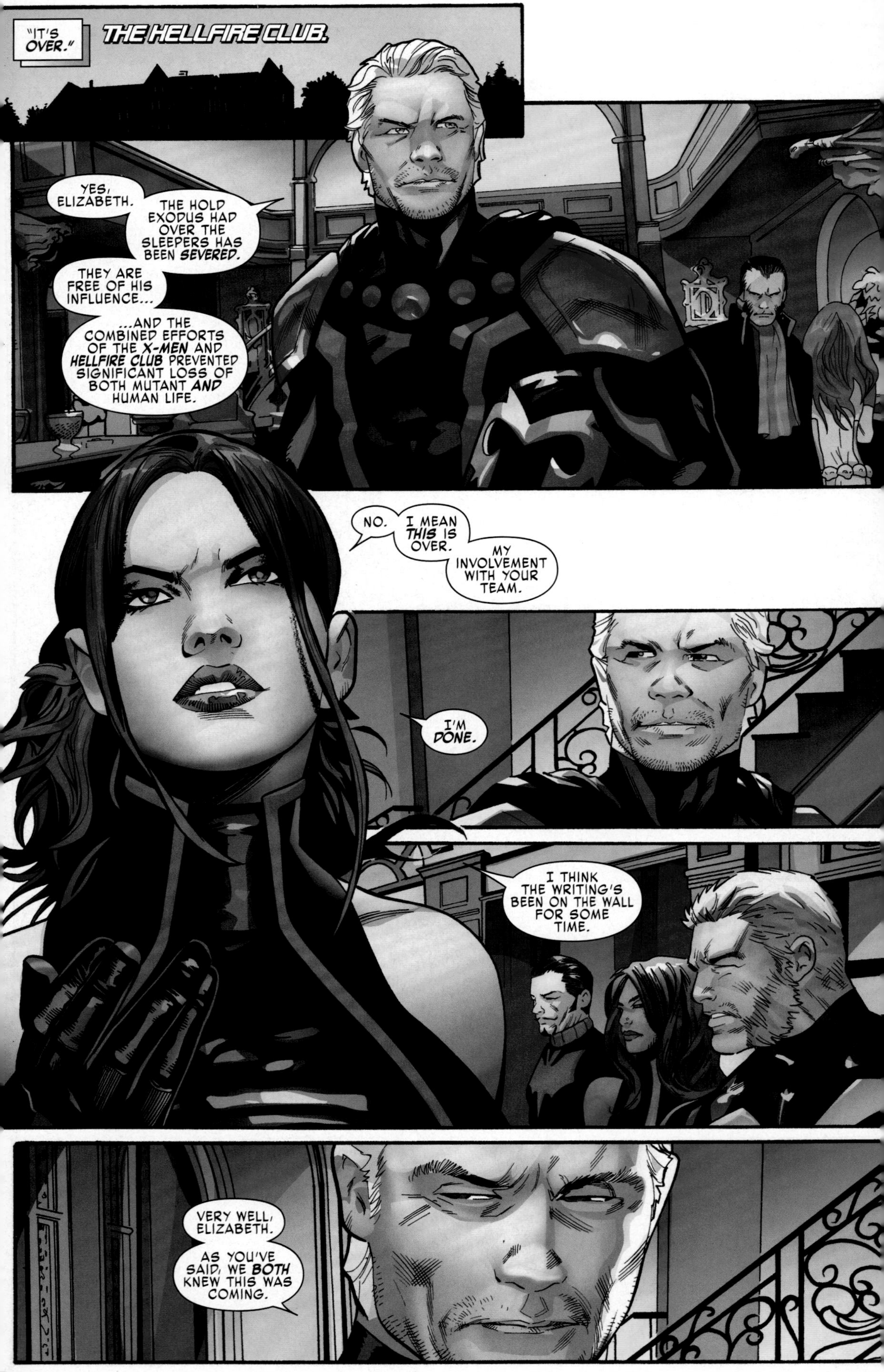
"IT'S OVER."
THE HELLFIRE CLUB.
YES, ELIZABETH.
THE HOLD EXODUS HAD OVER THE SLEEPERS HAS BEEN SEVERED.
THEY ARE FREE OF HIS INFLUENCE...
...AND THE COMBINED EFFORTS OF THE X-MEN AND HELLFIRE CLUB PREVENTED SIGNIFICANT LOSS OF BOTH MUTANT AND HUMAN LIFE.
NO.
I MEAN THIS IS OVER.
MY INVOLVEMENT WITH YOUR TEAM.
I'M DONE.
I THINK THE WRITING'S BEEN ON THE WALL FOR SOME TIME.
VERY WELL, ELIZABETH.
AS YOU'VE SAID, WE BOTH KNEW THIS WAS COMING.

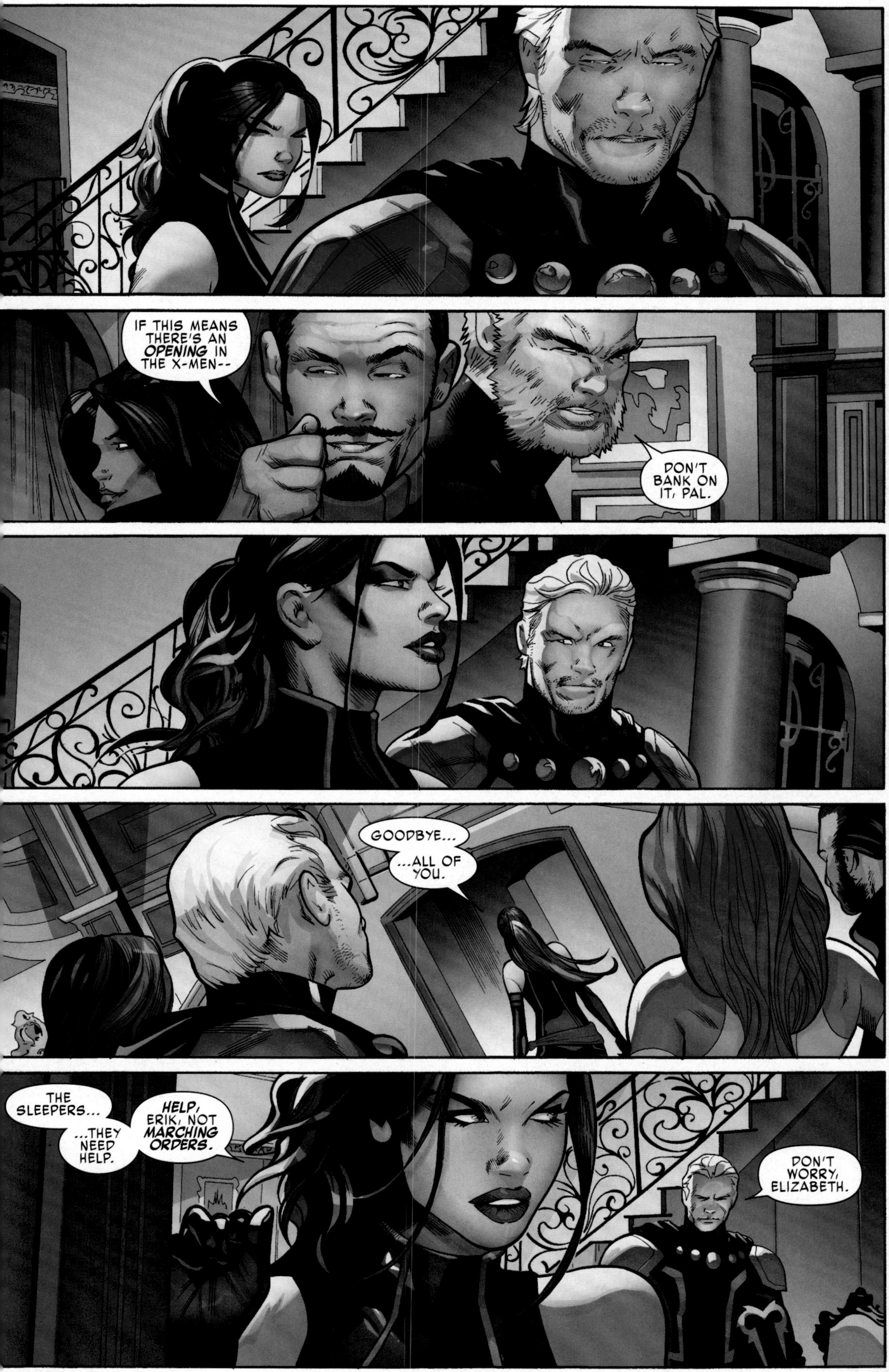

IF THIS MEANS THERE'S AN OPENING IN THE X-MEN--
DON'T BANK ON IT, PAL.
GOODBYE...
...ALL OF YOU.
THE SLEEPERS...
...THEY NEED HELP.
HELP, ERIK, NOT MARCHING ORDERS.
DON'T WORRY, ELIZABETH.

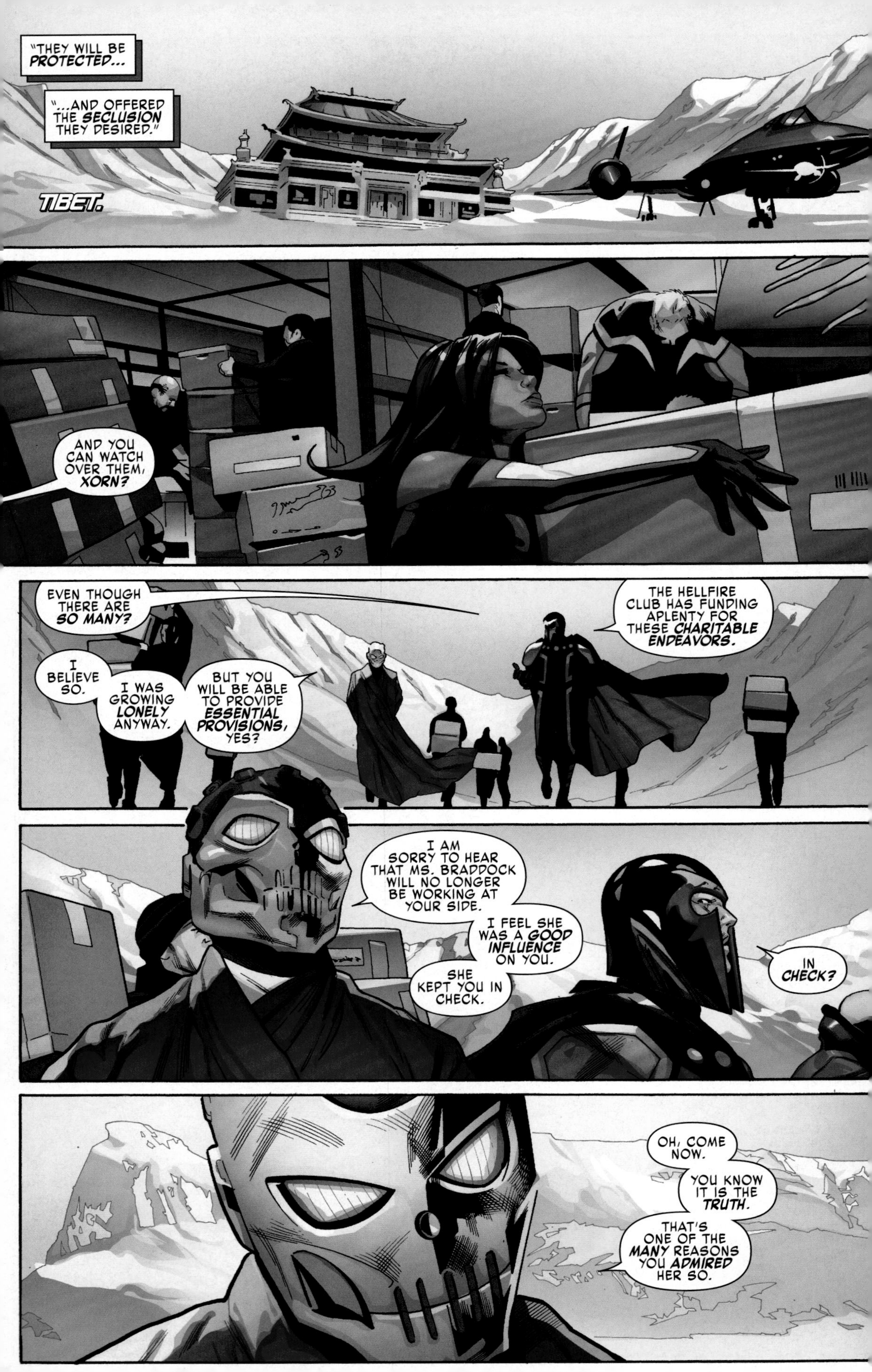
"THEY WILL BE PROTECTED...
"...AND OFFERED THE SECLUSION THEY DESIRED."
TIBET.
AND YOU CAN WATCH OVER THEM, XORN?
EVEN THOUGH THERE ARE SO MANY?
I BELIEVE SO.
I WAS GROWING LONELY ANYWAY.
BUT YOU WILL BE ABLE TO PROVIDE ESSENTIAL PROVISIONS, YES?
THE HELLFIRE CLUB HAS FUNDING APLENTY FOR THESE CHARITABLE ENDEAVORS.
I AM SORRY TO HEAR THAT MS. BRADDOCK WILL NO LONGER BE WORKING AT YOUR SIDE.
I FEEL SHE WAS A GOOD INFLUENCE ON YOU.
SHE KEPT YOU IN CHECK.
IN CHECK?
OH, COME NOW.
YOU KNOW IT IS THE TRUTH.
THAT'S ONE OF THE MANY REASONS YOU ADMIRED HER SO.

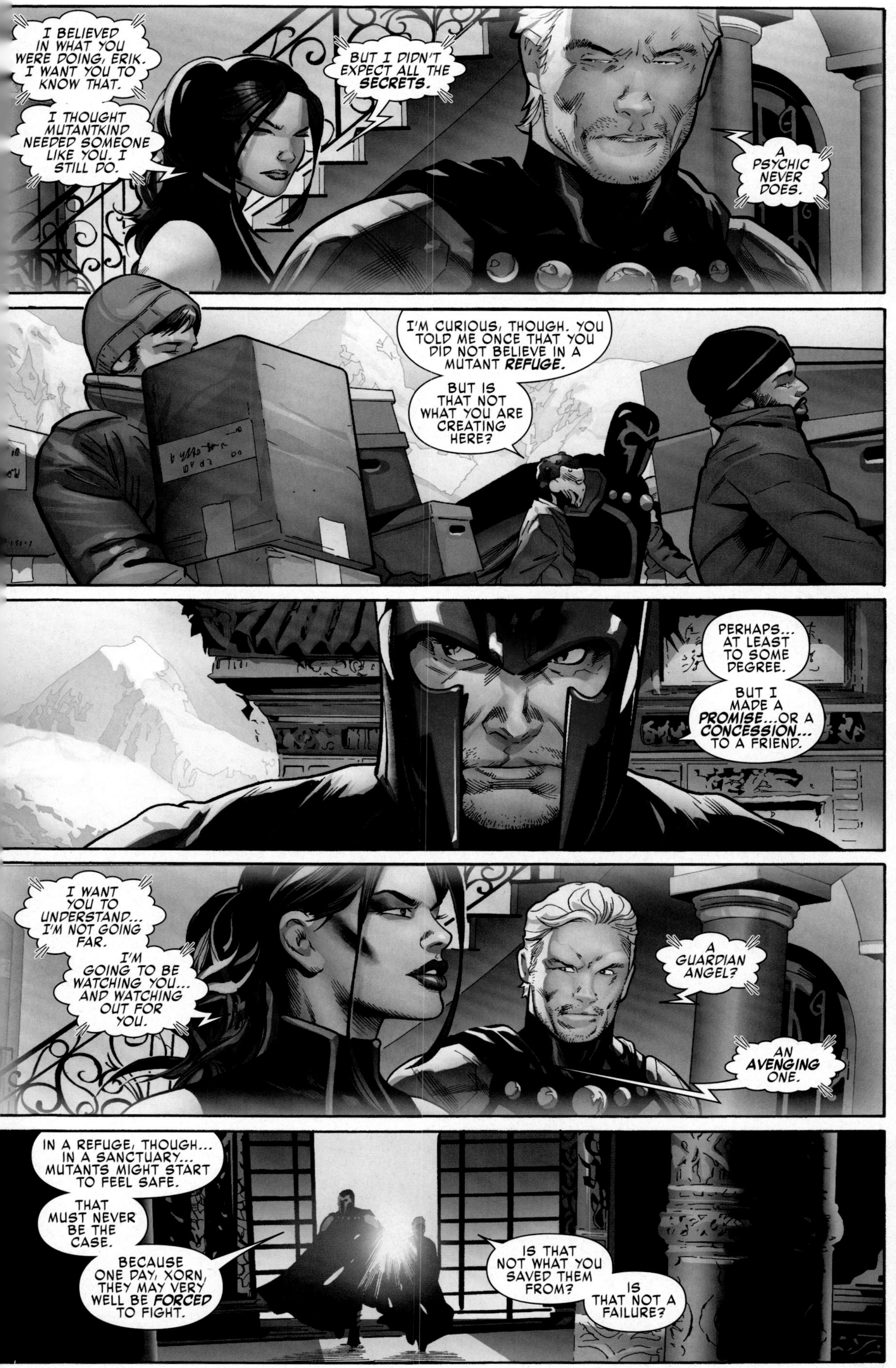
I BELIEVED IN WHAT YOU WERE DOING, ERIK. I WANT YOU TO KNOW THAT.
I THOUGHT MUTANTKIND NEEDED SOMEONE LIKE YOU. I STILL DO.
BUT I DIDN'T EXPECT ALL THE SECRETS.
A PSYCHIC NEVER DOES.
I'M CURIOUS, THOUGH. YOU TOLD ME ONCE THAT YOU DID NOT BELIEVE IN A MUTANT REFUGE.
BUT IS THAT NOT WHAT YOU ARE CREATING HERE?
PERHAPS... AT LEAST TO SOME DEGREE.
BUT I MADE A PROMISE...OR A CONCESSION... TO A FRIEND.
I WANT YOU TO UNDERSTAND... I'M NOT GOING FAR.
I'M GOING TO BE WATCHING YOU... AND WATCHING OUT FOR YOU.
A GUARDIAN ANGEL?
AN AVENGING ONE.
IN A REFUGE, THOUGH... IN A SANCTUARY... MUTANTS MIGHT START TO FEEL SAFE.
THAT MUST NEVER BE THE CASE.
BECAUSE ONE DAY, XORN, THEY MAY VERY WELL BE FORCED TO FIGHT.
IS THAT NOT WHAT YOU SAVED THEM FROM?
IS THAT NOT A FAILURE?

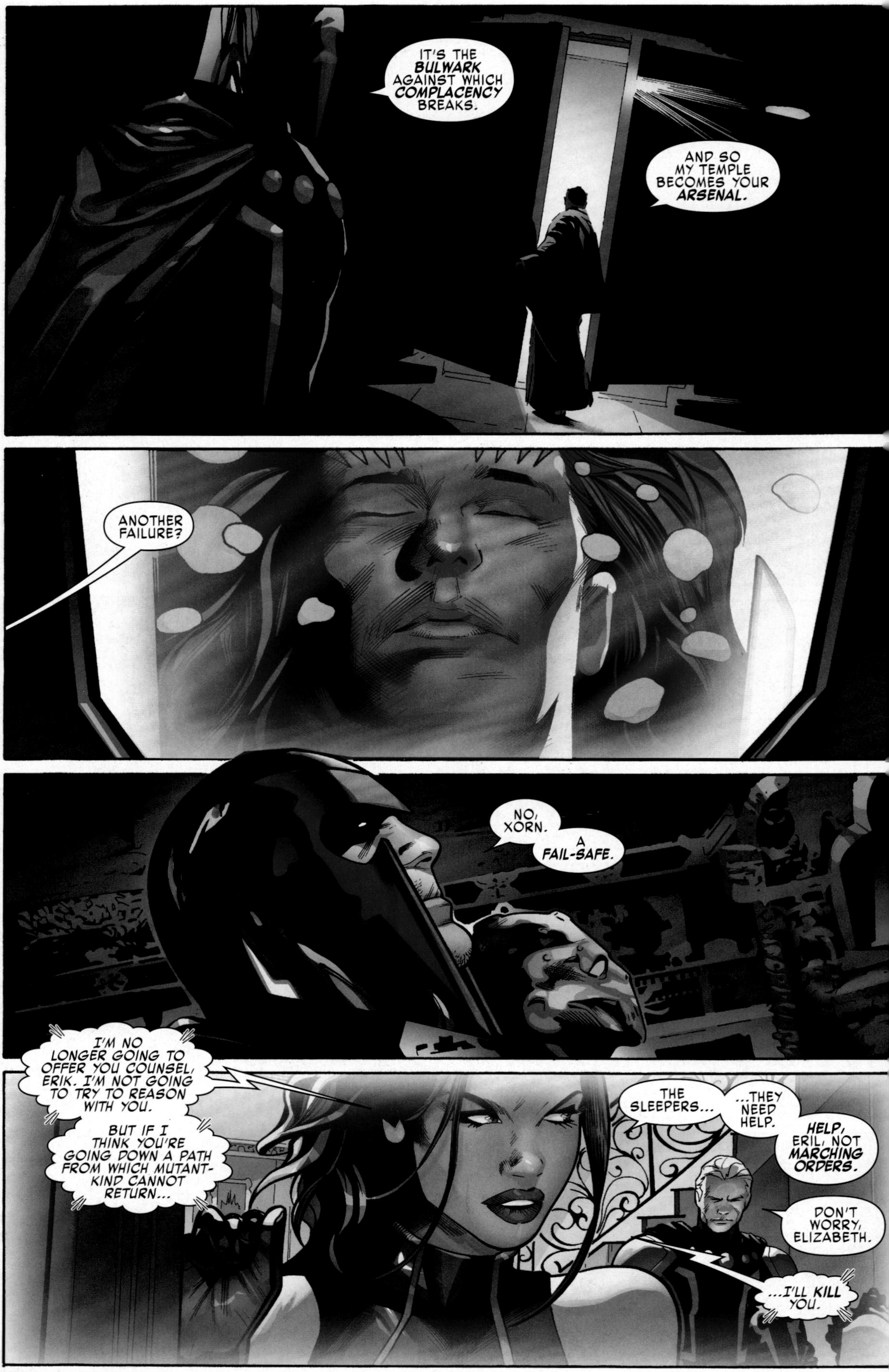
IT'S THE BULWARK AGAINST WHICH COMPLACENCY BREAKS.
AND SO MY TEMPLE BECOMES YOUR ARSENAL.
ANOTHER FAILURE?
NO, XORN.
A FAIL-SAFE.
I'M NO LONGER GOING TO OFFER YOU COUNSEL, ERIK. I'M NOT GOING TO TRY TO REASON WITH YOU.
BUT IF I THINK YOU'RE GOING DOWN A PATH FROM WHICH MUTANT-KIND CANNOT RETURN...
THE SLEEPERS...
...THEY NEED HELP.
HELP, ERIL, NOT MARCHING ORDERS.
DON'T WORRY, ELIZABETH.
...I'LL KILL YOU.

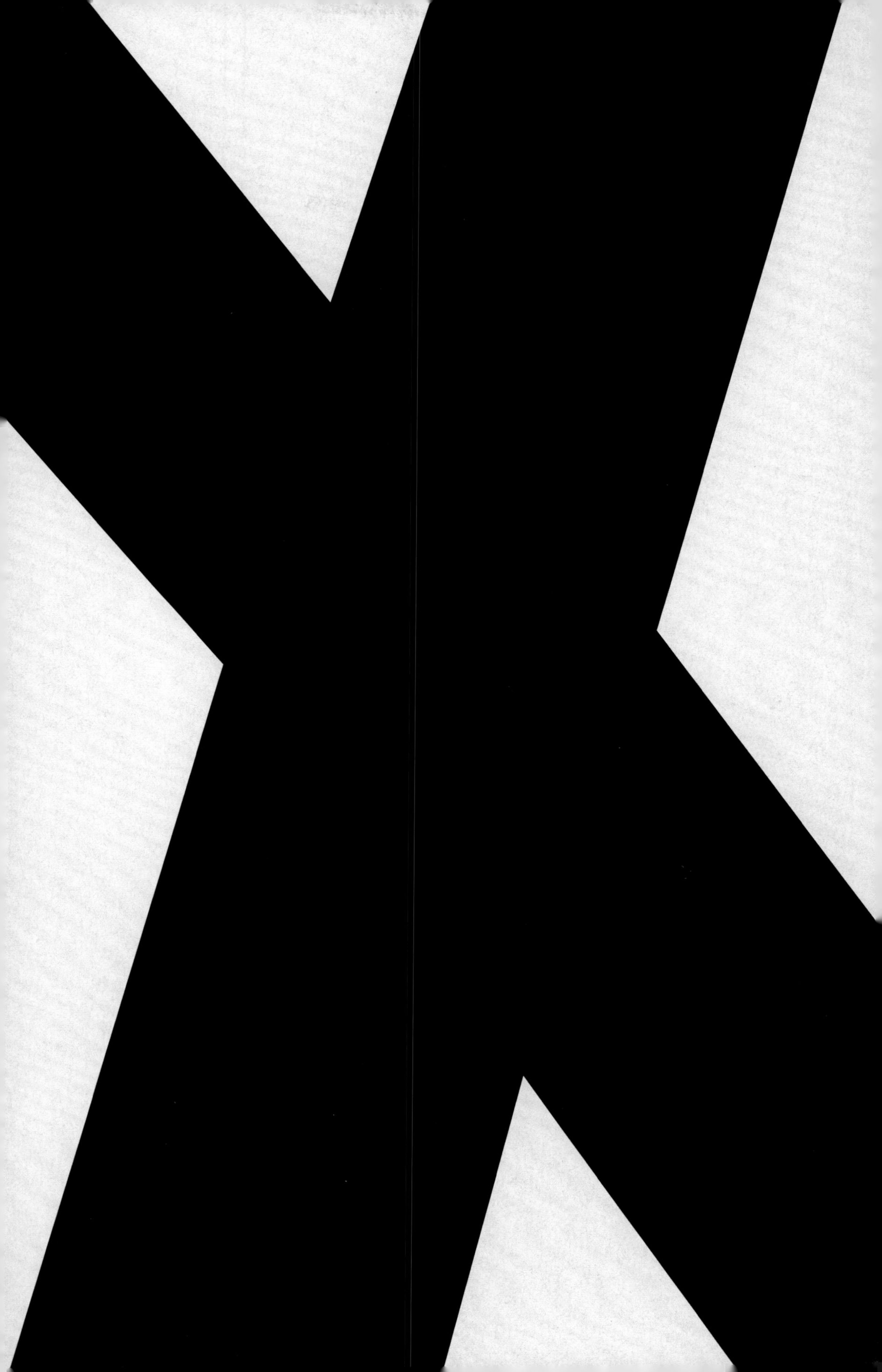

15

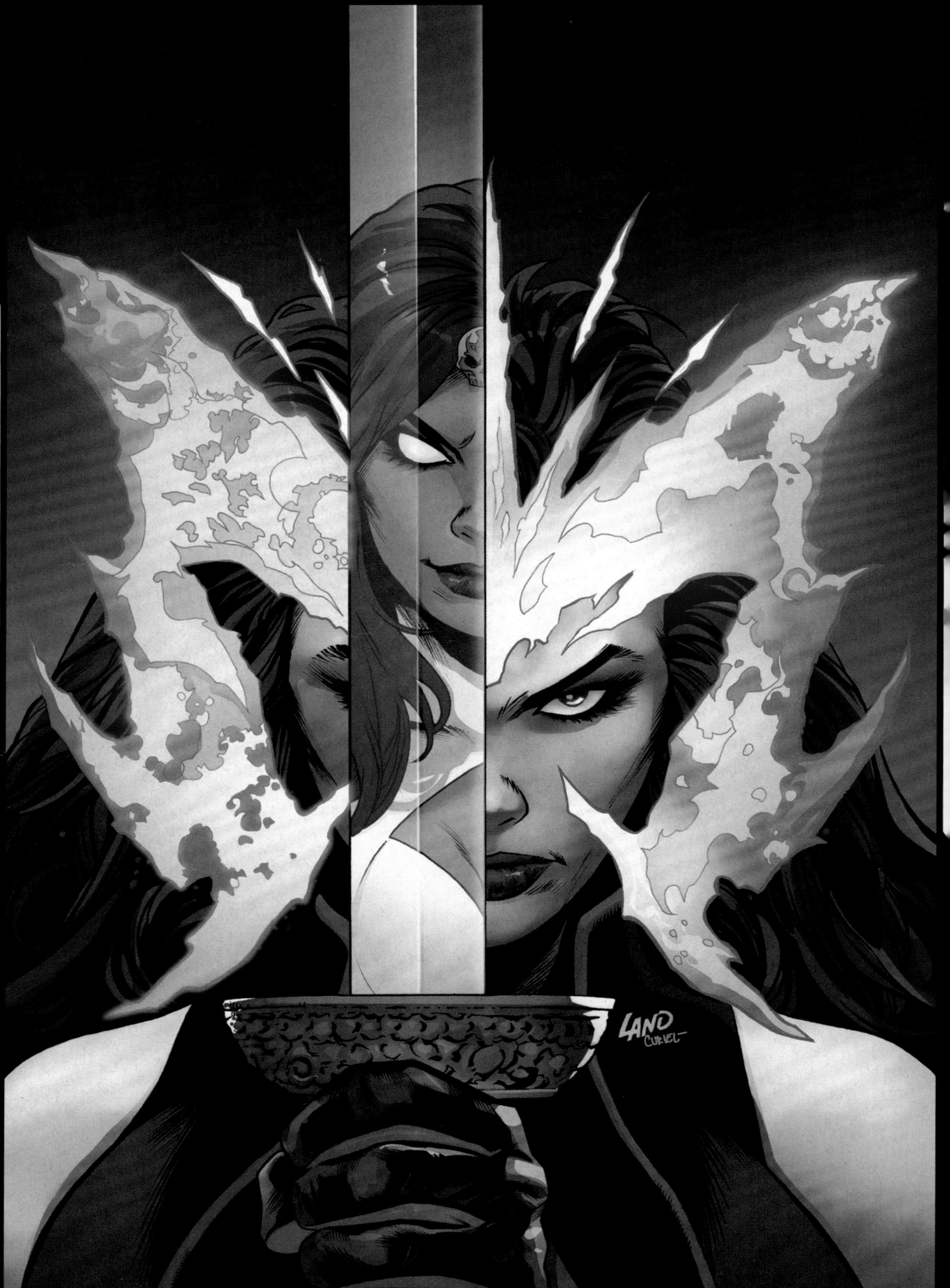
LAND
CURIEL

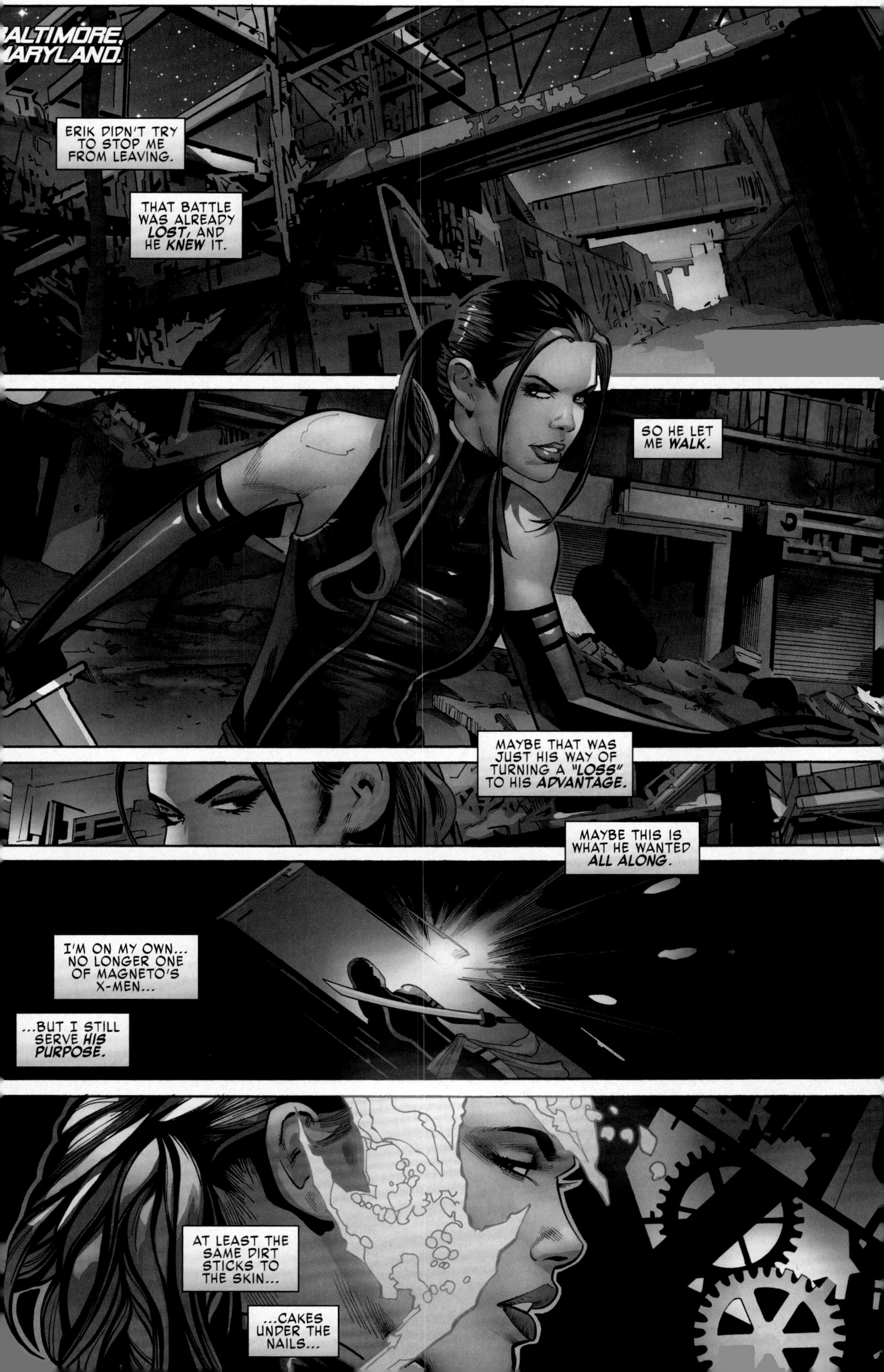

BALTIMORE, MARYLAND.
ERIK DIDN'T TRY TO STOP ME FROM LEAVING.
THAT BATTLE WAS ALREADY LOST, AND HE KNEW IT.
SO HE LET ME WALK.
MAYBE THAT WAS JUST HIS WAY OF TURNING A "LOSS" TO HIS ADVANTAGE.
MAYBE THIS IS WHAT HE WANTED ALL ALONG.
I'M ON MY OWN... NO LONGER ONE OF MAGNETO'S X-MEN...
...BUT I STILL SERVE HIS PURPOSE.
AT LEAST THE SAME DIRT STICKS TO THE SKIN...
...CAKES UNDER THE NAILS...

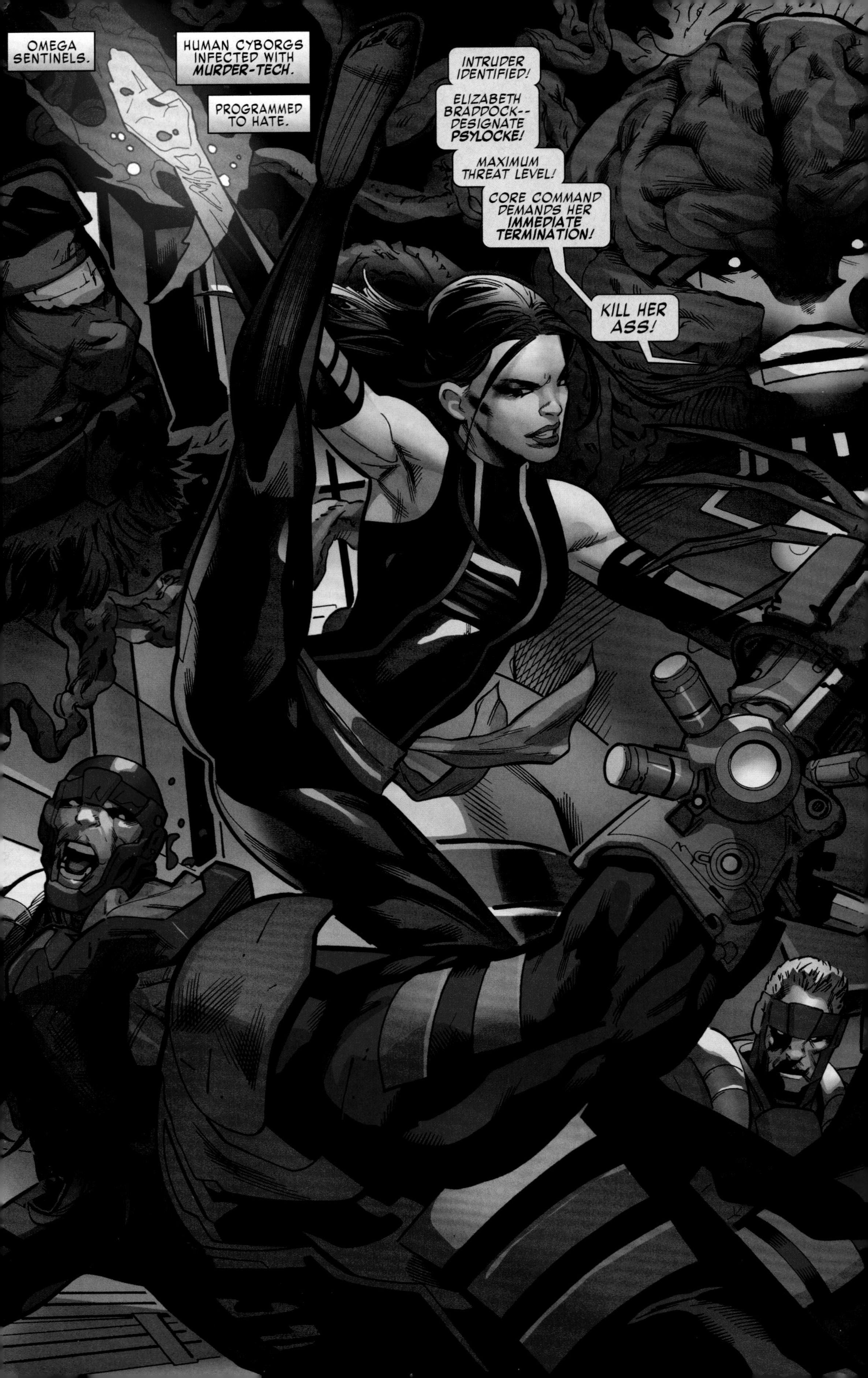
OMEGA SENTINELS.
HUMAN CYBORGS INFECTED WITH MURDER-TECH.
PROGRAMMED TO HATE.
INTRUDER IDENTIFIED!
ELIZABETH BRADDOCK--DESIGNATE PSYLOCKE!
MAXIMUM THREAT LEVEL!
CORE COMMAND DEMANDS HER IMMEDIATE TERMINATION!
KILL HER ASS!

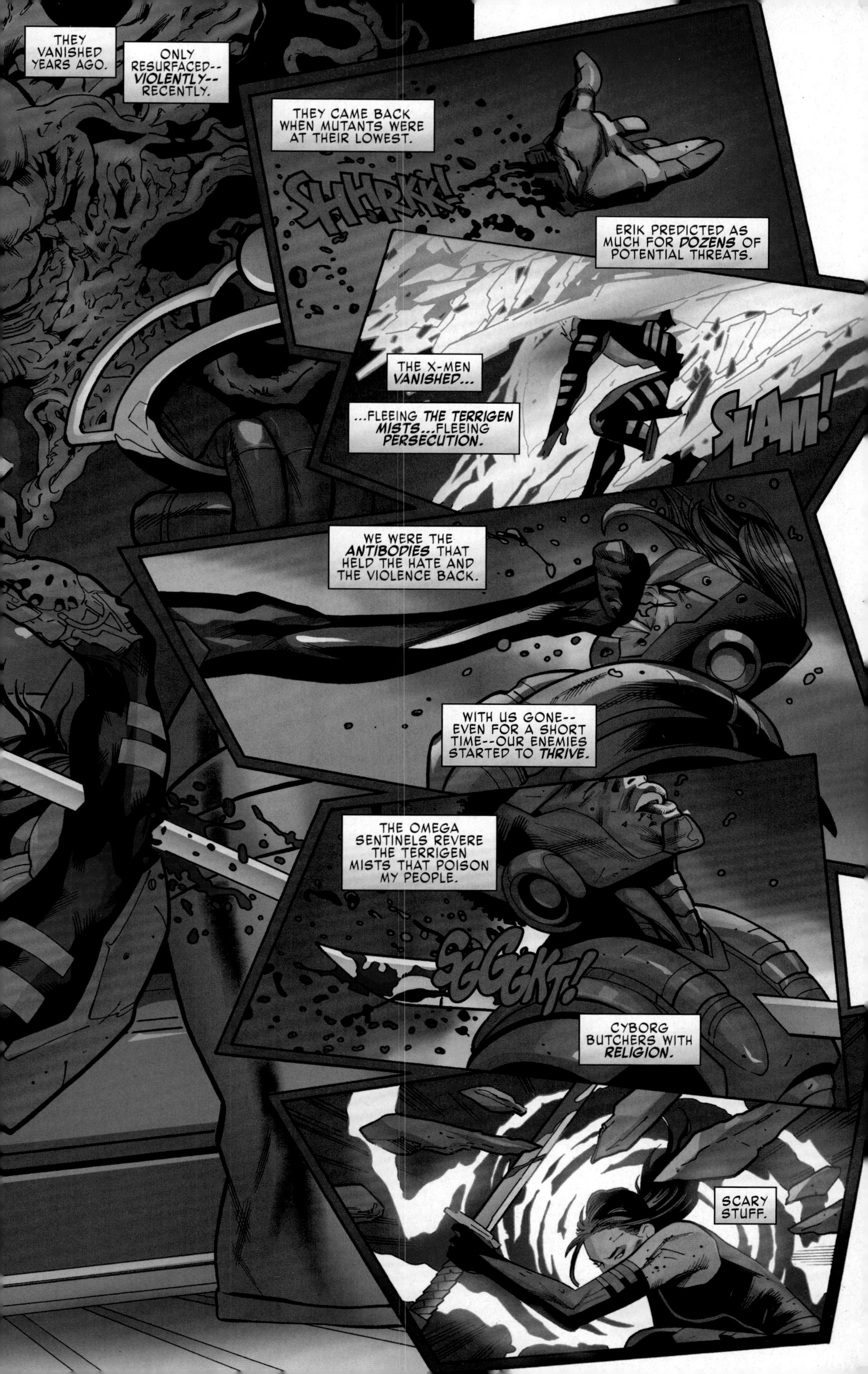

THEY VANISHED YEARS AGO.
ONLY RESURFACED-- *VIOLENTLY--* RECENTLY.
THEY CAME BACK WHEN MUTANTS WERE AT THEIR LOWEST.
SHHRKK!
ERIK PREDICTED AS MUCH FOR *DOZENS* OF POTENTIAL THREATS.
THE X-MEN *VANISHED...*
...FLEEING *THE TERRIGEN MISTS*...FLEEING *PERSECUTION.*
SLAM!
WE WERE THE *ANTIBODIES* THAT HELD THE HATE AND THE VIOLENCE BACK.
WITH US GONE-- EVEN FOR A SHORT TIME--OUR ENEMIES STARTED TO *THRIVE.*
THE OMEGA SENTINELS REVERE THE TERRIGEN MISTS THAT POISON MY PEOPLE.
SGGGKT!
CYBORG BUTCHERS WITH *RELIGION.*
SCARY STUFF.

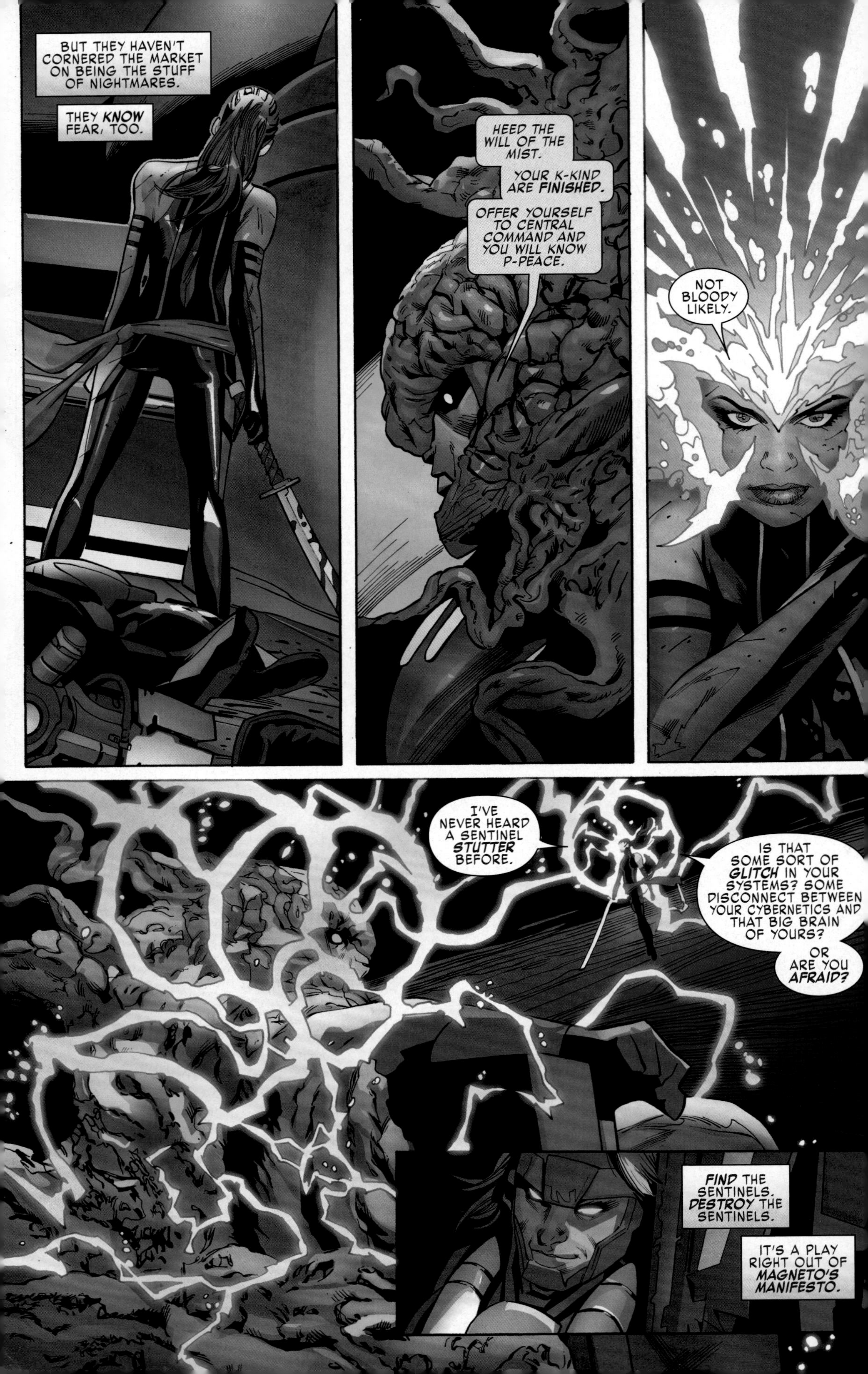
BUT THEY HAVEN'T CORNERED THE MARKET ON BEING THE STUFF OF NIGHTMARES.
THEY KNOW FEAR, TOO.
HEED THE WILL OF THE MIST.
YOUR K-KIND ARE FINISHED.
OFFER YOURSELF TO CENTRAL COMMAND AND YOU WILL KNOW P-PEACE.
NOT BLOODY LIKELY.
I'VE NEVER HEARD A SENTINEL STUTTER BEFORE.
IS THAT SOME SORT OF GLITCH IN YOUR SYSTEMS? SOME DISCONNECT BETWEEN YOUR CYBERNETICS AND THAT BIG BRAIN OF YOURS?
OR ARE YOU AFRAID?
FIND THE SENTINELS. DESTROY THE SENTINELS.
IT'S A PLAY RIGHT OUT OF MAGNETO'S MANIFESTO.

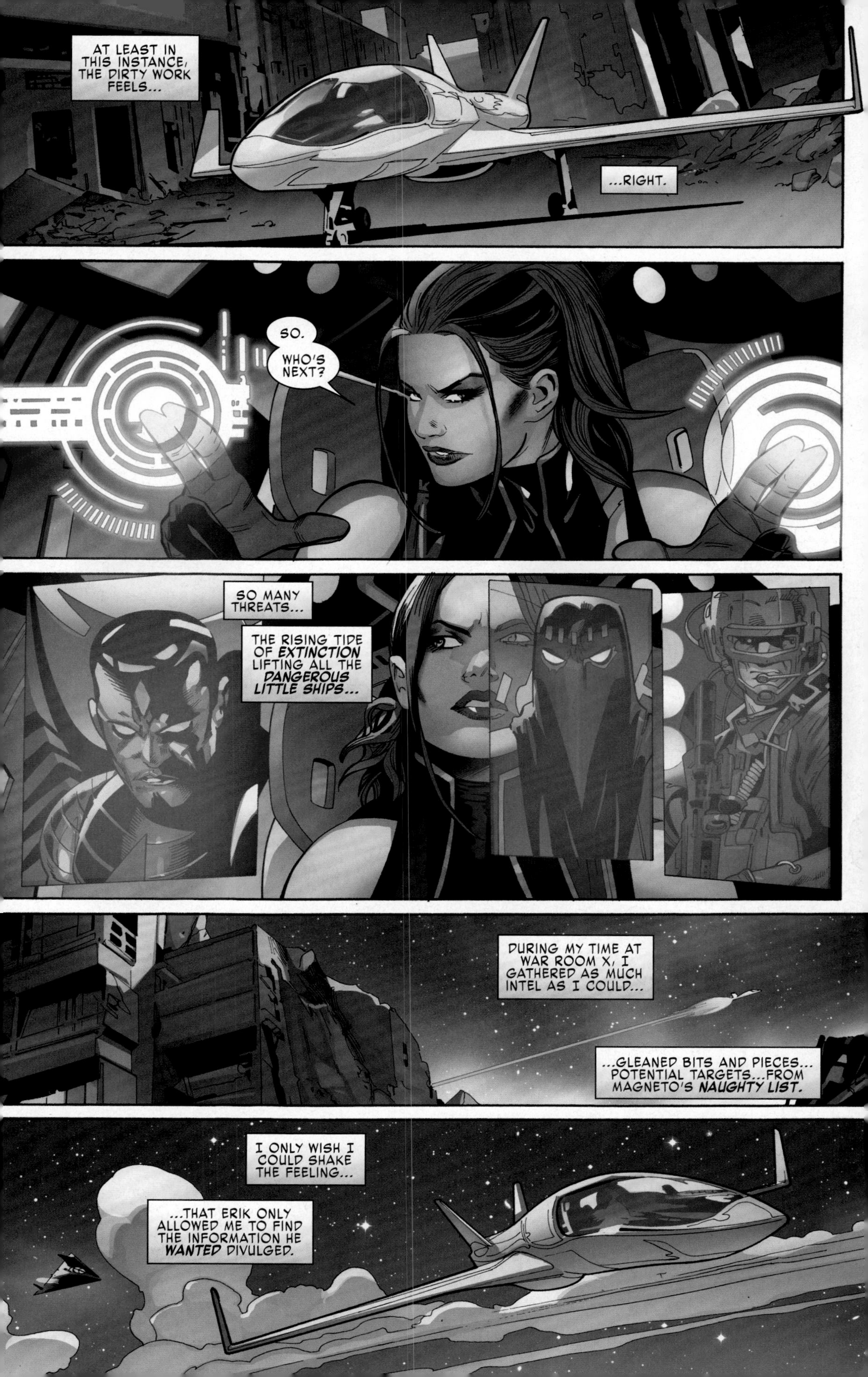
AT LEAST IN THIS INSTANCE, THE DIRTY WORK FEELS...
...RIGHT.
SO.
WHO'S NEXT?
SO MANY THREATS...
THE RISING TIDE OF EXTINCTION LIFTING ALL THE DANGEROUS LITTLE SHIPS...
DURING MY TIME AT WAR ROOM X, I GATHERED AS MUCH INTEL AS I COULD...
...GLEANED BITS AND PIECES... POTENTIAL TARGETS...FROM MAGNETO'S NAUGHTY LIST.
I ONLY WISH I COULD SHAKE THE FEELING...
...THAT ERIK ONLY ALLOWED ME TO FIND THE INFORMATION HE WANTED DIVULGED.

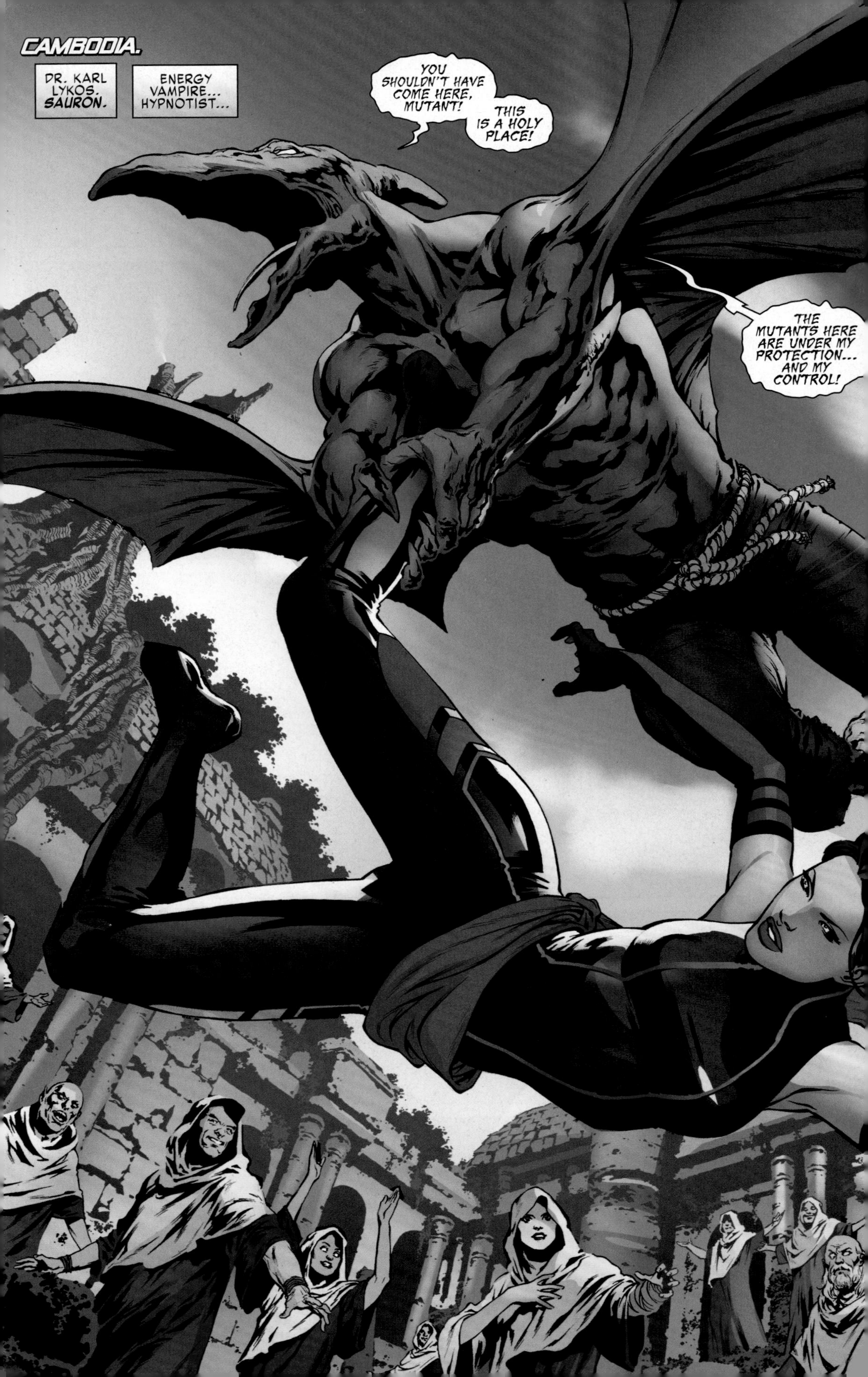
CAMBODIA.
DR. KARL LYKOS. SAURON.
ENERGY VAMPIRE... HYPNOTIST...
YOU SHOULDN'T HAVE COME HERE, MUTANT!
THIS IS A HOLY PLACE!
THE MUTANTS HERE ARE UNDER MY PROTECTION... AND MY CONTROL!

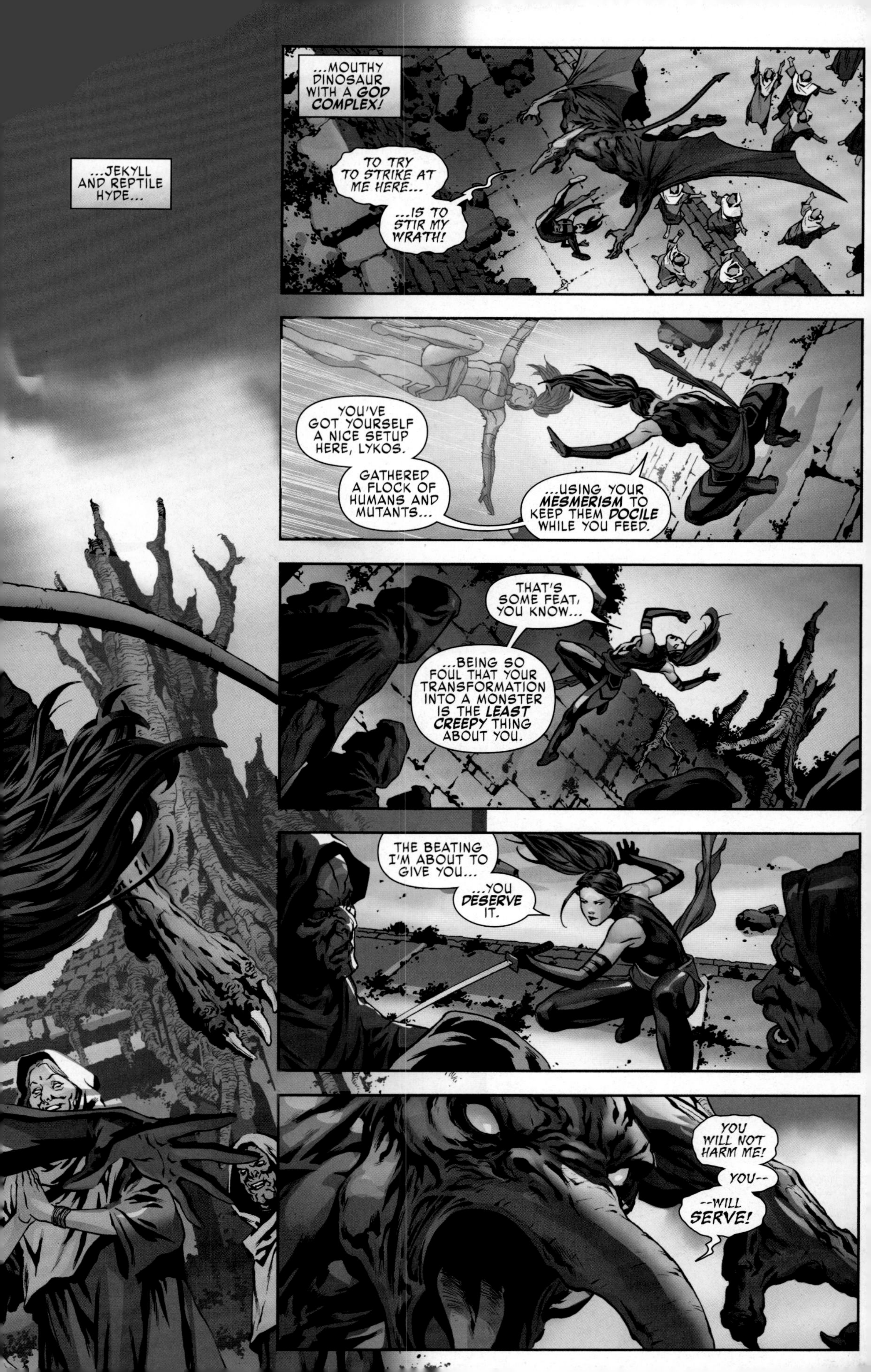
...JEKYLL AND REPTILE HYDE...
...MOUTHY DINOSAUR WITH A GOD COMPLEX!
TO TRY TO STRIKE AT ME HERE...
...IS TO STIR MY WRATH!
YOU'VE GOT YOURSELF A NICE SETUP HERE, LYKOS.
GATHERED A FLOCK OF HUMANS AND MUTANTS...
...USING YOUR MESMERISM TO KEEP THEM DOCILE WHILE YOU FEED.
THAT'S SOME FEAT, YOU KNOW...
...BEING SO FOUL THAT YOUR TRANSFORMATION INTO A MONSTER IS THE LEAST CREEPY THING ABOUT YOU.
THE BEATING I'M ABOUT TO GIVE YOU...
...YOU DESERVE IT.
YOU WILL NOT HARM ME!
YOU--
--WILL SERVE!

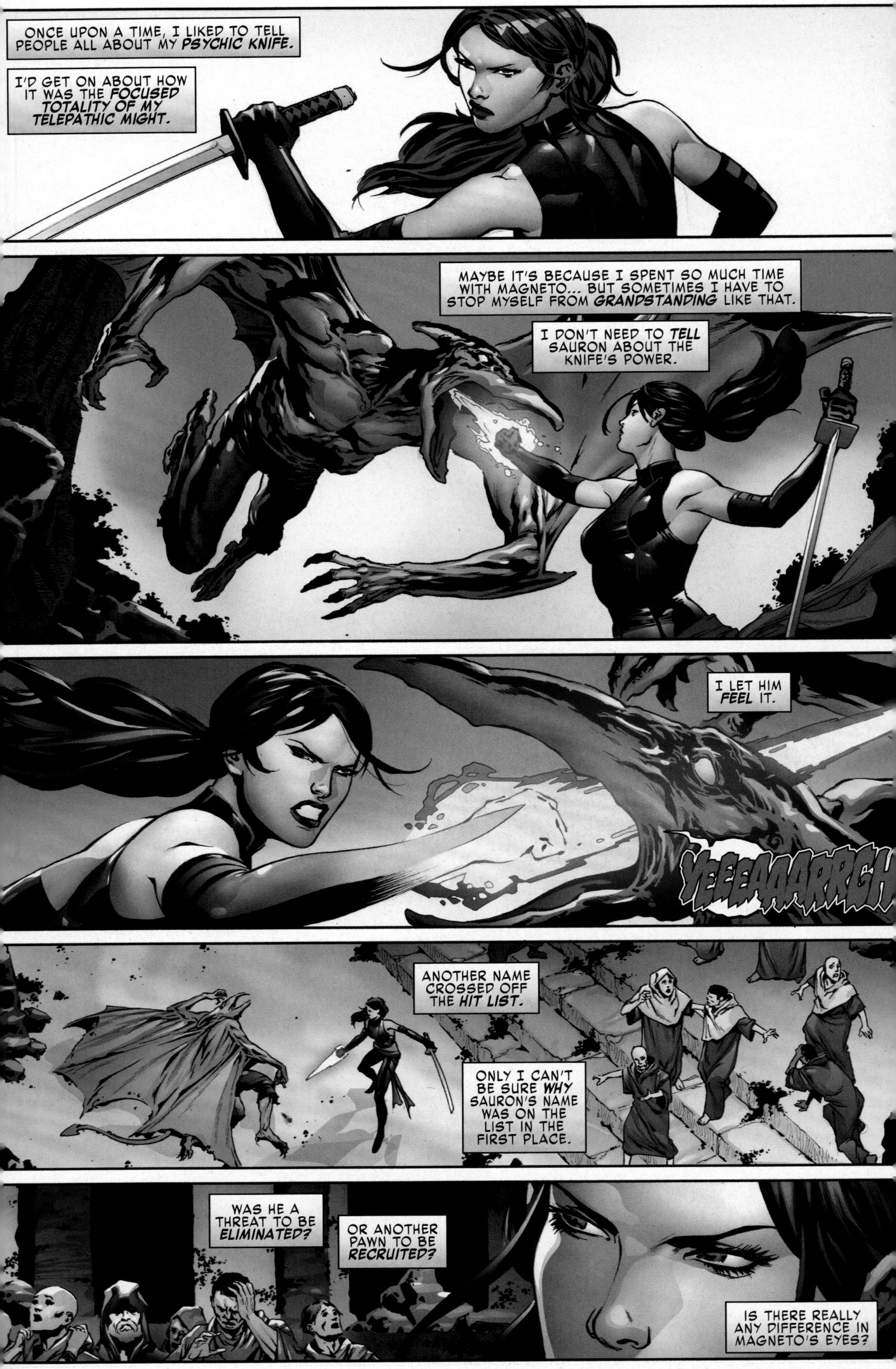
ONCE UPON A TIME, I LIKED TO TELL PEOPLE ALL ABOUT MY PSYCHIC KNIFE.
I'D GET ON ABOUT HOW IT WAS THE FOCUSED TOTALITY OF MY TELEPATHIC MIGHT.
MAYBE IT'S BECAUSE I SPENT SO MUCH TIME WITH MAGNETO... BUT SOMETIMES I HAVE TO STOP MYSELF FROM GRANDSTANDING LIKE THAT.
I DON'T NEED TO TELL SAURON ABOUT THE KNIFE'S POWER.
I LET HIM FEEL IT.
YEEEAAARRRGH
ANOTHER NAME CROSSED OFF THE HIT LIST.
ONLY I CAN'T BE SURE WHY SAURON'S NAME WAS ON THE LIST IN THE FIRST PLACE.
WAS HE A THREAT TO BE ELIMINATED?
OR ANOTHER PAWN TO BE RECRUITED?
IS THERE REALLY ANY DIFFERENCE IN MAGNETO'S EYES?

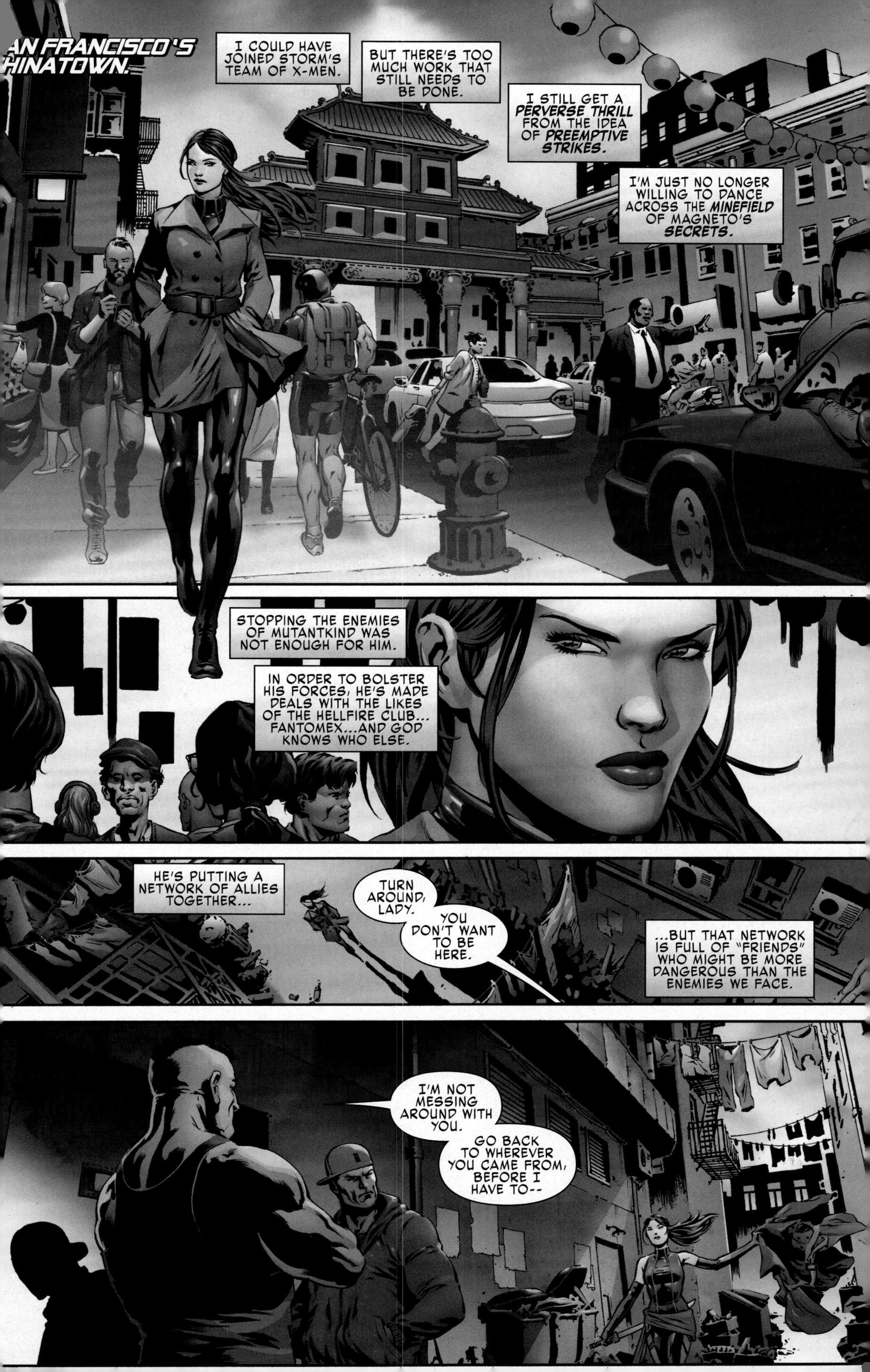
AN FRANCISCO'S
HINATOWN.
I COULD HAVE JOINED STORM'S TEAM OF X-MEN.
BUT THERE'S TOO MUCH WORK THAT STILL NEEDS TO BE DONE.
I STILL GET A PERVERSE THRILL FROM THE IDEA OF PREEMPTIVE STRIKES.
I'M JUST NO LONGER WILLING TO DANCE ACROSS THE MINEFIELD OF MAGNETO'S SECRETS.
STOPPING THE ENEMIES OF MUTANTKIND WAS NOT ENOUGH FOR HIM.
IN ORDER TO BOLSTER HIS FORCES, HE'S MADE DEALS WITH THE LIKES OF THE HELLFIRE CLUB... FANTOMEX...AND GOD KNOWS WHO ELSE.
HE'S PUTTING A NETWORK OF ALLIES TOGETHER...
TURN AROUND, LADY.
YOU DON'T WANT TO BE HERE.
...BUT THAT NETWORK IS FULL OF "FRIENDS" WHO MIGHT BE MORE DANGEROUS THAN THE ENEMIES WE FACE.
I'M NOT MESSING AROUND WITH YOU.
GO BACK TO WHEREVER YOU CAME FROM, BEFORE I HAVE TO--

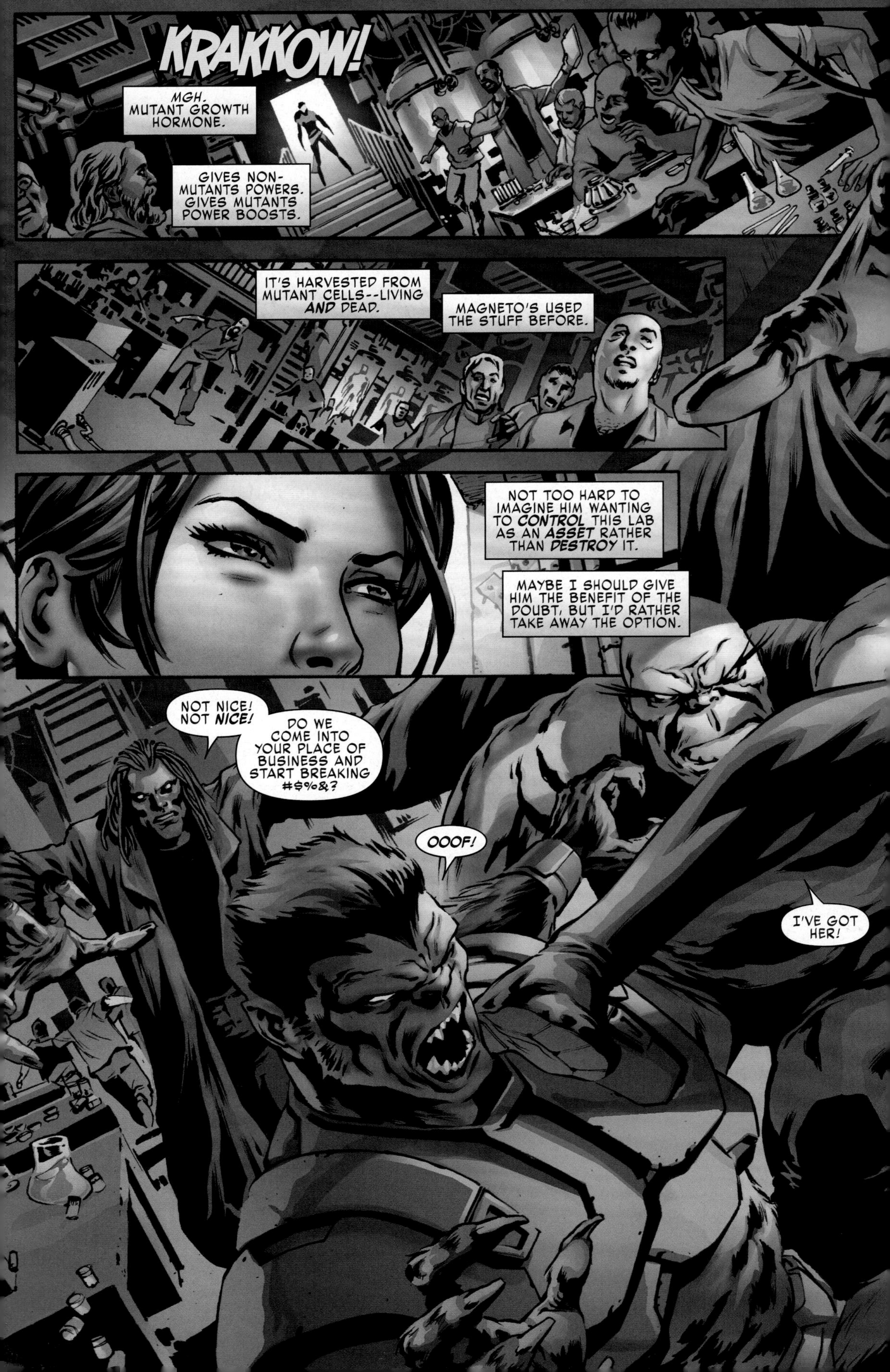
KRAKKOW!
MGH. MUTANT GROWTH HORMONE.
GIVES NON-MUTANTS POWERS. GIVES MUTANTS POWER BOOSTS.
IT'S HARVESTED FROM MUTANT CELLS--LIVING AND DEAD.
MAGNETO'S USED THE STUFF BEFORE.
NOT TOO HARD TO IMAGINE HIM WANTING TO CONTROL THIS LAB AS AN ASSET RATHER THAN DESTROY IT.
MAYBE I SHOULD GIVE HIM THE BENEFIT OF THE DOUBT, BUT I'D RATHER TAKE AWAY THE OPTION.
NOT NICE! NOT NICE!
DO WE COME INTO YOUR PLACE OF BUSINESS AND START BREAKING #$%&?
OOOF!
I'VE GOT HER!

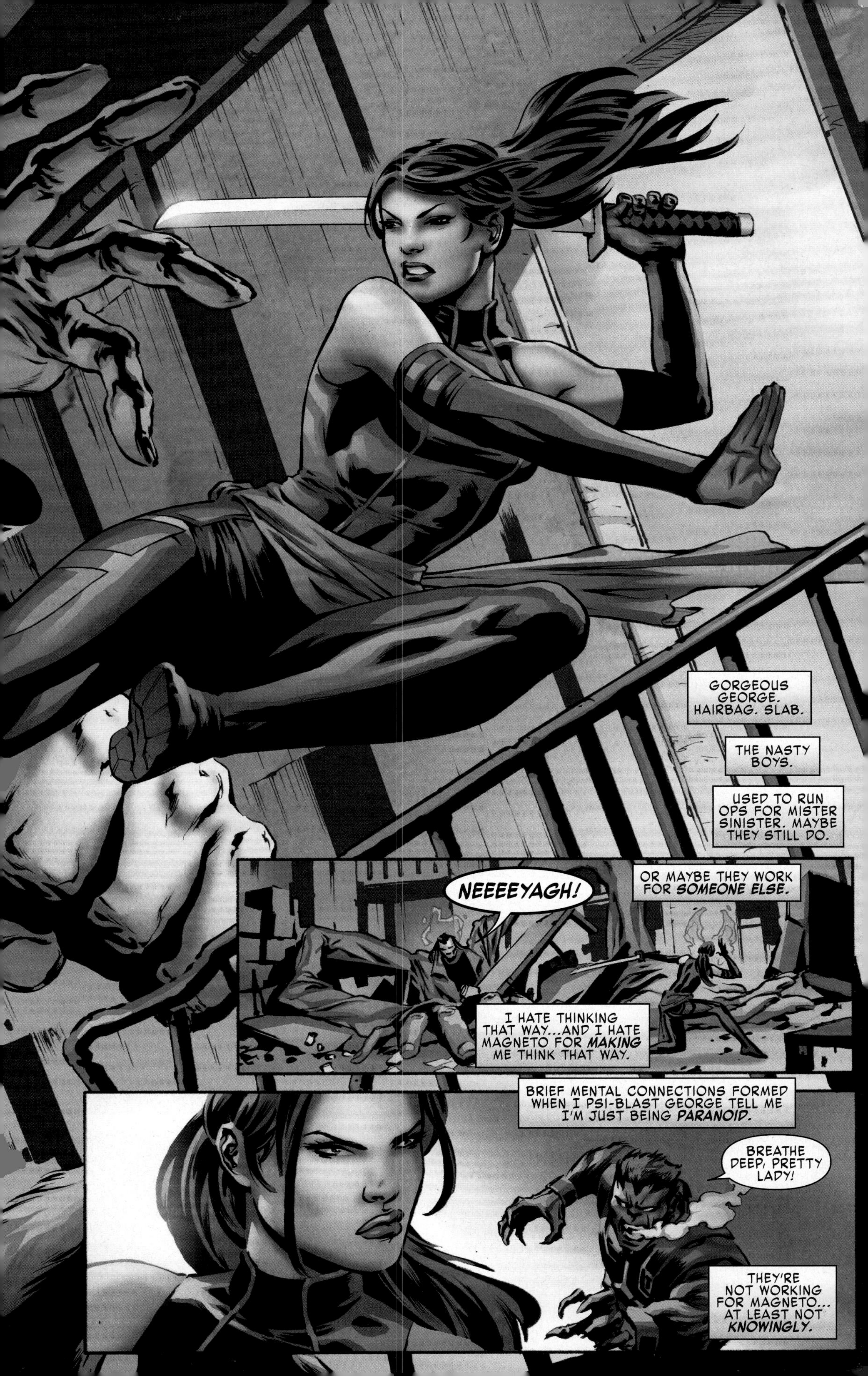
GORGEOUS GEORGE. HAIRBAG. SLAB.
THE NASTY BOYS.
USED TO RUN OPS FOR MISTER SINISTER. MAYBE THEY STILL DO.
NEEEEYAGH!
OR MAYBE THEY WORK FOR SOMEONE ELSE.
I HATE THINKING THAT WAY...AND I HATE MAGNETO FOR MAKING ME THINK THAT WAY.
BRIEF MENTAL CONNECTIONS FORMED WHEN I PSI-BLAST GEORGE TELL ME I'M JUST BEING PARANOID.
BREATHE DEEP, PRETTY LADY!
THEY'RE NOT WORKING FOR MAGNETO... AT LEAST NOT KNOWINGLY.

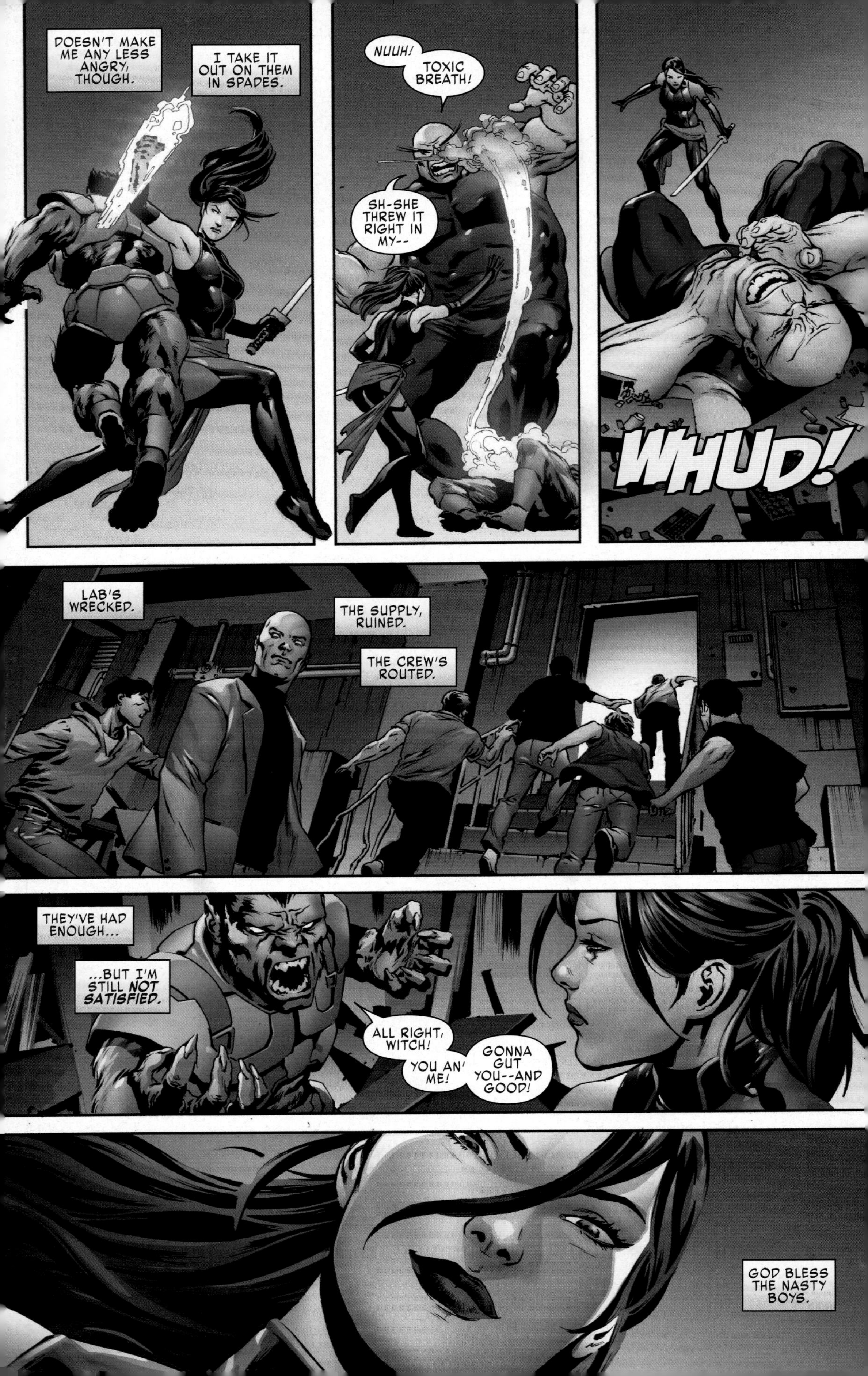
DOESN'T MAKE ME ANY LESS ANGRY, THOUGH.
I TAKE IT OUT ON THEM IN SPADES.
NUUH!
TOXIC BREATH!
SH-SHE THREW IT RIGHT IN MY--
WHUD!
LAB'S WRECKED.
THE SUPPLY, RUINED.
THE CREW'S ROUTED.
THEY'VE HAD ENOUGH...
...BUT I'M STILL NOT SATISFIED.
ALL RIGHT, WITCH!
YOU AN' ME!
GONNA GUT YOU--AND GOOD!
GOD BLESS THE NASTY BOYS.

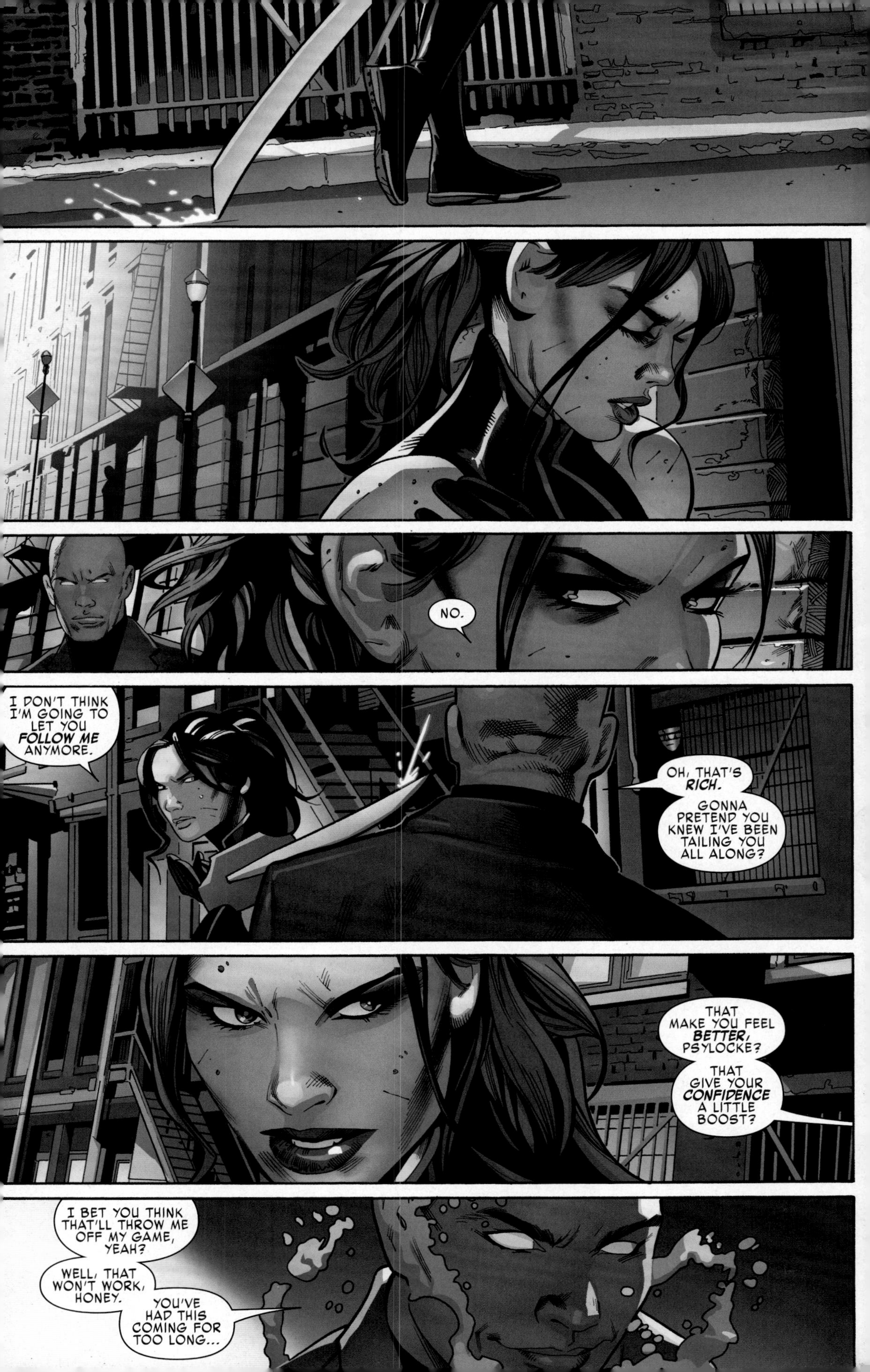
NO.
I DON'T THINK I'M GOING TO LET YOU FOLLOW ME ANYMORE.
OH, THAT'S RICH.
GONNA PRETEND YOU KNEW I'VE BEEN TAILING YOU ALL ALONG?
THAT MAKE YOU FEEL BETTER, PSYLOCKE?
THAT GIVE YOUR CONFIDENCE A LITTLE BOOST?
I BET YOU THINK THAT'LL THROW ME OFF MY GAME, YEAH?
WELL, THAT WON'T WORK, HONEY.
YOU'VE HAD THIS COMING FOR TOO LONG...

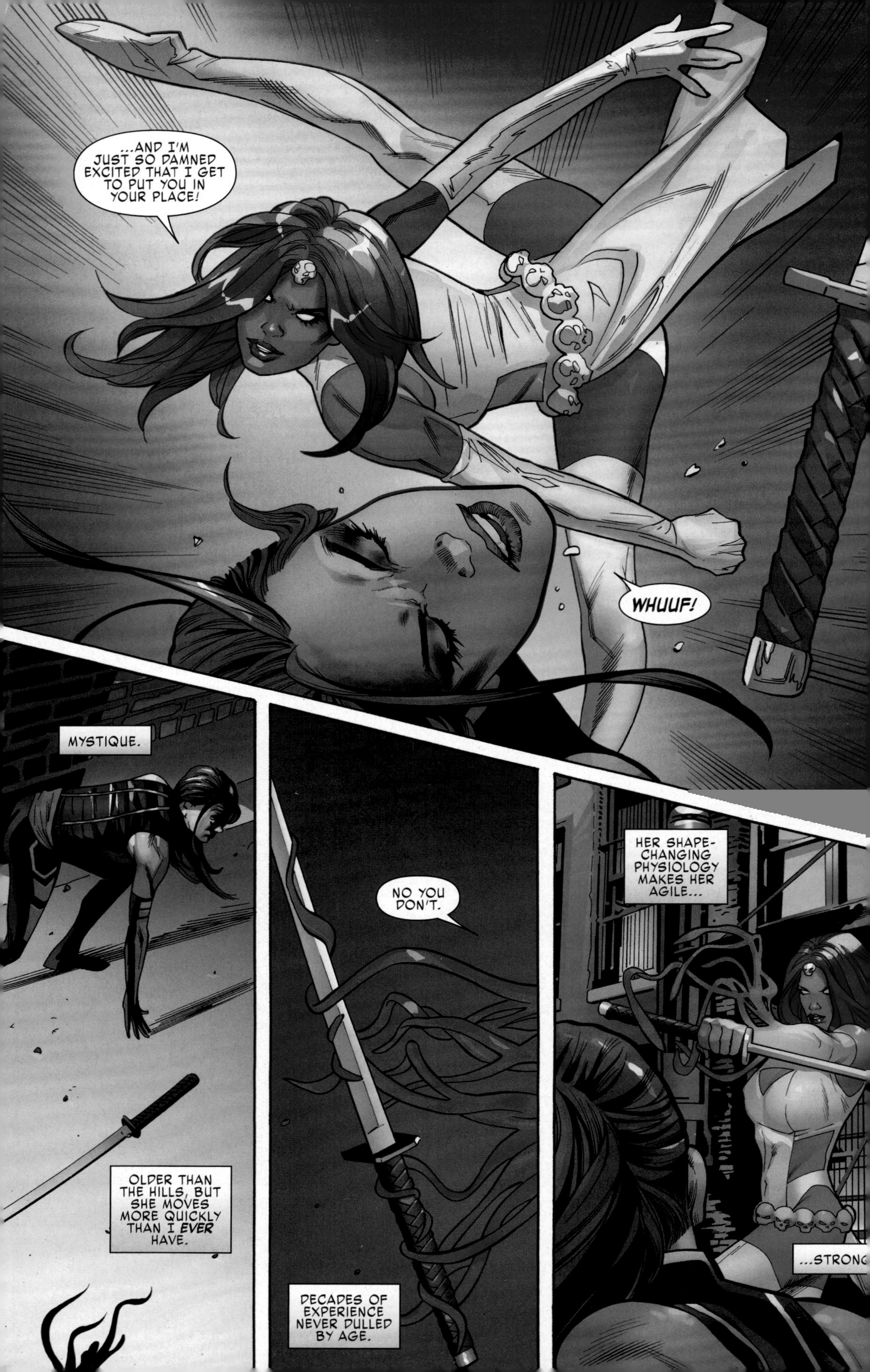
...AND I'M JUST SO DAMNED EXCITED THAT I GET TO PUT YOU IN YOUR PLACE!
WHUUF!
MYSTIQUE.
OLDER THAN THE HILLS, BUT SHE MOVES MORE QUICKLY THAN I *EVER* HAVE.
NO YOU DON'T.
DECADES OF EXPERIENCE NEVER DULLED BY AGE.
HER SHAPE-CHANGING PHYSIOLOGY MAKES HER AGILE...
...STRONG

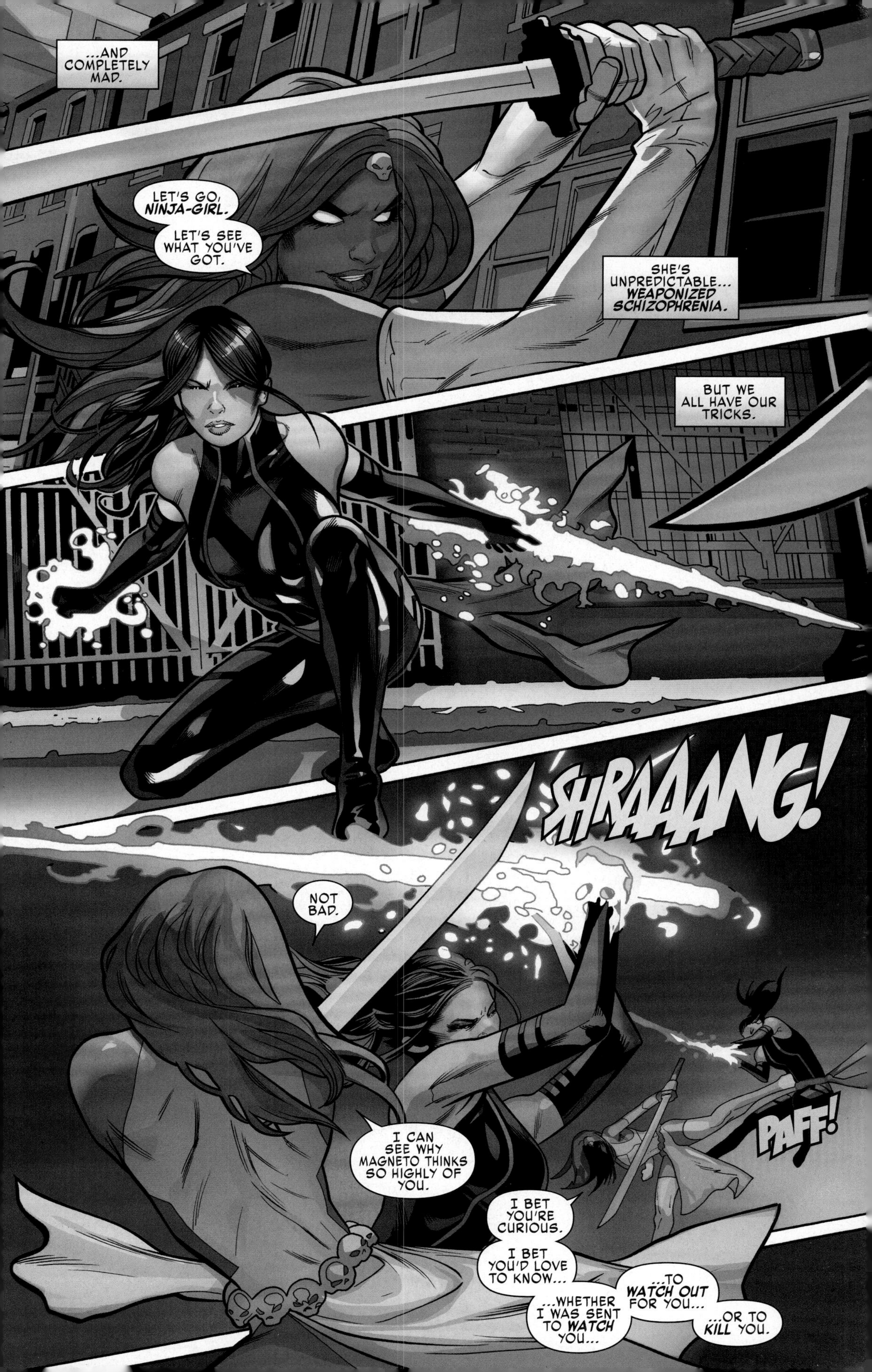
...AND COMPLETELY MAD.
LET'S GO, NINJA-GIRL.
LET'S SEE WHAT YOU'VE GOT.
SHE'S UNPREDICTABLE... WEAPONIZED SCHIZOPHRENIA.
BUT WE ALL HAVE OUR TRICKS.
SHRAAAANG!
NOT BAD.
PAFF!
I CAN SEE WHY MAGNETO THINKS SO HIGHLY OF YOU.
I BET YOU'RE CURIOUS.
I BET YOU'D LOVE TO KNOW...
...WHETHER I WAS SENT TO WATCH YOU...
...TO WATCH OUT FOR YOU...
...OR TO KILL YOU.

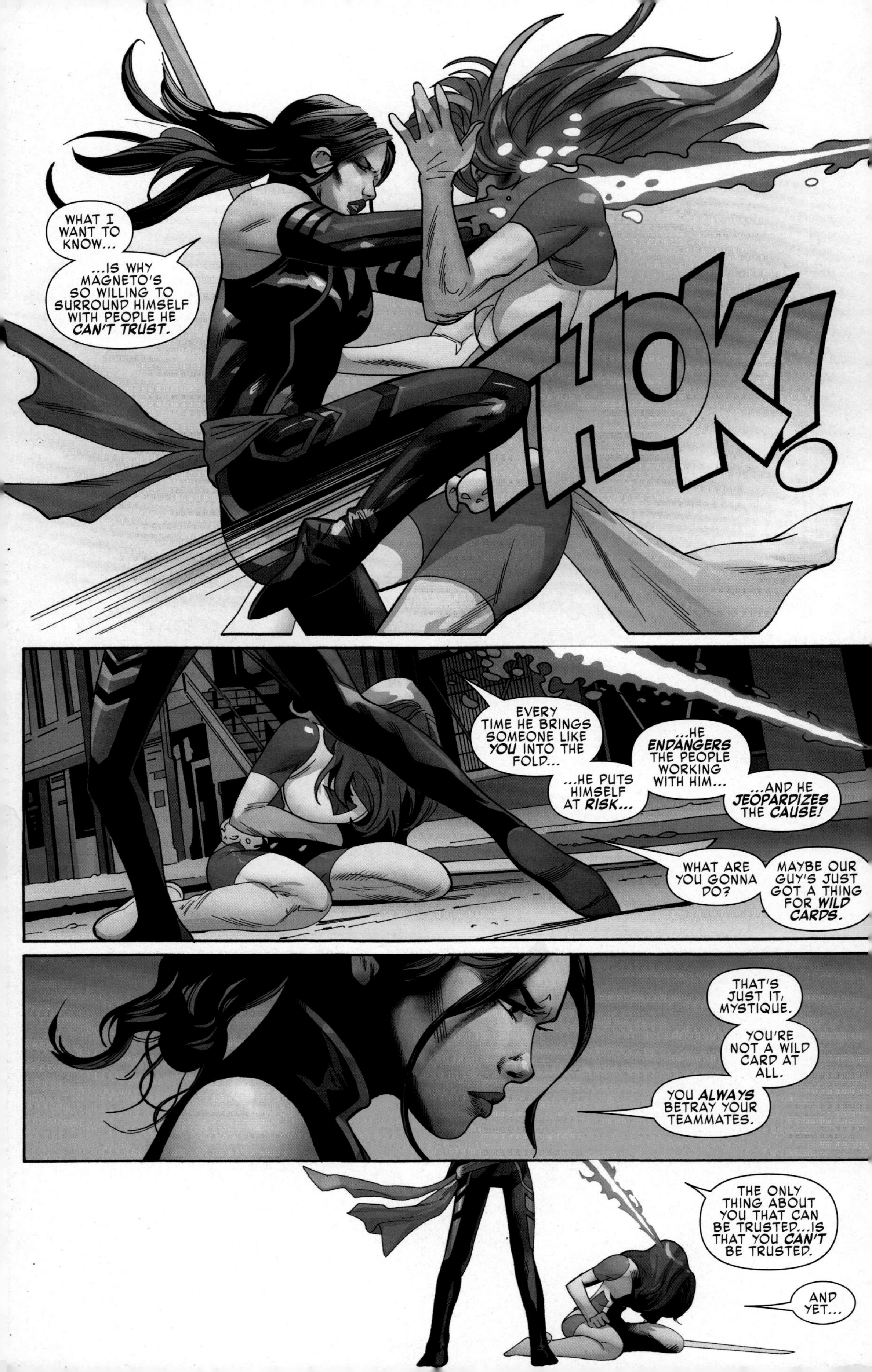

WHAT I WANT TO KNOW...
...IS WHY MAGNETO'S SO WILLING TO SURROUND HIMSELF WITH PEOPLE HE CAN'T TRUST.
THOK!
EVERY TIME HE BRINGS SOMEONE LIKE YOU INTO THE FOLD...
...HE PUTS HIMSELF AT RISK...
...HE ENDANGERS THE PEOPLE WORKING WITH HIM...
...AND HE JEOPARDIZES THE CAUSE!
WHAT ARE YOU GONNA DO?
MAYBE OUR GUY'S JUST GOT A THING FOR WILD CARDS.
THAT'S JUST IT, MYSTIQUE.
YOU'RE NOT A WILD CARD AT ALL.
YOU ALWAYS BETRAY YOUR TEAMMATES.
THE ONLY THING ABOUT YOU THAT CAN BE TRUSTED...IS THAT YOU CAN'T BE TRUSTED.
AND YET...

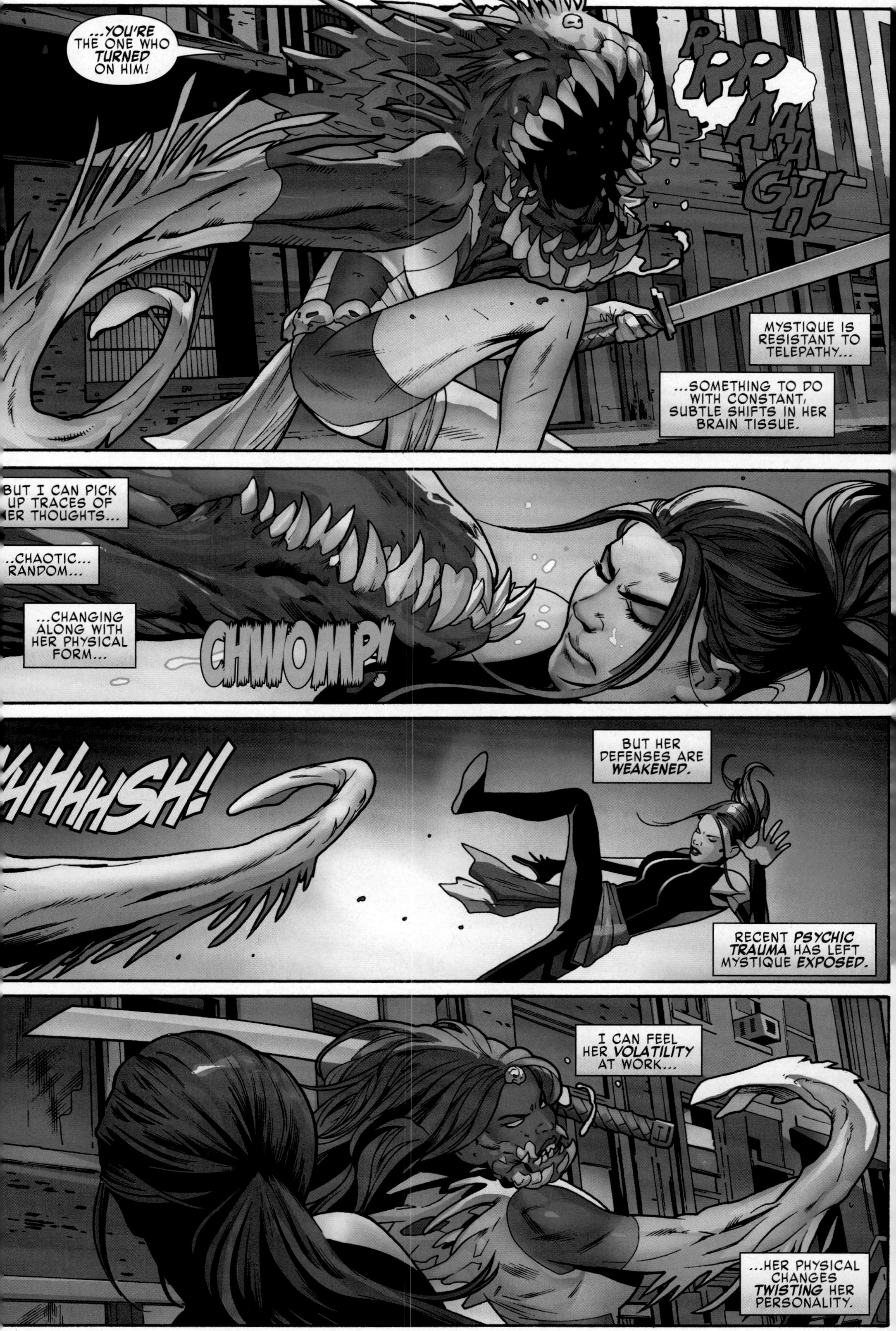
...YOU'RE THE ONE WHO TURNED ON HIM!
RRRAAAGH!
MYSTIQUE IS RESISTANT TO TELEPATHY...
...SOMETHING TO DO WITH CONSTANT, SUBTLE SHIFTS IN HER BRAIN TISSUE.
BUT I CAN PICK UP TRACES OF ER THOUGHTS...
..CHAOTIC... RANDOM...
...CHANGING ALONG WITH HER PHYSICAL FORM...
CHWOMP!
HHHHSH!
BUT HER DEFENSES ARE WEAKENED.
RECENT PSYCHIC TRAUMA HAS LEFT MYSTIQUE EXPOSED.
I CAN FEEL HER VOLATILITY AT WORK...
...HER PHYSICAL CHANGES TWISTING HER PERSONALITY.

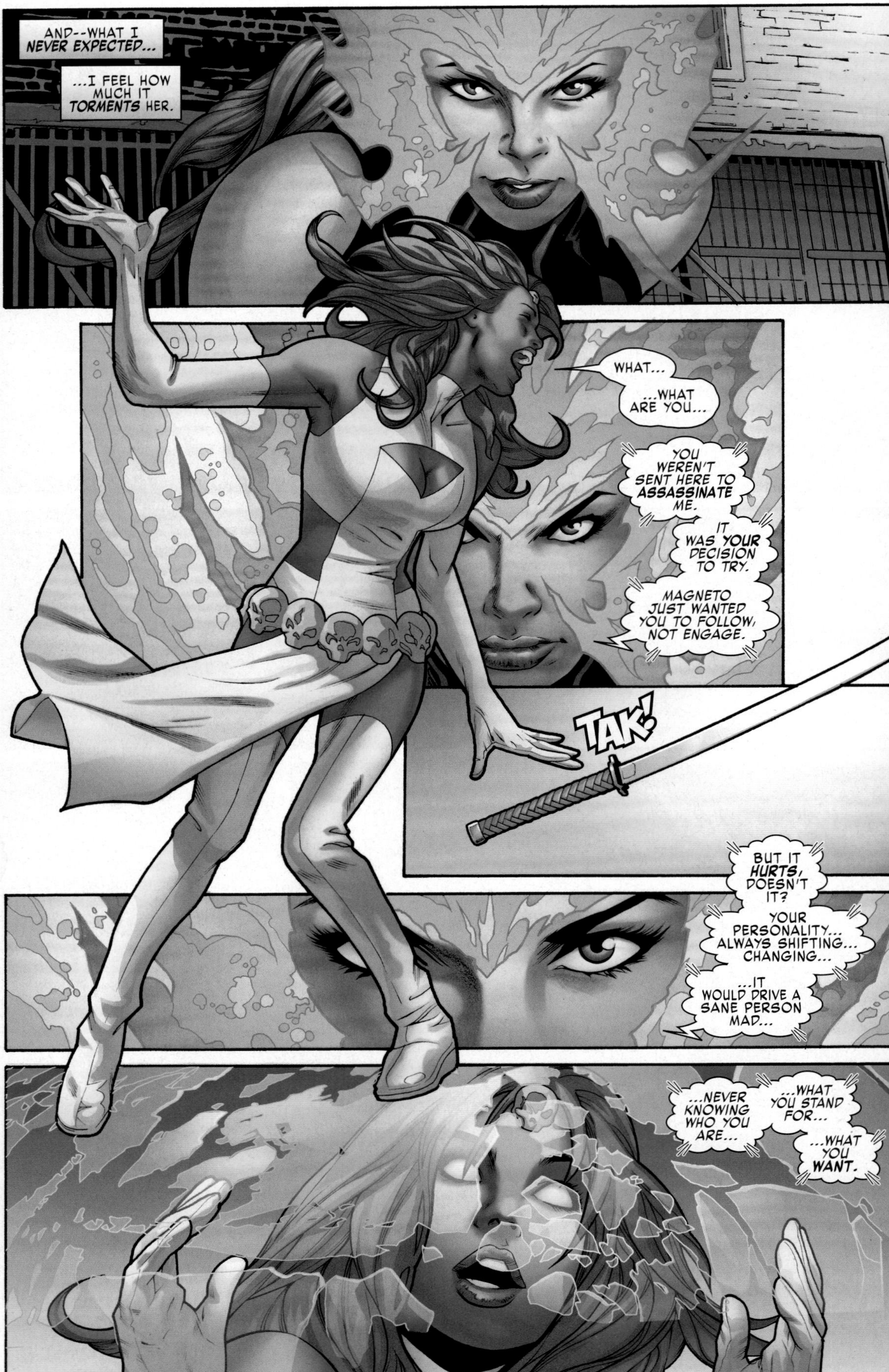
AND--WHAT I NEVER EXPECTED...
...I FEEL HOW MUCH IT TORMENTS HER.
WHAT...
...WHAT ARE YOU...
YOU WEREN'T SENT HERE TO ASSASSINATE ME.
IT WAS YOUR DECISION TO TRY.
MAGNETO JUST WANTED YOU TO FOLLOW, NOT ENGAGE.
TAK!
BUT IT HURTS, DOESN'T IT?
YOUR PERSONALITY... ALWAYS SHIFTING... CHANGING...
...IT WOULD DRIVE A SANE PERSON MAD...
...NEVER KNOWING WHO YOU ARE...
...WHAT YOU STAND FOR...
...WHAT YOU WANT.

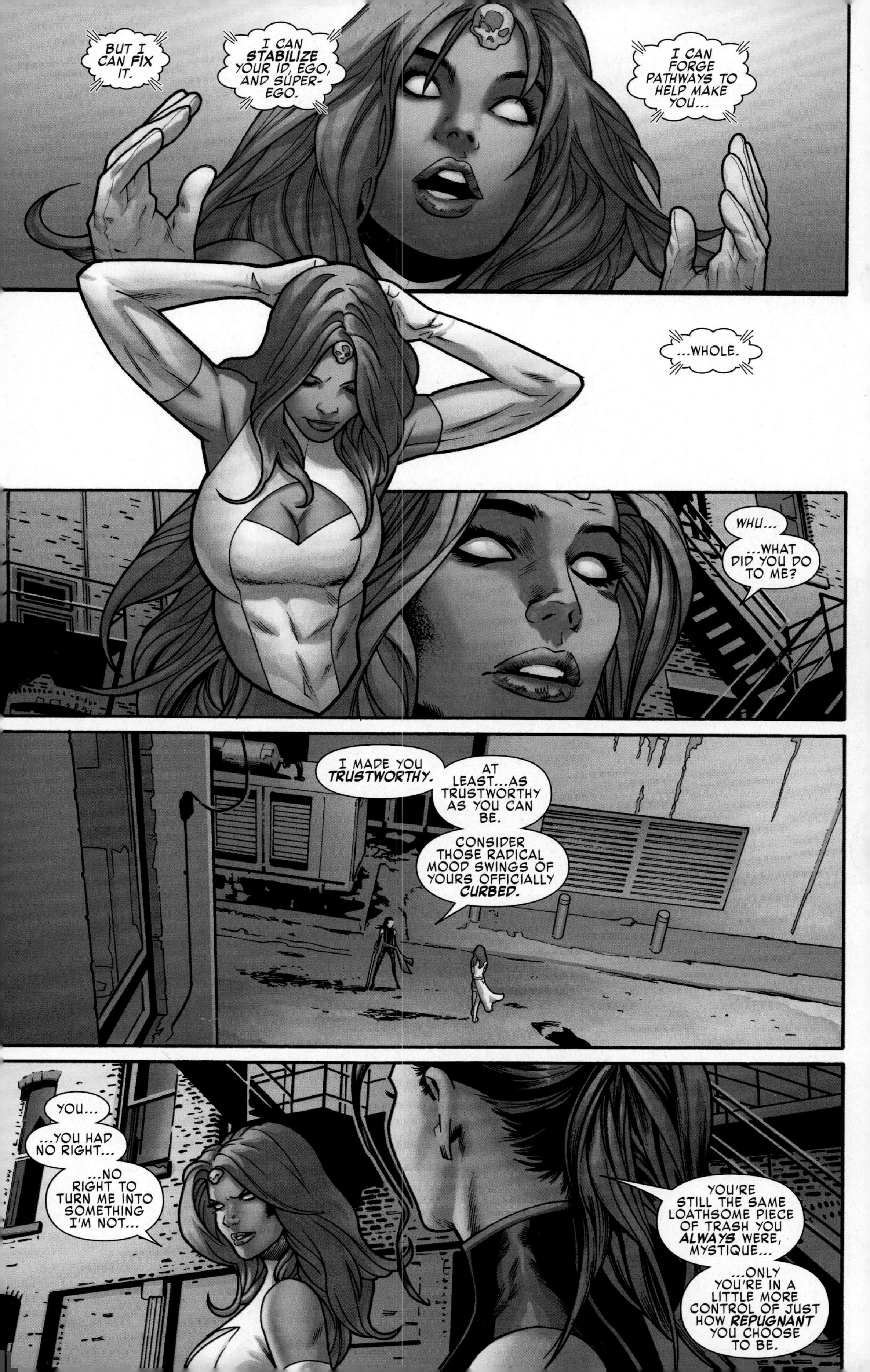
BUT I CAN FIX IT.
I CAN STABILIZE YOUR ID, EGO, AND SUPER-EGO.
I CAN FORGE PATHWAYS TO HELP MAKE YOU...
...WHOLE.
WHU...
...WHAT DID YOU DO TO ME?
I MADE YOU TRUSTWORTHY.
AT LEAST...AS TRUSTWORTHY AS YOU CAN BE.
CONSIDER THOSE RADICAL MOOD SWINGS OF YOURS OFFICIALLY CURBED.
YOU...
...YOU HAD NO RIGHT...
...NO RIGHT TO TURN ME INTO SOMETHING I'M NOT...
YOU'RE STILL THE SAME LOATHSOME PIECE OF TRASH YOU ALWAYS WERE, MYSTIQUE...
...ONLY YOU'RE IN A LITTLE MORE CONTROL OF JUST HOW REPUGNANT YOU CHOOSE TO BE.

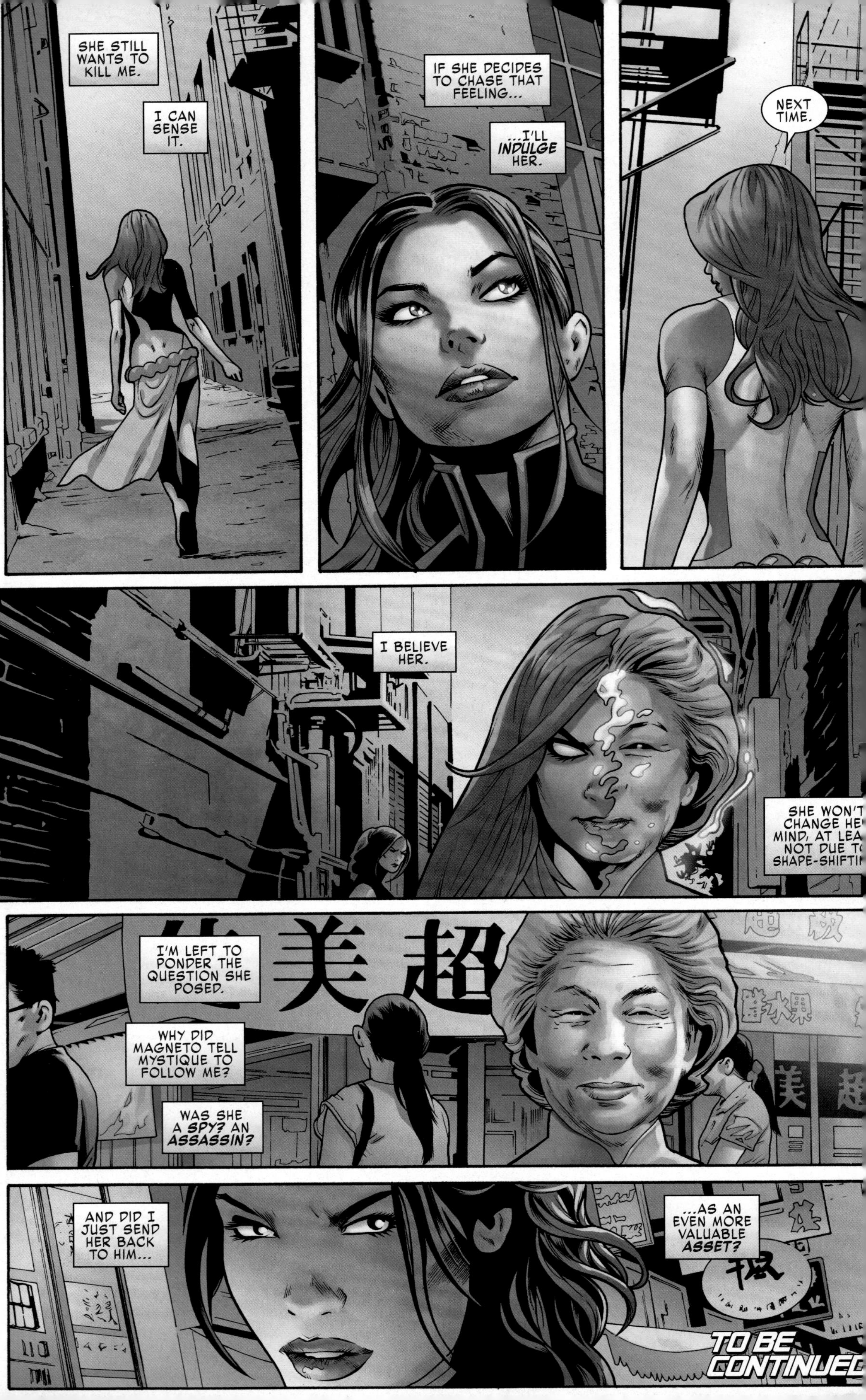
SHE STILL WANTS TO KILL ME.
I CAN SENSE IT.
IF SHE DECIDES TO CHASE THAT FEELING...
...I'LL INDULGE HER.
NEXT TIME.
I BELIEVE HER.
SHE WON'T CHANGE HE MIND, AT LEA NOT DUE TO SHAPE-SHIFTIN
I'M LEFT TO PONDER THE QUESTION SHE POSED.
WHY DID MAGNETO TELL MYSTIQUE TO FOLLOW ME?
WAS SHE A SPY? AN ASSASSIN?
AND DID I JUST SEND HER BACK TO HIM...
...AS AN EVEN MORE VALUABLE ASSET?
TO BE CONTINUED

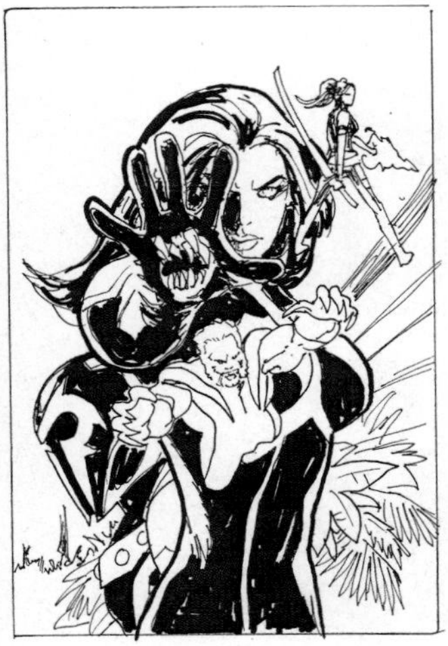

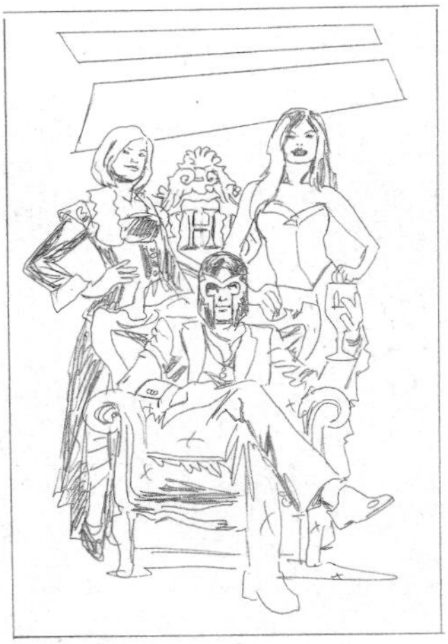

1

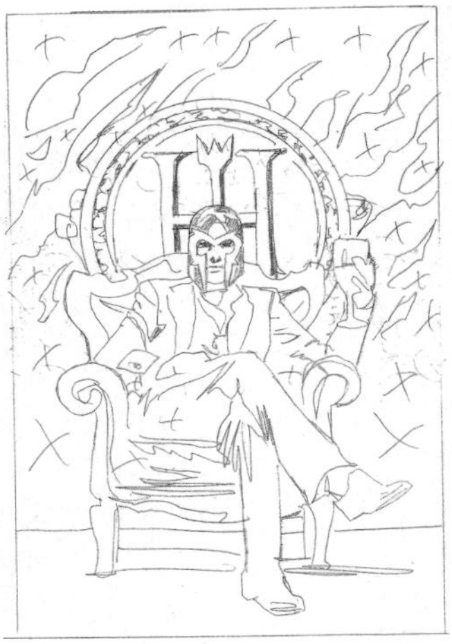

2

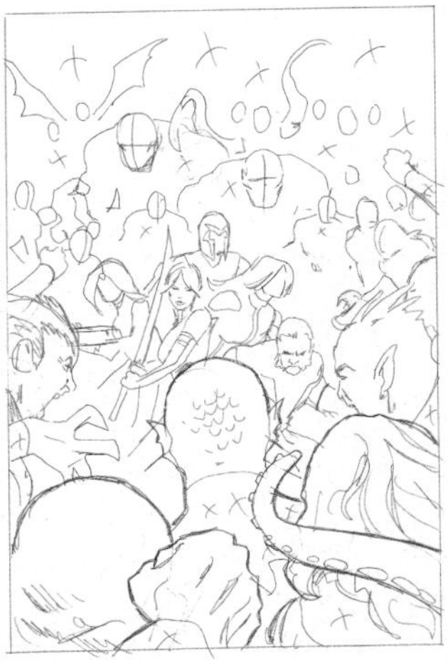

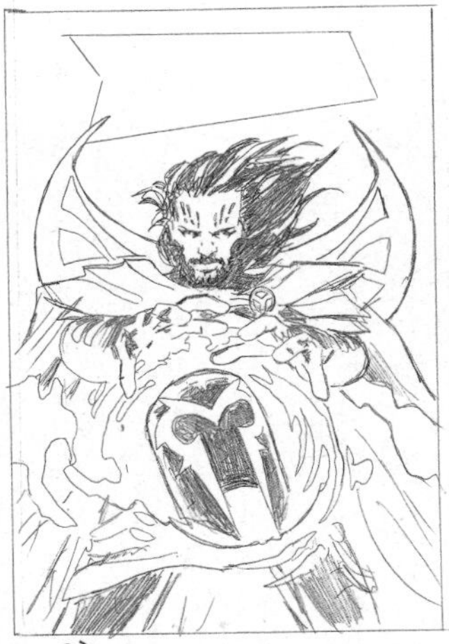

1

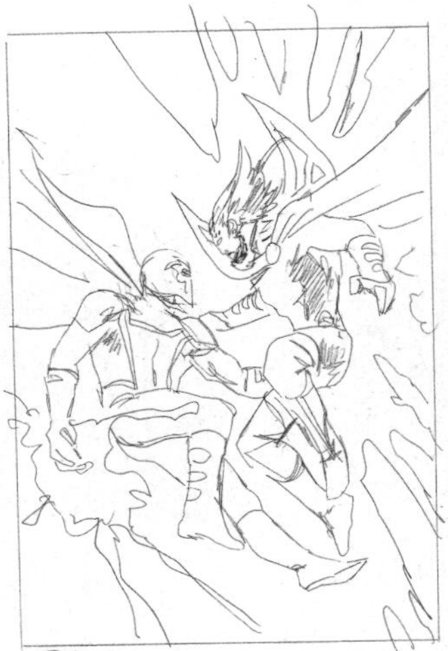

2

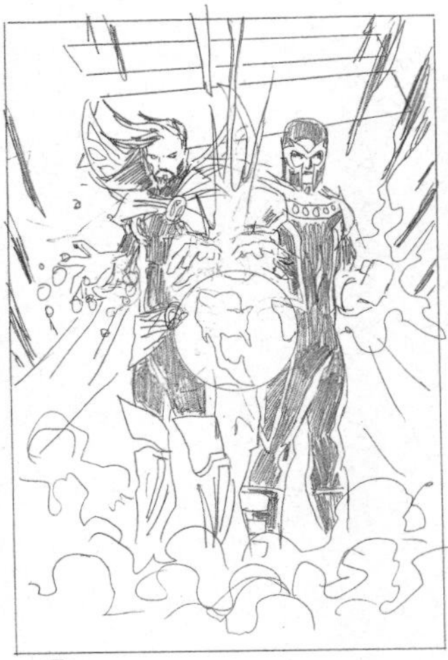

3

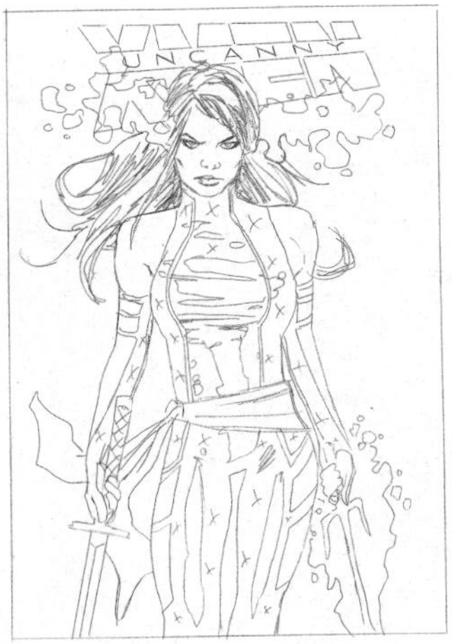
UNCANNY

1

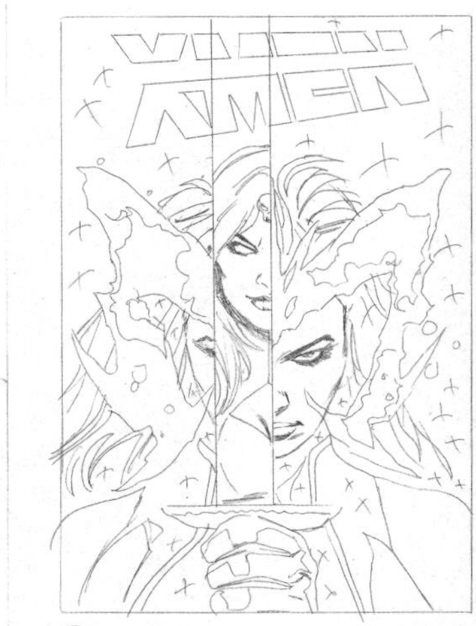

2

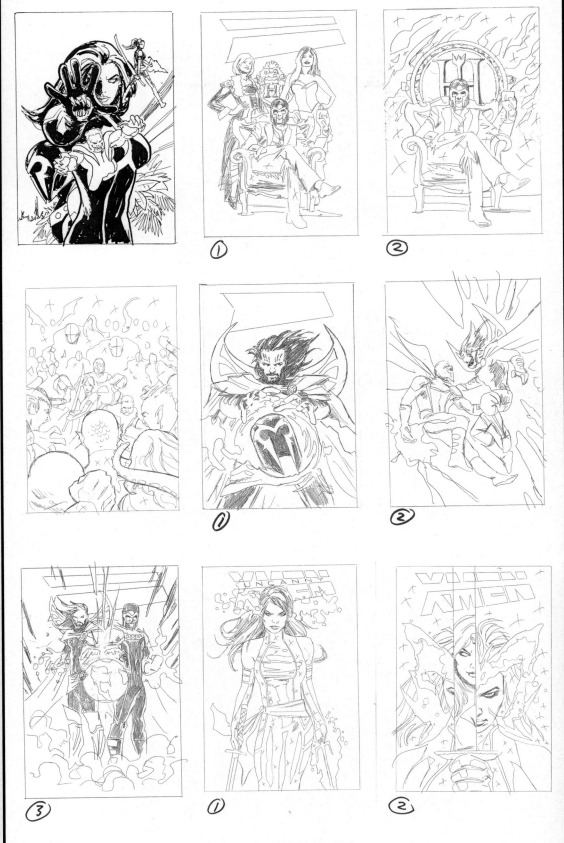

COVER SKETCHES BY **GREG LAND**

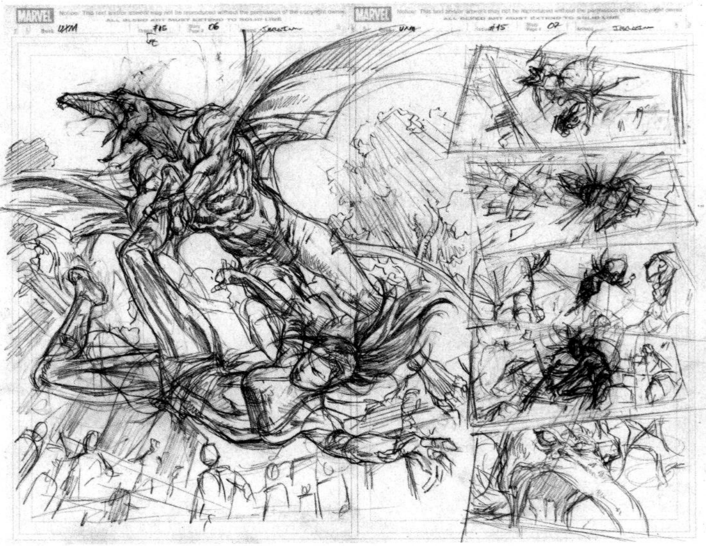

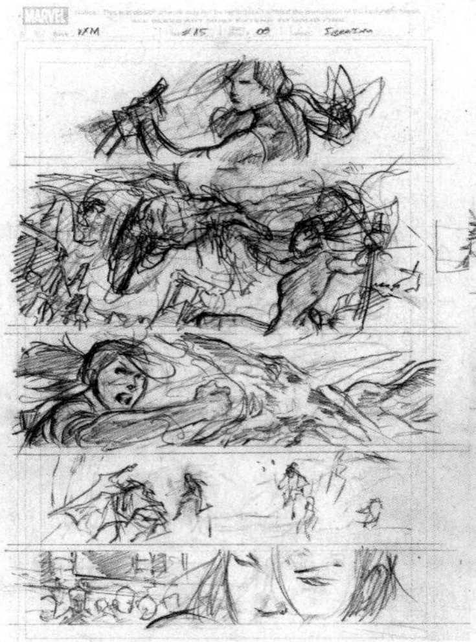

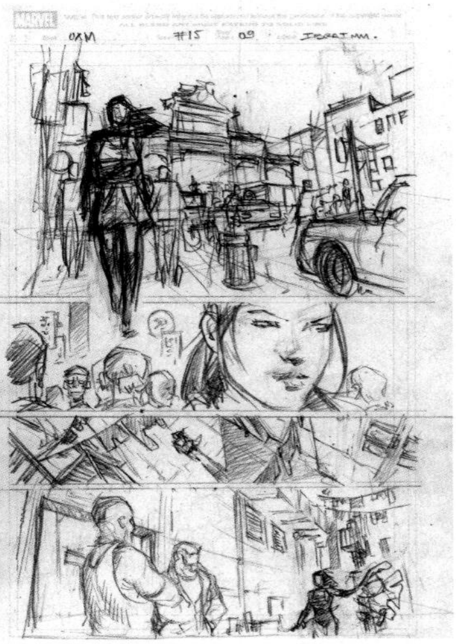

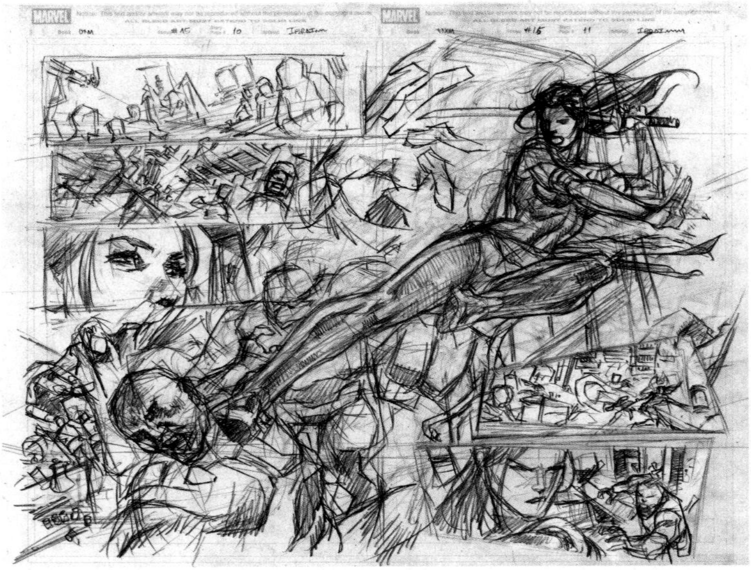

LAYOUTS BY ***IBRAIM ROBERSON***